Paddling Montana

A Guide to the State's Best Paddling Routes

Fourth Edition

Kit Fischer

FALCONGUIDES

GUILFORD, CONNECTICUT

To all those people who not only enjoy Montana's rivers but also work to conserve them.

FALCONGUIDES®

An imprint of The Rowman & Littlefield Publishing Group, Inc.
4501 Forbes Blvd., Ste. 200
Lanham, MD 20706
www.rowman.com
Falcon and FalconGuides are registered trademarks and Make Adventure Your Story is a trademark of
The Rowman & Littlefield Publishing Group, Inc.

Distributed by NATIONAL BOOK NETWORK

Library of Congress Cataloging-in-Publication Data available

ISBN 978-1-4930-5970-6 (paper: alk. paper)
ISBN 978-1-4930-5971-3 (electronic)

∞™ The paper used in this publication meets the minimum requirements of American National
Standard for Information Sciences—Permanence of Paper for Printed Library Materials, ANSI/NISO
Z39.48-1992.

Contents

Overview

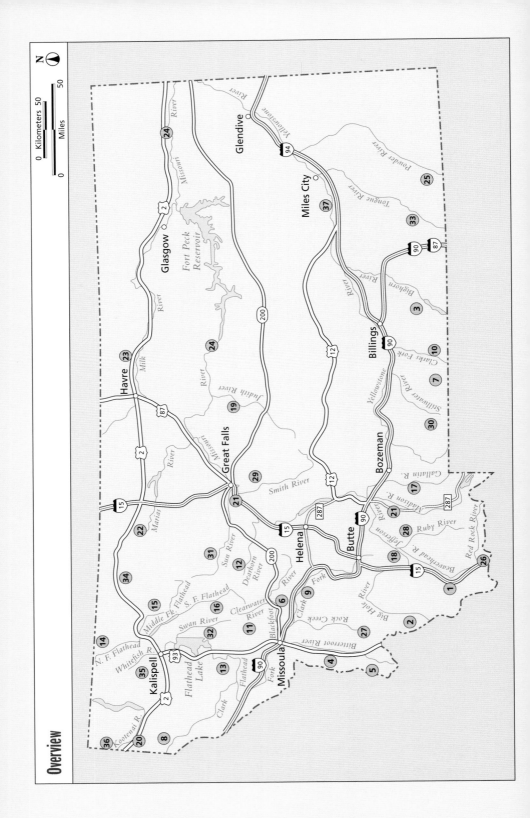

N

0 Kilometers 50

0 Miles 50

Lewis and Clark's Montana River Routes

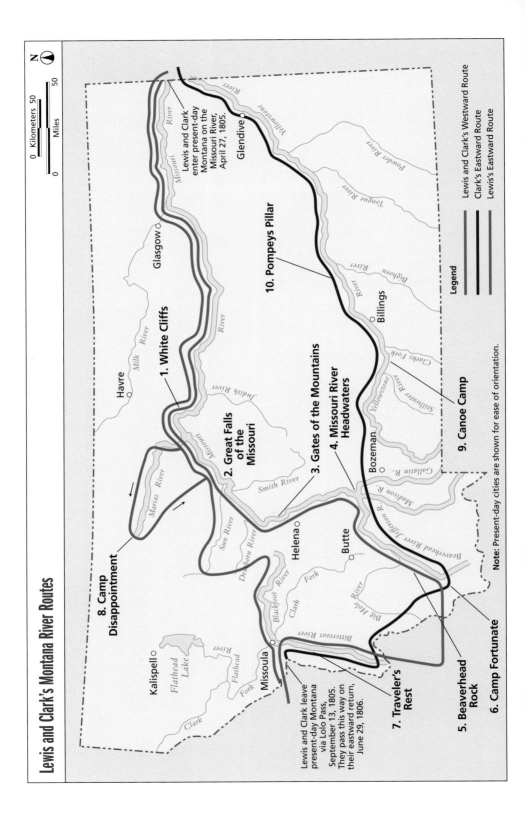

1. White Cliffs

2. Great Falls of the Missouri

3. Gates of the Mountains

4. Missouri River Headwaters

5. Beaverhead Rock

6. Camp Fortunate

7. Traveler's Rest

8. Camp Disappointment

9. Canoe Camp

10. Pompeys Pillar

Lewis and Clark enter present-day Montana on the Missouri River, April 27, 1805.

Lewis and Clark leave present-day Montana via Lolo Pass, September 13, 1805. They pass this way on their eastward return, June 29, 1806.

Note: Present-day cities are shown for ease of orientation.

Legend

Lewis and Clark's Westward Route

Clark's Eastward Route

Lewis's Eastward Route

0   Kilometers   50

0   Miles   50

N

Lewis and Clark: Paddling Montana, 1805–1806

These dates and events correspond to the labeled sites on the map on the preceding page. The map shows the routes Lewis and Clark followed on several Montana rivers on their way west and on their eastward return.

1. White Cliffs, May 31, 1805—A spectacular 35-mile section of the Missouri River, described by Captain Lewis in a journal entry as resembling "a thousand grotesque figures."
2. Great Falls of the Missouri, June 21–July 15, 1805—Termed a "sublimely grand spectacle" by Lewis; it took the Corps of Discovery nearly a month to make the 18-mile portage.
3. Gates of the Mountains, July 18, 1805—Lewis said this place had the most remarkable cliffs the expedition had seen to that point. "These clifts rise from the waters edge on either side perpendicularly to the height of 1200 feet. Every object here wears a dark and gloomy aspect. The tow(er)ing and projecting rocks in many places seem ready to tumble on us." A boat-tour excursion carries modern-day visitors to the site.
4. Missouri River Headwaters, July 27–29, 1805—Lewis described the place where the Jefferson, Madison, and, a short distance upstream, the Gallatin Rivers merge as "an essential point in the geography of the western world."
5. Beaverhead Rock, August 8, 1805—Sacagawea recognized this landmark, which resembles a swimming beaver, and knew her tribe, the Shoshones, would not be far away.
6. Camp Fortunate, August 17, 1805—Sacagawea found the Shoshones here, and they provided horses for the Corps' trip over the mountains.
7. Traveler's Rest, September 9–10, 1805; June 30–July 2, 1806—The Corps of Discovery rested here in preparation for what turned out to be an arduous passage over the mountains. On their return trip the expedition camped here again and separated into two parties. Lewis headed for the Blackfoot River; Clark led his party down the Bitterroot River.
8. Camp Disappointment, July 22–25, 1806—The northernmost point reached by Lewis on an exploration of the Marias River; this is close to the spot where Lewis and his party had a hostile encounter with Blackfeet Indians. Two braves were killed.
9. Canoe Camp, July 19–23, 1806—Clark and his men built two canoes at this site for their return down the Yellowstone River.
10. Pompeys Pillar, July 25, 1806—Named for Sacagawea's son, this sandstone pillar holds the only physical evidence of Lewis and Clark's passage through Montana: Clark's name and the date carved into the rock.

Introduction

By such a river it is impossible to believe that one will ever be tired or old. Every sense applauds it. Taste it, feel its chill on the teeth: it is purity absolute. Watch its racing current, its steady renewal of force: it is transient and eternal. And listen again to its sounds: get far enough away so that the noise of falling tons of water does not stun the ears, and hear how much is going on underneath—a whole symphony of smaller sounds, hiss and splash and gurgle, the small talk of side channels, the whisper of blown and scattered spray gathering itself and beginning to flow again, secret and irresistible, among the wet rocks.
—Wallace Stegner, *The Sound of Mountain Water*

Montana's Rivers

Most people carry an "escape" dream, an idyllic plan for the time when life becomes too harried or complicated. For some the dream takes them on a long wilderness trek. Others hope to sail off to sea. For many the fantasy is simpler: Put a canoe, kayak, or raft in the nearest river, lie back, let the sun warm the body, trail a hand in the water, and drift away. With over 20,000 miles of streams in Montana, a lifetime of exploring can be had without ever leaving the state.

It's a dream that started with the excursions of early river explorers like Lewis and Clark and John Wesley Powell. It has been kept alive by writers like Mark Twain, Ernest Hemingway, and Bernard DeVoto, and now it is being relived by modern-day river runners.

Montana's rivers have a special kind of historical significance, as the waterways played a key role in the Treasure State's early development. In early times the rivers carried only Indians and intrepid explorers. Later they brought miners, loggers, cowboys, sodbusters, soldiers, and shopkeepers. Indian bullboats and French pirogues were gradually replaced by flatboats and even steamships. It was only with the coming of the railroads in the late 1800s that Montana's rivers faded in importance.

One reason the rivers were so important is that they are easily navigated. Despite the cold waters and rapid flow, most Montana rivers can be floated by people with only moderate river skills. Those who have seen Montana's towering mountains often find this hard to believe, as did Meriwether Lewis of the Lewis and Clark Expedition. He noted in his journal of 1805:

I can scarcely form an idea of a river running to great extent through such a rough mountainous country without having it's stream intersepted by some difficult and dangerous rappids or falls, we daily pass a great number of small rappids or riffles which descend one to or 3 feet in 150 yards but we are rarely incommoded with fixed or standing rocks and altho' strong rapid water are nevertheless quite practicable & by no means dangerous.

The majority of Montana's rivers lie in the mountainous western portion of the state, where they flow down broad valleys between mountain ranges. In arid eastern Montana, where only a few major rivers flow, the streams are generally broad and flat as they cut through open grassland and sagebrush country. While the sparkling western streams may be more spectacular, the eastern rivers have a quiet beauty and offer better opportunities for solitude.

On most Montana rivers, whitewater sections occur primarily in narrow canyons and last only a few miles. While much of the whitewater is extremely challenging, most runs can be covered in a day. Unlike some western states, Montana has few rivers suitable for extended whitewater trips.

Montana rivers have a distinctly different appeal. They offer a deep sense of history and adventure that can still be felt today. In many instances, floaters can follow the river routes of early explorers and, if diligent enough, can seek out the same campsites that were used long ago. The countryside surrounding some rivers has changed only slightly since the days of westward expansion; floaters may travel for a week and see only a few bridges and farmhouses. Despite a landscape that has changed little, the popularity of floating has increased dramatically. Luckily, it's still quite easy to find solitude as approximately 75 percent of floating occurs on fewer than ten rivers in the state.

As the rivers wind through secluded canyons, heavily timbered bottomlands, or isolated marshes, one can observe eagles, deer, bighorn sheep, osprey, bears, and waterfowl. More than anything else, wildlife sightings define Montana float trips. Watching an osprey catch a fish, floating past a great blue heron rookery, or seeing a deer with newborn fawns creates memories long remembered. Quiet floaters often won't disturb wildlife as they drift by, allowing excellent opportunities for observation and photography.

Outstanding trout fishing lures many people to Montana rivers. Fisheries biologists report that some streams contain more than a ton of trout for each mile of stream; other rivers hold a trout 2 pounds or larger for every 10 feet of streambank and a 4-pounder or larger for every 20 feet. Montana has about 450 miles of blue-ribbon trout water, and most of it can be floated. Many fishermen opt for professional guides to row them into trout, although a greater number opt for a do-it-yourself adventure.

Canoes, kayaks, and rafts allow a quiet approach and can take anglers to secluded portions of rivers not often visited on foot. Float anglers often become addicted to this style of angling.

This book was written in hopes that everyone who experiences Montana's rivers will become addicted to them. Anyone who has floated a free river, relished its natural beauty, fished for its wild trout, or challenged its whitewater should become an advocate for its protection. Hopefully, getting to know Montana's sparkling streams will give people a personal stake in the rivers' future.

Use It, but Don't Abuse It

If floaters are careful, rivers can be floated again and again without showing signs of use. Your attentiveness to caring for the river could prevent the need for permit systems that limit use. Currently only one river in Montana requires a permit for noncommercial use. Floaters on overnight trips should be especially mindful of their activities. Here are a few suggestions.

Plan Ahead and Prepare

- Know and respect the regulations for the river you plan to visit.
- Prepare for extreme weather conditions and emergencies.
- Float in small groups to reduce social conflicts and impacts.
- Plan river trips that are compatible with the skill level of everyone in the group.

Camp on Durable Surfaces

- Durable surfaces include designated campsites, rock, gravel, and dry grasses.
- Concentrate use on existing campsites; avoid places where impacts are just beginning.
- Water-saturated soil and wet vegetation are particularly vulnerable to impact from recreational users.

Dispose of Waste Properly

- Littering degrades Montana's rivers. Police your campsite before leaving, and pack out all litter.
- While some rivers have established toilets, most do not. Deposit solid human waste in a "cat hole" 6 to 8 inches deep at least 200 feet from water sources, campsites, and trails. Fill in and disguise the cat hole when finished. Better yet, bring a "groover" or disposable sanitary bags to collect your waste and leave no trace.
- Strain and scatter dishwashing and cooking water.

Leave What You Find

- Preserve the past: Examine but do not touch or remove archaeological, historical, or paleontological resources.
- Leave rocks and plants and other natural objects as you find them.
- Avoid introducing or transporting nonnative aquatic invasive species. Floaters are required to stop at various checkpoints to have their boats checked for invasive plants and animals.
- Do not build structures or furniture or dig trenches around campsites.

Minimize Campfire Impacts

- Campfires cause long-lasting impacts on our rivers. If you must have a campfire, contain all fires in established rock fire rings, metal fire grates, or your own portable fire pan.

- Check local burn restrictions if you plan on using a fire.

- Do not construct new rock fire rings—they blacken rocks, sterilize the soil, and leave lasting impacts. If you do construct fire rings, scatter remaining wood, ashes, and rocks to avoid establishing new sites.

- Collect only down and dead firewood that can be broken by hand, or pack in your own firewood.

- Keep fires small, and burn all wood down to white ash. Ensure that fires are completely extinguished before leaving.

Respect Wildlife

- Observe wildlife from a distance. Do not follow or intentionally approach them.

- Feeding wildlife is harmful to their health, alters natural behavior, and exposes them to predators and other dangers. It is also unsafe and unlawful.

- Protect wildlife and your food by securing rations and trash properly.

- Be Bear Aware. Grizzly bears have expanded their range significantly in the state. Carrying bear spray, securing your food, and remaining vigilant is important to remain safe.

Floating and the Law

Montana has one of the most progressive stream access laws in the West. This legislation was precipitated by lawsuits involving access disputes on the Beaverhead, Dearborn, and Ruby Rivers. In 1984 the Montana Supreme Court ruled that the public has a right to recreational use of the state's waters up to the high-water mark.

In 1985 the Montana Legislature further defined stream access rules. The law provides that rivers and streams capable of recreational use may be used by the public, up to the high-water mark, regardless of streambed ownership. The law does dictate, however, that certain activities require landowner permission and that camping and other recreational activities must take place 500 yards away from occupied dwellings.

The law defines "recreational use" as floating, fishing, upland and waterfowl hunting, swimming, and other water-related pleasure activities. It defines the ordinary high-water mark as the line the water impresses on land by covering it for a sufficient time to cause different characteristics below the line, such as deprivation of the soil of substantially all its terrestrial vegetation and destruction of its value for agricultural vegetation.

The law divides the state's rivers and streams into two categories, Class I and Class II. These classes are not to be confused with the international system of rating rivers and streams according to difficulty and recommended skill level. That system is thoroughly explained in the *How to Use This Guide* section.

Class I streams are capable of recreational use and have been declared navigable or are capable of certain kinds of commercial activity, including commercial outfitting. All other Montana rivers are Class II. For the most part the rivers discussed in this book are Class I streams, with the exception of the Clarks Fork of the Yellowstone, Clearwater, Judith, Milk, Powder, Red Rock, Ruby, Stillwater, and Whitefish. Review appendix D for further details on the classifications and the regulations regarding each.

Recreationists should also be aware of trespass law passed by the Montana Legislature in 1985. This law states that lands can be closed to the public either by verbal communication or by actual posting. Do not trespass on posted land. When in doubt, ask permission. A special brochure is available from Montana Fish, Wildlife and Parks that explains important provisions of the stream access law.

One aspect of stream access remains controversial. Private landowners on the Blackfoot and Ruby Rivers have challenged whether rights-of-way associated with county bridges constitute legal access to streams and rivers. The State of Montana has argued that they do, and floaters typically use county bridges without seeking permission. In fact, the Montana Department of Transportation has started to construct access for floaters on new and repaired bridges. In 2014 the Montana Supreme Court affirmed that a public prescriptive road, established through a historical easement, may be legally used by the public for all uses, including accessing streams and rivers. As a result, many bridges now have designated access points to minimize landowner conflict and ease access.

Have a Safe Trip

Although few people like to talk about it, floating in Montana can be dangerous. Not only are many streams powerful and fast, but they are also quite cold, even in summer. Hypothermia can be as serious a danger as drowning. With proper caution and appropriate clothing, however, these problems can be overcome.

Several people die in Montana each year due to floating-related accidents. Statistics show that the overwhelming number of floating deaths occur in May and June, when rivers are running at three to four times their normal flow. Beginners should be extremely wary about taking trips during the high-water period or in cold weather. Know your limitations, and respect the rivers.

In addition, make sure you leave for every floating trip with the proper equipment. The following checklist suggests the essentials and some optional items. You'll want to add items if you're planning an overnight or extended trip.

Paddling Checklist

Basics

- ❏ spare paddles/oars
- ❏ life jacket (personal flotation device, PFD)
- ❏ ropes for bowline and for securing gear
- ❏ drinking water or water filter
- ❏ waterproof storage bags with extra dry clothes
- ❏ flotation bags (optional)
- ❏ maps in a watertight map case (or a Ziploc bag)
- ❏ repair kit for boats

Emergency Equipment

- ❏ knife
- ❏ whistle
- ❏ waterproof matches, lighter, fire starter
- ❏ multipurpose tool (Leatherman-type)
- ❏ throw bag (optional)
- ❏ duct tape
- ❏ extra rope
- ❏ cellphone
- ❏ GPS
- ❏ first-aid kit
- ❏ first-aid book
- ❏ adhesive bandages
- ❏ butterfly closures
- ❏ sterile compresses
- ❏ gauze roll
- ❏ adhesive tape
- ❏ Ace bandage
- ❏ triangular bandage
- ❏ first-aid and burn ointment

- ❐ skin lotion
- ❐ Vaseline
- ❐ safety pins
- ❐ aspirin and pain pills
- ❐ tweezers
- ❐ needle
- ❐ moleskin and blister kit

Clothing

- ❐ shorts (fast drying)
- ❐ short-sleeve polypropylene shirt
- ❐ long-sleeve polypropylene shirt
- ❐ wind parka
- ❐ rain parka and pants
- ❐ baseball cap
- ❐ waterproof sandals and/or aqua socks

Miscellaneous

- ❐ sunglasses with strap
- ❐ water bottles
- ❐ sunblock
- ❐ lip balm/block
- ❐ insect repellent
- ❐ fishing license either in paper form or on cellphone
- ❐ food and beverages
- ❐ trash bag
- ❐ camera
- ❐ binoculars

How to Use This Guide

This book's intent isn't to provide a mile-by-mile guide to Montana's rivers. To the contrary, our purpose is to tell the minimum amount necessary for a safe, enjoyable trip. Knowing everything in advance is like having someone tell you how a movie ends. Discovery and exploration are essential components of any river trip. Put-in and take-out locations should be scouted in advance as some can be difficult to identify from the water.

Additionally, this book only includes what we regard as the major Montana rivers for floating. Other small streams in the state have boating potential, although usually only for short stretches or during high-water periods.

Every river trip begins with a brief summary of the river and its unique features. Basic information for each river can then be found in the at-a-glance section. The information includes several headings.

Vital statistics: The total length of the river, where it begins, and where it ends.

Level of difficulty: The difficulty of the river according to the international system of river rating described in the sidebar in this section.

Flow: Provides average annual flow in cubic feet per second (cfs), explains whether the river is generally floatable year-round, and estimates the minimum flow for floating (below which continual hauling over shallow spots is required) and the maximum flow for safety (the flow over which only experts should be on the river). (*Caution:* The maximum and minimum flows can vary significantly based on your craft and skill level.)

Recommended watercraft: Some rivers flow fast and deep; others flow broad and shallow. Picking the proper boat to match your float will make for safer, more enjoyable floats.

Hazards: The specific hazards for each river. Pay special attention to these. They include portages, diversions, and known logjams.

Where the crowd goes: The most popular stretch on each river.

Avoiding the scene: The most isolated spots on each river.

Inside tip: Special information gleaned from our experience.

Maps: A listing of maps that are more detailed than the ones in this book. The book's maps are only meant to provide a general idea of the course of the rivers, the most challenging rapids, dams, or other hazards, and the points of access that can help you plan a trip. These maps are not intended to be used as navigational tools. Please refer to the *About the Maps* section to learn where you can get more detailed maps to help you navigate these rivers.

Shuttle information: While shuttle companies tend to come and go with the seasons, a few have stood the test of time and will save you valuable time on the water.

River rules: Regulations to be followed while traveling on the river. Most are enforced by Montana Fish, Wildlife and Parks (FWP) or, for rivers that flow through Tribal Lands, contact local tribal law enforcement organizations.

For more information: Lists the names of agencies or offices that can provide additional help to readers planning a river trip. Contact information for these organizations can be found in appendix A.

The paddling: A narrative description of the river.

We use the international scale of river difficulty (which rates rivers on a I to VI scale) in the vital statistics and in some of the whitewater descriptions. In the general text, however, we use three grades of ability level to help readers determine if the river is suitable for their skills: beginner, intermediate, or expert.

INTERNATIONAL SCALE OF RIVER DIFFICULTY

This is the American version of a rating system used to compare river difficulty throughout the world. This system is not exact; rivers do not always fit easily into one category, and regional or individual interpretations may cause misunderstanding. It is no substitute for a guidebook or accurate firsthand descriptions of a run.

Paddlers attempting difficult runs in an unfamiliar area should act cautiously until they get a feel for the way the scale is interpreted locally. River difficulty may change each year due to fluctuations in water level, downed trees, recent floods, geological disturbances, or bad weather. Stay alert for unexpected problems!

As river difficulty increases, the danger to swimming paddlers becomes more severe. As rapids become longer and more continuous, the challenge increases. There is a difference between running an occasional Class IV rapid and dealing with an entire river of this category. Allow an extra margin of safety between skills and river ratings when the water is cold or if the river itself is remote and inaccessible.

The six difficulty classes:

Class I: Easy. Fast-moving water with riffles and small waves. Few obstructions, all obvious and easily missed with little training. Risk to swimmers is slight; self-rescue is easy.

Class II: Novice. Straightforward rapids with wide, clear channels that are evident without scouting. Occasional maneuvering may be required, but rocks and medium-size waves are easily missed by trained paddlers. Swimmers are seldom injured, and group assistance, while helpful, is seldom needed.

Class III: Intermediate. Rapids with moderate, irregular waves that may be difficult to avoid and that can swamp an open canoe. Complex maneuvers in fast current and good boat control in tight passages or around ledges are often required; large waves or strainers may be present

This approach has limitations. First, it doesn't account for drastic changes in river conditions caused by spring runoff. Cold water, heavy current, and potential river debris characterize peak stream flows. During May and June, beginners and even intermediates should be extremely cautious about taking river trips and should pay close attention to flow levels. Probably nine out of ten river deaths occur at this time of year. Second, beginning rafters can negotiate some rivers that beginning canoeists cannot, simply because of the inherent stability and buoyancy of good inflatable crafts. On the other hand, rafters might want to avoid some of the small, winding streams

but are easily avoided. Strong eddies and powerful current effects can be found, particularly on large-volume rivers. Scouting is advisable for inexperienced parties. Injuries while swimming are rare; self-rescue is usually easy, but group assistance may be required to avoid long swims.

Class IV: Advanced. Intense, powerful but predictable rapids requiring precise boat handling in turbulent water. Depending on the character of the river, it may feature large, unavoidable waves and holes or constricted passages demanding fast maneuvers under pressure. A fast, reliable eddy turn may be needed to initiate maneuvers, scout rapids, or rest. Rapids may require "must" moves above dangerous hazards. Scouting is necessary the first time down. Risk of injury to swimmers is moderate to high, and water conditions may make self-rescue difficult. Group assistance for rescue is often essential but requires practiced skills. A strong Eskimo roll is highly recommended.

Class V: Expert. Extremely long, obstructed, or very violent rapids that expose a paddler to above-average danger. Drops may contain large, unavoidable waves and holes or steep, congested chutes with complex, demanding routes. Rapids may continue for long distances between pools, demanding a high level of fitness. What eddies exist may be small, turbulent, or difficult to reach. At the high end of the scale, several of these factors may be combined. Scouting is recommended but difficult. Swims are dangerous, and rescue is difficult even for experts. A very reliable Eskimo roll, proper equipment, extensive experience, and practiced rescue skills are essential.

Class VI: Extreme. One grade more difficult than Class V. These runs often exemplify the extremes of difficulty, unpredictability, and danger. The consequences of errors are very severe and rescue may be impossible. For teams of experts only, at favorable water levels, after close personal inspection and taking all precautions. This class does not represent drops thought to be unrunnable, but may include rapids which are only occasionally run.

Reprinted by permission of American Whitewater

where canoeists do fine. We try to suggest what style of boat works best for each river, but it's often personal choice.

Here's how we rate the different levels of paddling skill:

Beginner—Knows the basic strokes (for canoeists: front paddle, back paddle, draw stroke, and pry stroke) and can handle the craft competently in smooth water. Knows how to bring the boat to shore safely in fast current, can negotiate sharp turns in fast current, can avoid logjams, and understands the difficulty of the stream he or she intends to float. A beginner is not a person who is picking up a paddle for the first time. Novices should get some practice on a lake or with an experienced floater before taking their first trip alone.

Intermediate—Knows basic strokes and uses them effectively. Can read water well and can negotiate fairly difficult rapids with confidence (knows how to safely catch an eddy). Won't panic and knows what to do in the event of an upset. For canoeists, knows how to coordinate strokes between bow and stern and can paddle at either end. Can come to shore quickly to inspect dangerous spots and knows when to portage.

Expert—Has mastered all strokes and uses them instinctively. Confident of own ability even in difficult situations. Skillful in heavy water or complex rapids. Knows when a rapid is unrunnable and has a deep respect for all safety precautions. Doesn't need to read guidebooks but does anyway.

Remember, this guide only contains the minimum information needed for a safe trip. Rivers are living, dynamic systems that change constantly. A channel free of barriers one year may contain a dangerous logjam the next, or there may be a diversion dam or a new barbed-wire fence. Thoroughly check out the stretch of river you plan to float before launching your craft.

Carefully check water conditions before starting any trip. US Geological Survey (USGS), Montana Fish, Wildlife and Parks (FWP), Bureau of Reclamation (BOR), and USDA Forest Service offices are usually good sources of information. Sporting goods stores or fishing shops can often provide information as well.

While the river adventurer won't face the perils of Odysseus—Sirens, Cyclops, or giant whirlpools—floaters should be aware of the hazards that await them. These include diversion dams, fallen trees and logs, weirs, and fast water studded with rocks. Know in advance how to deal with each hazard, and know what to do in the event of an upset. Consult a swiftwater rescue guide for recommended rescue techniques, and buy the appropriate gear to rescue and repair your craft in advance of every season. For inflatables, check your repair kit often to make sure your glue isn't dried up!

About the Maps

The maps that accompany the text provide a general picture of the location of access points. We suggest you use them in combination with either electronic or paper maps to plan trips. Under the Maps heading, which precedes each narrative, we suggest the best maps to use if you want detail and the ability to chart mile-by-mile progress. Appendix C includes contact information for acquiring these maps.

When using the maps in this guide, pay careful attention to the scale as shown in the upper right-hand corner, as it varies considerably. A map of an 80-mile river gives more detail than one of a 200-mile river.

We've included most bridges and all official public access points on the maps. A triangular arrow marks all public access points—USDA Forest Service; Bureau of Land Management; Montana Fish, Wildlife and Parks; county; and municipality.

Some county bridges that are poor accesses have not been included. Some access points where roads run next to the river or where old roads and trails lead to the river also haven't been included. Many of these "local" access points are privately owned, so ask permission before launching. Again, consult appendix C for obtaining maps that show all roads and landownership.

Finding Detailed Maps

There are several basic sources for floaters who want detailed maps of rivers and the surrounding lands: the Montana Afloat series; Bureau of Land Management (BLM); USDA Forest Service (USFS); Montana Fish, Wildlife and Parks (FWP); US Geological Survey (USGS); and online map sources such as onXmaps. While the USGS provides the most detailed maps, you could go broke buying all the maps needed for a long river trip. The standard BLM and USFS maps have an advantage over USGS maps because of their smaller scale and their well-defined landownership patterns, roads, trails, and access points. The most useful maps for strictly river floating are the privately produced Montana Afloat maps and the River Rat Maps, which show access points, river miles, bridges, and interesting historical information. OnXmaps is also a useful option for those who prefer to use their cellphone for navigation. You can download the appropriate area in advance of your float and can accurately track your progress and mileage. You will find the maps you need for a particular river under the Maps heading at the beginning of each river description.

The Montana Afloat series covers fifteen rivers with large foldout maps. Although these maps don't necessarily include the entire river, they do include the sections most often floated, with excellent information on history, topography, and fishing. The maps clearly show access points, bridges, roads, and river hazards. The rivers included in this series are the Beaverhead, Big Hole, Bighorn, Bitterroot, Blackfoot, Clark Fork, Gallatin, Jefferson, Madison, Middle Fork of the Flathead, Missouri,

Whether you are seeking a day trip for a quick escape or preparing for a multiday adventure, proper planning ensures a successful float.

North Fork of the Flathead, Rock Creek, Smith, and Yellowstone. Maps are available at most outdoor stores, from FWP, and from FalconGuides.

The River Rat Maps series is somewhat new on the market and produced locally in the Bitterroot valley. Currently these sturdy maps include the Beaverhead, Bighorn, Big Hole, Bitterroot, Blackfoot, Clark Fork, Gallatin, Jefferson, Madison, Rock Creek, Smith, Missouri, and Yellowstone. The River Rat series can be found at most fishing shops in Montana or on their website at riverratmaps.com.

Most BLM printed maps have been discontinued due to ever-changing landownership and much more reliable and affordable maps available online. The BLM does offer several specialty maps for notable rivers such as the Yellowstone and the Missouri.

The Forest Service's Forest Visitors Series maps each cover one national forest or a part of a national forest (some large forests have more than one map) and have essentially the same features as BLM maps. The scale is 0.5 inch per mile. These maps are available for purchase at most Forest Service offices or by writing to the USDA Forest Service in Missoula (see address in appendix C). Make your check for the amount of purchase only; it's not necessary to include postage. The Forest Service has maps of wilderness areas available as well. The only disadvantage of these maps is that the forests don't block up to one another, which can result in annoying gaps in coverage.

Montana FWP offers an excellent online resource for paddlers looking for detailed information and locations of fishing access sites at https://fwp.mt.gov/gis/maps/fishingGuide/. Throughout this book, and especially on the maps, we have used the abbreviation "FAS" to indicate fishing access sites.

For those who want more detail than the Forest Service or BLM maps provide, or for those sections of rivers that just can't be found elsewhere, USGS topographic maps (7.5-minute series) are the best bet. An index for these maps is printed on the Forest Service maps. The scale of these maps is 1:24,000, so they can be a bit bulky if you're planning a long trip—it may take four or five maps to cover a 30-mile section of river. Be prepared to cut and paste. You can purchase these maps online at the USGS website listed in appendix C, or locally from drafting or blueprint offices and sporting goods stores. USGS also has a 1 x 2 degree series (1:250,000). Twenty-five of these maps cover all of Montana, but you obviously lose a lot of detail. These are the maps listed under "USGS" for each river in this guidebook. In between these two series is the 3 x 60 series (1:100,000).

Perhaps the best tool for researching floating trips can be found online through the online app onXmaps, which provides up-to-date GIS mapping of landownership and watersheds statewide, camping sites, and FWP Fishing Access Sites.

For Lewis and Clark buffs, an excellent map is available that shows the explorers' route and campsites in Montana. To purchase this map, write or email the Portage Route Chapter of the Lewis & Clark Trail Heritage Foundation, Inc. at the address listed in appendix C. There are also excellent pullout maps of Lewis and Clark campsites along the Beaverhead, Jefferson, and upper Missouri Rivers in the book *Lewis and Clark in the Three Rivers Valley* (see appendix C).

Legend

Transportation

═⟨15⟩═	Interstate Highway
═⟨12⟩═	U.S. Highway
═⟨287⟩═	State Highway
═══	Paved Road
══ ══	Unpaved Road
-------	Trail
+—+—+	Railroad

Political Boundaries

■··—··■	International
---·---	State/Province

Water Features

⬭	Body of Water
∿	River or Creek
//	Waterfall/Rapid

Symbols

Symbol	Description
↘	Access Site
∿∿	Diversion Dam
/	Dam
)(	Bridge
⛺	Campground
24	Mileage Marker
■	Structure/Point of Interest
◄	Scenic View/Overlook
⇶	Boat Launch
🏠	Ranger Station
🌲	State Park
○	Towns and Cities

Land Management

▭	National Park/Forest
▭	Wilderness/Wildlife Area
▭	Miscellaneous Boundary

River Trips

The Bitterroot River (Paddle 4) is floatable for nearly 12 months a year and the shoulder seasons are a great time to find some solitude. Alec Underwood

1 Beaverhead River

Slow and serpentine with a jungle of vegetation, the Beaverhead meanders through rock canyons and broad valleys, and offers much of interest for Lewis and Clark aficionados.

Vital statistics: 80 miles from Clark Canyon Dam to the Jefferson River.

Level of difficulty: Almost all Class I water. Suitable for intermediates south of Dillon, practiced beginners north of town.

Flow: Annual mean flow: 408 cfs near Twin Bridges. Above Barrett's Dam flows are usually adequate all year. Below Barrett's (especially north of Dillon) may be too low in dry years. Flows of 75 cfs are a bare minimum for canoes, with flows above 300 cfs being optimum.

Recommended watercraft: Suitable for all crafts when above 300 cfs; below 300 cfs stick to canoes and smaller boats.

Hazards: Bends, narrow channels, and swift currents in the upper 20 miles. Numerous irrigation jetties, diversions, low bridges, fences, and logjams. A low bridge (Hildreth Bridge) about 2 miles below High Bridge FAS and another near Tash. Three diversion dams require portages: Barrett's, Dillon, and a diversion dam 1 mile below Twin Bridges.

Where the crowd goes: Outfitters and non-residents are limited to what sections they are allowed to float; see river rules below and plan your float accordingly.

Avoiding the scene: Downstream from Dillon.

Inside tip: Excellent bird-watching or waterfowl hunting in season north of Dillon.

Maps: BLM: #33 (Butte South), #34 (Dillon); USFS: Beaverhead Interagency Travel Plan (East and West); USGS: Dillon, MT; Montana Afloat: #7 (The Beaverhead River).

Shuttle information: One More Bend Shuttle & Service, Dillon, (406) 925-2575; Frontier Anglers, (406) 683-5276.

River rules: Complex fishing and floating regulations are in place to alleviate crowding and overfishing. Many sections restrict the number of outfitted boats in any given reach. In particular, FWP rules state: "Float fishing by nonresidents and float outfitting is limited as follows on the Beaverhead River from the third Saturday in May through Labor Day: a) each Saturday float fishing by nonresidents and float outfitting is not permitted on the river reach from High Bridge fishing access site to Henneberry fishing access site; and b) each Sunday float fishing by nonresidents and float outfitting is not permitted on the river reach from Henneberry fishing access site to Pipe Organ fishing access site." In addition, Clark Canyon to Pipe Organ is closed to fishing November 30th until the third Saturday in May.

For more information: Frontier Anglers, Dillon; Four Rivers Fishing Company, Twin Bridges; FWP, Bozeman; BOR, Billings.

The Paddling

The Beaverhead River flows for only 43 air miles, but if the US Army Corps of Engineers ever decided to straighten it (and we're certainly not recommending it), the Beaverhead probably would stretch halfway across Montana. Sinuous and serpentine, from the air it looks like a swimming snake. The Beaverhead today is much the same as Meriwether Lewis described it in 1805: "from 35 to 40 yards wide very crooked many short bends constituting large and general bends; insomuch that altho' we travel briskly and a considerable distance yet it takes us only a few miles on our general course or rout." Expect to travel about 3 river miles for every air mile. When the wind picks up on this river, it will only be at your back for a short time.

Not only does the Beaverhead meander a great deal, it also supports a jungle of vegetation along its banks. The combination of deeply undercut banks and thick brush provides the habitat that makes the Beaverhead one of the best trout streams in the country, and one best fished from a boat. Biologists estimate that some sections of the river contain more than 400 2- to 4-pound trout per mile and another 100 over 5 pounds.

The Beaverhead originates at the confluence of the Red Rock River and Horse Prairie Creek, at the present site of Clark Canyon Dam (about 20 miles south of Dillon). The upper section of the river flows through a highly scenic but arid canyon; however, it is flanked by Interstate 15 until below Barrett's Dam. The upper section is amicably known as the "fish ditch" as its banks are well rip-rapped and in some places feels more like an irrigation ditch. By the time the river reaches Dillon, the valley opens up and the Pioneer and Ruby ranges provide a scenic backdrop.

Floaters north of Dillon can orient themselves the same way that Lewis and Clark did—by looking for Beaverhead Rock. This notable landmark, located just upstream from the Highway 41 bridge, juts about 150 feet above the river. It's the place where Sacagawea first recognized her homeland while guiding Lewis and Clark through the Rockies. Viewed from many angles in the large valley—particularly from near Sheridan—the rock resembles a swimming beaver. The land around Beaverhead Rock is publicly owned, so feel free to explore.

Beaverhead floaters shouldn't expect to find crystal-clear water. Often it's downright murky, due to a combination of irrigation returns, heavy livestock grazing, and natural siltation. Nevertheless, the river's rich load of nutrients produces the insects that make trout fat and trout anglers happy.

Clark Canyon Dam regulates the flow of the Beaverhead, and it can create unusual water conditions. Early in the floating season (May, June, and July), flows can be moderate, particularly in dry years. When most rivers are blown out with spring runoff, the Beaverhead may have excellent floating conditions. But then during the fall, when floating conditions are normally ideal on most Montana rivers, the Beaverhead may have high flows if it has been a wet year and water is being released from the reservoir. Heavy irrigation demands can result in extremely low flows in dry years, and floating may not be possible north of Dillon. It's always smart to call a local source or to check water levels on the internet. (Check the USGS website for flows near Twin Bridges and Barrett's.)

The upper section of the Beaverhead offers the easiest access and the best fishing. Predictably, it receives the heaviest floating pressure, including many outfitters. In summer it isn't a place for solitude.

If fishing is secondary, however, the river between Dillon and Twin Bridges may be more to your liking, since it receives much less floating pressure. Access is limited but adequate. This is an excellent stretch for wildlife viewing. Expect to see white-tailed deer, great blue herons, beaver, and waterfowl. Sandhill cranes are common here, particularly at migration times. In spring these ungainly birds perform their unique courtship rituals in open meadows. Tundra swans can be another Beaverhead migratory treat, and great horned owls like the willow bottoms.

Floaters can camp near the actual campsites, numbering more than a dozen, that Lewis and Clark used on the Beaverhead. It's fun to read the journals and then try to locate the precise campsites. One historic spot you can try to find is a place Lewis and Clark named Three Thousand Mile Island. Located a few miles downstream from Anderson Lane Bridge, it's the place where the Corps of Discovery estimated they were exactly 3,000 miles from the mouth of the Missouri River.

Floaters on the Beaverhead south of Dillon must be able to negotiate sharp turns and maneuver down narrow channels, particularly above Pipe Organ Rock. The current is quite swift in the upper 20 miles of the river and frequently runs right into the brushy banks. This isn't a place for beginners in a raft or canoe. Low bridges also provide challenges, especially at higher flows. Beware of two low bridges between Barrett's and Dillon that can cause problems for rafts and drift boats.

Intermediate rafters and canoeists shouldn't have any trouble with the upper 20 miles of the river. Canoeists must be sure not to overload their boats on winding rivers like the Beaverhead. Three people in a canoe or too much gear can result in lost maneuverability, which translates into dangerous situations and possible upsets.

Floating gets easier north of Dillon. The river still meanders repeatedly, but the current isn't as swift. When the water is low, beginners can handle this part of the Beaverhead all the way to Twin Bridges. At low water, keep your eyes peeled for occasional barbed wire across the stream, as well as the occasional diversion dam.

Float fishing: Float fishing is extremely popular on the Beaverhead, as the deep runs and brushy banks make wading difficult. As a result the Beaverhead has adopted specific rules restricting nonresident and outfitter float fishing to minimize conflict of the resource (see river rules). According to biologists, some sections of the Beaverhead support one trout weighing 4 pounds or better for every 20 feet of bank. But before you rush off with your boat in tow, read a little more. The Beaverhead offers some of the most frustrating and expensive fishing imaginable. The roots and bushes that extend into the water act like a safety screen for the fish, and a magnet for flies and lures. Anyone with plans to fish the Beaverhead should have a full fly box, a fat wallet, and a cheerful disposition.

The fly box should contain a few venerable Girdle Bugs, one of the most successful creations for catching canny Beaverhead trout. Developed by a Dillon angler particularly for the Beaverhead, this strange fly looks like it might be more at home on a lazy, southern bass pond. Consisting of a black or brown chenille body with trembling rubber legs, it reputedly was originally tied with the materials from a woman's girdle.

The Beaverhead below Clark Canyon Reservoir is an extremely popular fishery; however, Interstate 15 does detract from the scenic beauty. ALEC UNDERWOOD

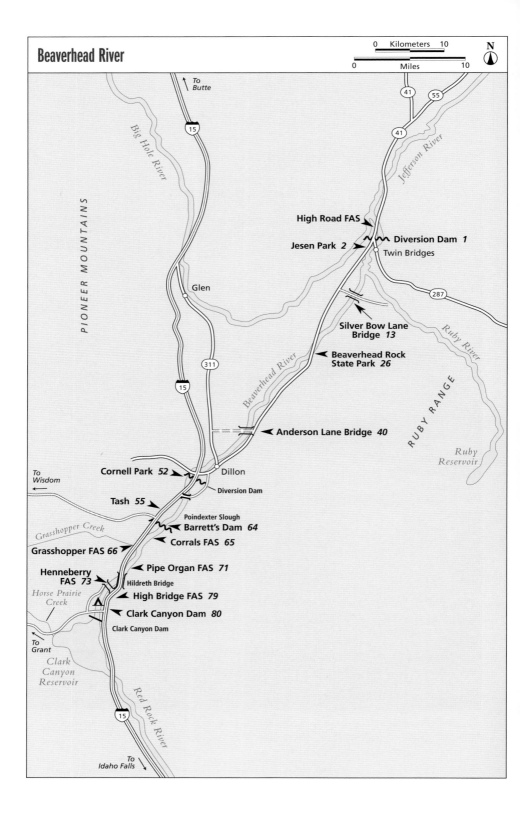

Beaverhead River

0 Kilometers 10
0 Miles 10

N

To Butte

Big Hole River

PIONEER MOUNTAINS

15

41

55

41

Jefferson River

High Road FAS

Jesen Park 2

Diversion Dam 1

Twin Bridges

Glen

287

Silver Bow Lane Bridge 13

Ruby River

311

Beaverhead River

Beaverhead Rock State Park 26

RUBY RANGE

Ruby Reservoir

15

Anderson Lane Bridge 40

To Wisdom

Cornell Park 52

Dillon

Diversion Dam

Tash 55

Poindexter Slough

Grasshopper Creek

Barrett's Dam 64

Corrals FAS 65

Grasshopper FAS 66

Pipe Organ FAS 71

Henneberry FAS 73

Hildreth Bridge

Horse Prairie Creek

High Bridge FAS 79

Clark Canyon Dam 80

Clark Canyon Dam

To Grant

Clark Canyon Reservoir

Red Rock River

15

To Idaho Falls

While some purists view this bundle of fuzz and rubber nymph with disdain, it does resemble a stonefly nymph, a long-legged insect that hatches on the Beaverhead in late summer. Knowledgeable locals also use a rig called a dropshot. Think two size 20 nymphs on 5x and a sinker on top. When in doubt, check in with the local fly shop. Anderson & Platt Outfitters know their stuff and they're even nice folks (406-683-2692)!

Key Access Points along the Beaverhead River

Access Point	Access Type	(River Mile)
Clark Canyon Dam	Ramp	(80)
High Bridge FAS	Hand Launch	(79)
Henneberry FAS	Ramp	(73)
Pipe Organ FAS	Ramp	(71)
Grasshopper FAS	Ramp	(66)
Corrals FAS	Walk-In	(65)
Barrett's Dam	Ramp	(64)
Tash Bridge	Hand Launch (55)	
Cornell Park	Ramp	(52)
Anderson Lane Bridge	Ramp	(40)
Beaverhead Rock Hwy 41 bridge	Ramp	(26)
Silver Bow Lane Bridge	Hand Launch	(13)
Jesen Park	Ramp	(2)

2 Big Hole River

Amber waters flowing over cobbled bottoms and through scenic valleys create one of Montana's most famous fishing rivers.

Vital statistics: 156 miles from Skinner Lake near Jackson to the Jefferson River.

Level of difficulty: Mostly Class I water except for the canyon between Wise River and Divide, which is Class II and even Class III at high flows. Swift flows, numerous snags, and obstructions make this river too difficult for beginners except between Wisdom and Wise River.

Flow: Annual mean flow: 1,121 cfs near Melrose. Upper sections may be unfloatable in August and early September in dry years. Flows of 250 cfs are minimum on the upper river. The lower sections below Melrose are floatable down to 300 cfs. Stay away if flows exceed 8,000 cfs.

Recommended watercraft: Suitable for all crafts at lower flows. Above 1,000 cfs, rafts and drift boats reign supreme.

Hazards: Fences, sharp bends, and overhanging branches in the upper river. Logjams and numerous channels in the last 25 miles of the lower river. Dangerous diversions at Divide and Pennington, especially at higher flows, can swamp a skiff.

Where the crowd goes: Divide to Melrose.

Avoiding the scene: Glen to the Big Hole's confluence with the Beaverhead.

Inside tip: Try fishing in late March or April—before runoff—to avoid crowds. Try birding from a raft or canoe between Wisdom and Wise River during spring migration. Take note of non-outfitting float sections to avoid the hordes.

Maps: BLM: #23 (Wisdom), #24 (Salmon), #33 (Butte South), #34 (Dillon); USFS: Beaverhead Interagency Travel Plan (East and West); USGS: Dillon, MT; Montana Afloat: #8 (Big Hole River).

Shuttle information: Sunrise Fly Shop, Melrose, (406) 835-3474.

River rules: No motors allowed. Complex fishing and floating regulations. Many sections restrict the number of outfitted boats in any given reach. In particular, FWP rules state: "Starting on the third Saturday in May through Labor Day, recreational use of the Big Hole River from its headwaters to Notch Bottom fishing access site shall be allowed and restricted by defining eight river zones with one zone closed to float outfitting each day and with the zone that is restricted on Saturday and the zone that is restricted on Sunday also closed to nonresident float fishing." Check with FWP for specific regulations.

For more information: FWP, Bozeman; Four Rivers Fishing Company, Twin Bridges; Sunrise Fly Shop, Melrose, (406) 835-3474; Big Hole Lodge, Wise River.

The Paddling

Perhaps nobody explained their time on the Big Hole better than local author Jim Harrison, who wrote, "I hope to define my life, whatever is left, by migrations, south and north with the birds and far from the metallic fever of clocks, the self staring at the clock saying, 'I must do this.' I can't tell the time on the tongue of the river in the cool morning air, the smell of the ferment of greenery, the dust off the canyon's rock walls, the swallows swooping above the scent of raw water."

Between Divide and Melrose, the Big Hole's canyon section is a popular full-day floating option.
MATT SCHMIDT

The Big Hole received its name from early trappers, who called all valleys "holes." Since this one was substantial, it earned the name Big Hole. The valley has had many other names. The Shoshone Indians called it Ground Squirrel Valley. Lewis and Clark labeled it Hot Springs Valley, due to nearby thermal features.

Few Montana rivers have as many enthusiastic devotees as the Big Hole. This delightful river has a cult of followers that make Reverend Moon's disciples look downright apathetic. George Grant, lifelong Butte resident and ardent conservationist, was the undesignated leader of this contingent. He fished the river from the 1920s until his one-hundredth birthday in 2006 (sadly he passed away in 2008). A dedicated river rat, Grant allegedly spent more time on the Big Hole than any other person. Grant once wrote, "In the nine great trout states of the western United States, it would be difficult to find a single stream that exceeds the overall quality of the Big Hole River. It must be classified as a big river, but it is certainly not as large or impersonal as the Yellowstone or Missouri, nor as barren-banked and monotonous as the famous Madison. The Big Hole rises at high altitude and flows clear and cold through wide valleys and narrow canyons, seldom presenting similar water or scenery throughout its entire 150 fascinating miles."

Adventuresome floaters can start as high in the Big Hole drainage as Jackson, where the river is small and sinuous with many channels and obstacles. Barbed-wire fences are common, and sharp bends into overhanging branches are the rule. At high water it's a challenge to stay out of the bushes; at low water it's a challenge to stay off the bottom. Nevertheless, the section from Jackson to Wisdom is isolated, interesting, and navigable by intermediates in canoes or kayaks. It's mighty small for rafts larger than 12 feet. The journals of Lewis and Clark mention the Big Hole and the Corps'

Near Wise River, the upper Big Hole River is a popular weekend destination with numerous camping options. MATT SCHMIDT

difficulty in navigating by boat in low water. On Saturday, August 3, 1805, the journal reads, "The men were so much fortiegued today that they wished much that navigation was at an end that they might go by land." Like the Corps of Discovery, we've all been there. Be sure to check the flows of the upper river before launching.

A Big Hole tributary that merits exploration (for those who don't mind carrying their boats occasionally) is the North Fork of the Big Hole in the vicinity of the Big Hole Battlefield. Best explored in a canoe or smaller craft, the river snakes through a maze of willow thickets and beaver ponds. It's not hazardous except during peak flows. At normal flows there are no rapids, just an unrelenting current that always cuts into the bank and under the bushes. From year to year, there may be beaver dams to ford. During spring and fall migration periods, ducks, geese, sandhill cranes, and all kinds of interesting songbirds use this rich habitat. It's also a great place to see moose.

About 10 miles north of Wisdom, the main stem river changes from a braided, winding stream to a broad, flat river. From here to the town of Wise River, the Big Hole flows peaceably and presents few obstacles. This scenic section flows through high-altitude meadows where colorful wildflowers dot the landscape. The sky-scraping peaks of the Anaconda-Pintler Wilderness complete the scene. This is a good section for beginners in canoes or rafts, as it has easy access and few hazards. The upper river has some good fishing and rarely gets discolored, even during runoff.

This section of the river supports not only brook and rainbow trout but also the occasional grayling. The upper Big Hole is virtually the only large river in the Lower 48 where grayling can still be caught with regularity. The native stream-dwelling grayling has been petitioned for listing as an endangered species and must be released if caught. Handle them quickly and carefully to ensure a successful release. These beautiful fish, with their large dorsal fin and delicate black spots, are truly spectacular.

Because the river between Wisdom and Wise River is wide and shallow, it can experience high water temperatures in summer. While fishing may tail off, rafting and swimming come into their own, making this an ideal spot for a family float.

Below Wise River, the Big Hole increases in velocity and gets narrower as it approaches Divide. In the canyon between Wise River and Divide, there are some large waves and moderate rapids. Intermediates can handle this section, although open canoes may get swamped by high waves at peak flows. The most difficult water can be scouted from the highway. Watch carefully for the diversion dam at the Big Hole Pumping Station about 0.5 mile above the highway bridge before Divide. If you're looking to avoid this hazard completely, make sure to take out at Powerhouse FAS. Although it was recently renovated in 2010, at high flows this diversion can still be quite dangerous. During high water, FWP recommends to float through the center of the diversion dam. Portaging is possible on the south side of the river, but no easy route exists.

The most heavily floated section of the Big Hole lies between Divide and Glen. It's a beautiful, isolated canyon where bighorn sheep graze along rocky outcroppings and golden eagles soar on the thermals. Unofficial estimates run as high as 150 floaters per day during peak periods. Unquestionably, the peak of the high-use period occurs when the salmon fly hatch starts in mid-June. When these large insects hatch, big trout become less wary and can be taken more readily on dry flies. This hatch is one of the state's most poorly kept secrets, however, and outfitters from all over haul their dudes in to get a piece of the action. The canyon section between Divide and Melrose can be too rough for even intermediate canoeists at high or medium flows. Intermediates in rafts and riverboats do fine, despite occasional downed trees and logjams. Melrose to Glen is easier, although it still has plenty of snags. Beginners in rafts or canoes can handle Melrose to Glen at low flows, but watch out for those logjams!

From Glen to the Big Hole's confluence with the Beaverhead, floating pressure is lighter and access is more difficult. The river meanders through thick cottonwood bottoms, changing its course from year to year. While it doesn't have many rapids, the river braids and winds and has some troublesome logjams and fallen trees. It's a little too much for beginner canoeists or rafters. Fishing remains good, particularly for brown trout. The lower part of the river is an excellent spot to see mink and river otters. Glen to Notch Bottom is an excellent option to avoid the crowds and still have great fishing.

As popular and delightful as the Big Hole may be, it has problems. Dewatering of the river is the Big Hole's most serious issue, as farmers and ranchers compete with fish and wildlife for water. In recent years FWP has closed the river to fishing during a portion of the summer because of severe drought conditions, and might do so in the future under similar conditions. Floaters and anglers should voluntarily limit use during these times of drought.

Montana has no state law that guarantees minimum stream flows. Depleted river flows not only have the obvious impact of less water in the river, they also cause

Big Hole River

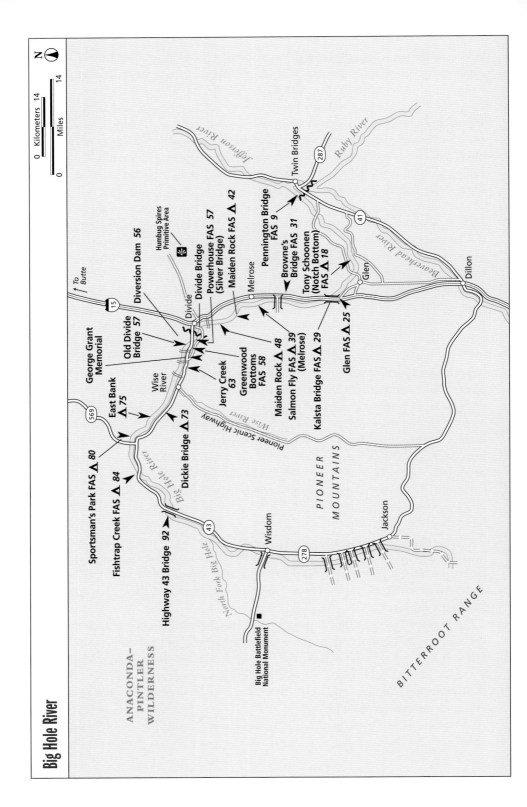

ANACONDA–
PINTLER
WILDERNESS

Sportsman's Park FAS ▲ 80

Fishtrap Creek FAS ▲ 84

Highway 43 Bridge 92

George Grant Memorial

Old Divide Bridge 57

East Bank ▲ 75

Wise River

Dickie Bridge ▲ 73

Diversion Dam 56

Divide Bridge

Powerhouse FAS 57

Maiden Rock FAS ▲ 42

Divide

Jerry Creek 63

Greenwood Bottoms FAS 58

Maiden Rock ▲ 48

Salmon Fly FAS ▲ 39 (Melrose)

Kalsta Bridge FAS ▲ 29

Pioneer Scenic Highway

Melrose

Pennington Bridge FAS 9

Browne's Bridge FAS 31

Tony Schoonen (Notch Bottom) FAS ▲ 18

Glen FAS ▲ 25

Glen

Humbug Spires Primitive Area

To Butte

15

569

North Fork Big Hole

Big Hole River

Wise River

Wisdom

Jackson

43

278

Big Hole Battlefield National Monument

PIONEER MOUNTAINS

BITTERROOT RANGE

Jefferson River

Jefferson River

Twin Bridges

Ruby River

287

41

Beaverhead River

Dillon

0 Kilometers 14

0 Miles 14

N

higher water temperatures and less dissolved oxygen in the stream. Montana sorely needs adequate in-stream water reservations to protect its rivers. The Big Hole River Foundation is a watchdog group looking out for the river. If you want to help, the foundation's address is in appendix B.

Float fishing: Because of the intensive fishing pressure, FWP has designed special fishing regulations geared toward protecting trophy trout. Although FWP has designated specific days for residents, nonresidents, and outfitters to float and fish, the problem is somewhat self-regulating: When the crowds get too thick, those who want solitude go elsewhere, knowing that in a few weeks fishing pressure will decrease.

Because many Big Hole anglers fish on foot, floaters need to be courteous and considerate to wade anglers. Keep as far away from anglers as you can, and go behind them when possible.

Biologists estimate that below Glen the river hosts a wild brown trout population maximum of about 2,000 fish per mile. As you move upriver, brown trout populations decrease but size increases. It's just the opposite for rainbows. In the lower reaches they're scarce, but they increase to a maximum of 2,000 per mile as you move upriver. While the trout may not always bite, the Big Hole mosquitoes are pretty dependable, especially in June and July. Take some repellent and wear long sleeves. If you're looking for big browns, try throwing tan or yellow streamers or dead drifting wooly buggers during high water and just off the bank.

Key Access Points along the Big Hole River

Access Point	Access Type	(River Mile)
Highway 43 bridge	Hand Launch	(92)
Fishtrap Creek FAS	Ramp	(84)
Sportsman's Park FAS	Ramp	(80)
East Bank	Ramp	(75)
Dickie Bridge	Ramp	(73)
Jerry Creek	Ramp	(63)
George Grant Memorial FAS	Ramp	(59)
Greenwood Bottoms FAS	Walk-In	(58)
Old Divide Bridge	Ramp	(57)
Powerhouse FAS	Ramp	(57)
Maiden Rock	Ramp	(48)
Maiden Rock FAS	Walk-In	(42)
Salmon Fly FAS	Ramp	(39)
Browne's Bridge FAS	Ramp	(31)
Kalsta Bridge FAS	Walk-In	(29)
Glen FAS	Ramp	(25)
Tony Schoonen FAS	Ramp	(18)
Pennington Bridge	Ramp	(9)

3 Bighorn River

An oasis of green slicing through parched land, the Bighorn rushes past scenic bluffs and thick cottonwood bottoms, providing anglers with some of Montana's most legendary tailwater trout fishing.

Vital statistics: 84 miles from Yellowtail Dam to its juncture with the Yellowstone River near Custer.

Level of difficulty: Class I, suitable for practiced beginners.

Flow: Annual mean flow: 3,482 cfs near St. Xavier. Dam-controlled, floatable all year. Can have excellent conditions in May and June when other rivers are high with runoff. Optimal flows for fishing are 3,500 to 4,000 cfs.

Recommended watercraft: Drift boats and canoes. When the wind picks up, you'll want to make sure you can make it to your take-out.

Hazards: Snags and occasional logjams, swift flows in the upper section. Sudden high winds associated with storms. Three diversion dams (portage necessary). Erratic flows because of Yellowtail Dam releases.

Where the crowd goes: Afterbay to Bighorn.

Avoiding the scene: Downstream from Hardin.

Inside tip: Good fishing on warm winter days and in early spring. One of Montana's warmest areas.

Maps: BLM: #79 (Hysham), #80 (Hardin), #81 (Lodge Grass); USGS: Billings, MT; Hardin, MT; Forsyth, MT; Montana Afloat: #14 (The Bighorn River).

Shuttle information: Bighorn Fly & Tackle Shop, Fort Smith, (406) 666-2375.

River rules: No motorboats from Afterbay to Bighorn. A National Park Service per-vehicle user fee or annual fee is required for floating between Afterbay and Bighorn. Permits can be purchased from automated fee machines and iron "ranger boxes" located at the south and north entrances to Bighorn Canyon.

For more information: Bighorn Fly & Tackle Shop, Fort Smith; Bighorn Angler, Fort Smith; Quill Gordon Fly Fishers, Sheridan; FWP, Billings; National Park Service, Fort Smith; BOR, Billings.

The Paddling

Steeped in history and shrouded in controversy, the magnificent Bighorn River springs from the glaciers of the Wind River Range in western Wyoming. It was long famed the best river in the United States for trout fishing; however, recently, because of unusually high flows out of the dam, fish numbers have plummeted. With tributaries including the Wind, Shoshone, and Little Bighorn Rivers, this is a big river, nearly as large as the Yellowstone when the two merge near Custer.

As the Bighorn flows from Wyoming into Montana, it carves a rugged and scenic canyon that extends for nearly 50 miles. This great chasm winds and twists through the mountains along a tortuous course, its limestone and sandstone cliffs exuding the same brilliant colors and hues as the Grand Canyon of the Yellowstone in Yellowstone National Park.

Before the days of rock riprap, junked cars were used to stablize banks along the Bighorn.
Scott Heywood

According to a 1932 newspaper account, the Bighorn Canyon once contained formidable rapids: "This river is one of the most dangerous in America to traverse. Many have lost their lives in attempts to go down the rapids, while a few others succeeded in accomplishing the feat." Famous mountain man Jim Bridger claimed he shot the Bighorn Canyon on a raft made of driftwood logs. Bridger, however, was known to stretch the truth. He also said the rivers in Yellowstone Park steamed because they flowed so fast they got the river bottom hot.

Yellowtail Dam transformed the treacherous Bighorn Canyon into a flatwater paddle. The 525-foot-high dam, completed in 1967, backs up 71 miles of river. While a canoe paddle through the canyon remains extremely scenic, the area is used primarily by powerboaters and water-skiers.

Jim Bridger was only one of the dozens of mountain men who trudged up the Bighorn on their way to outstanding fur-producing areas along the Wind and Green Rivers. This river valley is alive with Montana history. While Lewis and Clark did not explore the Bighorn, it's obvious from Captain Clark's journals that the Corps of Discovery knew the approximate length of the Bighorn and some of its tributaries. The river was named for its healthy population of bighorn sheep in the canyon area.

Construction of Yellowtail Dam changed the entire character of the Bighorn River in Montana. The river once carried a heavy silt load to the Yellowstone. Now the dam traps the dirt. Below the dam the Bighorn winds through arid benchlands and thick cottonwood groves. The river is an oasis in the middle of a parched land, a belt of green that attracts many species of wildlife, including deer, beaver, and songbirds. Migrating waterfowl flock to the Bighorn.

The combination of less sediment and regular flows means the river no longer braids or creates islands. In fact, about 1,500 acres of islands have disappeared since 1967, a 50 percent decrease. While this habitat loss is especially significant to beaver, muskrat, and geese, other native wildlife associated with the river have also suffered.

On the other hand, the combination of less sediment and cold flows from the reservoir has created an outstanding trout fishery. The river is not only rich in vegetation, but it squirms with aquatic life, including freshwater shrimp and caddis fly larvae. The river flows through limestone country, and the water is quite mineralized and rich in nutrients, which makes for excellent insect life. Such a favorable climate creates extraordinary growing conditions for trout. For instance, a 7-inch Bighorn River rainbow trout can grow to 14 inches in a year, about three times the normal growth rate. A fingerling brown trout can grow to 16 inches in 3 years. Only the Beaverhead can match the Bighorn for productivity.

Float fishing: The Bighorn's reputation rests on its abundance of trout and their exceptional size. The record Bighorn trout is a 29-inch, 16-pound rainbow. Although few trout exceed 21 inches, the average trout is 8–15 inches. Since 2017, high water discharges from the Yellowtail Dam have reportedly impacted spawning success in the river and fish numbers have plummeted. Angler pressure is also an issue on the Bighorn as the river can be choked with drift boats. The good news is a collaborative effort is underway to explore flow regimes that will better sustain the fishery long-term.

During the peak periods of July, August, and September, the popular sections of the river may see well over one hundred boats a day. Fortunately, this river has good fishing almost all year, so it is possible to avoid the crowds if you are willing to brave inclement weather. A National Park Service per-vehicle user fee is required for floaters between Afterbay and Bighorn. Purchase permits at Quill Gordon Fly Fishers in Sheridan or at the National Park Service Afterbay access. No permits are required for those boating downstream from Bighorn.

Summertime moss and algae buildups can frustrate anglers—especially those with spinning gear. But the copious amounts of river vegetation attract wildlife, and the bird life along the Bighorn can be spectacular. Shorebirds pass through this drainage in large numbers, and the river sees heavy waterfowl use during migration. Up to 20,000 mallards winter on the river, and these ducks attract raptors like bald eagles and, occasionally, peregrine falcons. Afterbay is a favorite winter and spring spot for serious bird-watchers.

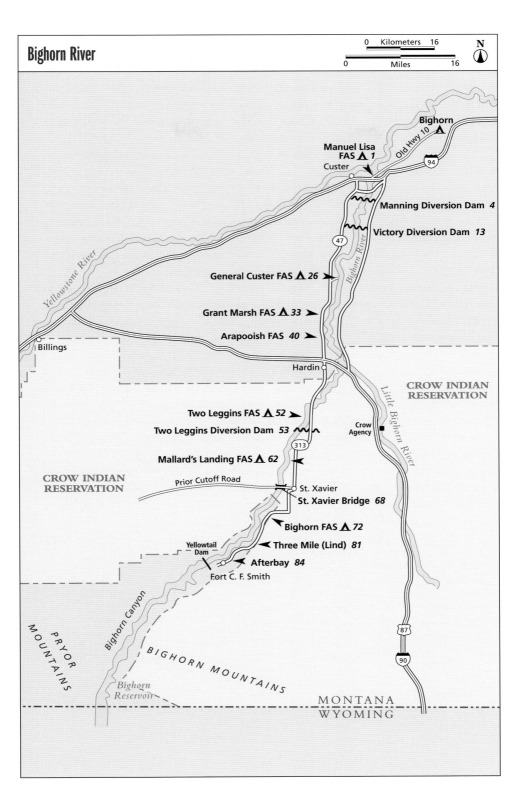

Bighorn River

0   Kilometers   16
0   Miles   16

N

Bighorn ▲

Old Hwy 10

Manuel Lisa
FAS ▲ 1

Custer

94

Manning Diversion Dam 4

Victory Diversion Dam 13

47

Bighorn River

General Custer FAS ▲ 26 ➤

Grant Marsh FAS ▲ 33 ➤

Arapooish FAS 40 ➤

Billings

Hardin

CROW INDIAN
RESERVATION

Little Bighorn River

Yellowstone River

Two Leggins FAS ▲ 52 ➤

Two Leggins Diversion Dam 53 ∿∿∿

Crow
Agency

313

Mallard's Landing FAS ▲ 62 ◄

CROW INDIAN
RESERVATION

Prior Cutoff Road

St. Xavier

St. Xavier Bridge 68

Bighorn FAS ▲ 72

Yellowtail
Dam

Three Mile (Lind) 81 ◄

Afterbay 84 ◄

Fort C. F. Smith

Bighorn Canyon

PRYOR
MOUNTAINS

BIGHORN MOUNTAINS

Bighorn
Reservoir

87

90

MONTANA
WYOMING

The upper 44 miles of the river in Montana flow through the Crow Indian Reservation. Recreational use of this portion of the Bighorn, particularly for fishing and hunting, has been a controversial topic for several decades. In 1976 the Crow Tribe declared the river off-limits to non–tribal members. This initiated a legal debate that was resolved by a 1978 Supreme Court decision that ruled the riverbed belongs to the State of Montana, not the Crow Tribe.

The state reopened the section of the Bighorn that flows through the reservation to public fishing in 1981. Be aware that on the reservation, recreational use is only permissible below the high-water mark. Hunting big game is not allowed by non–tribal members and upland bird and waterfowl hunting require special tribal licenses.

Access to the Bighorn is limited but adequate. Most floating occurs immediately below the dam in the 12-mile section between Afterbay and the Bighorn access. While the trout habitat between Bighorn and Mallard's Landing isn't as good, the fishing pressure is considerably lower and the fishing still excellent.

For flies, think small. When it's happening on top, look for PMD cripples, sparkle duns, tricos, and If you're lucky, caddis. And these fish are smart, so bring your light tippet material. When the bugs aren't flying, you will be relegated to dunking San Juan worms and midges.

Below Hardin it is a warmwater fishery with limited populations of sauger, channel catfish, burbot, and smallmouth bass. This section also has good waterfowl concentrations and receives some hunting pressure. The Crow Reservation stops at Hardin. Floating pressure below Hardin is light. Access can be difficult, however, as the river flows mostly through private land.

Floaters use all kinds of crafts on the Bighorn, including motorboats and jet boats (no motors allowed above the Bighorn access). Practiced beginners can handle the Bighorn. The main channel splits occasionally, and snags in the river can cause problems for the unwary. High winds can be a problem too. Watch for the low diversion dam on the downstream side of the old Two Leggins Bridge. Below Hardin, watch for the Victory and Manning diversion dams.

Key Access Points along the Bighorn River

Access Point	Access Type	(River Mile)
Afterbay	Ramp	(84)
Three Mile	Ramp	(81)
Bighorn FAS	Ramp	(72)
St. Xavier Bridge	Hand Launch	(68)
Mallard's Landing FAS	Ramp	(62)
Two Leggins FAS	Ramp	(52)
Arapooish FAS	Ramp	(40)
Grant Marsh FAS	Ramp	(33)
General Custer FAS	Ramp	(26)
Manuel Lisa FAS	Ramp	(1)

4 Bitterroot River

You might as well expect rivers to run backwards as any man born free to be contented penned up.

—Chief Joseph of the Nez Perce Tribe

With a wide floodplain, the Bitterroot flows over graveled bottoms and through cottonwood bottoms in a picturesque valley. Excellent access and a productive fishery make the Bitterroot a favorite among anglers.

Vital statistics: 80 miles from Conner to its confluence with the Clark Fork River near Missoula.

Level of difficulty: All Class I, but swift water, frequent logjams, and occasional snags above Stevensville require intermediate skills. Beginners can try below Stevensville, but avoid high flows and be aware of diversion dams.

Flow: Annual mean flow: 876 cfs near Darby. May get too low in exceptionally dry years, especially between Corvallis and Stevensville. Minimum flow is 175 cfs (Darby gauge). Stay home when the river is above 2,200 cfs at Darby.

Recommended watercraft: Stick to rafts and drift boats until the flows drop below 1,000 cfs.

Hazards: Logjams and snags, narrow channels, and sharp bends. Five diversion dams (miles 65, 60, 54, 45, 44).

Where the crowd goes: The Bitterroot sees heavy use from Darby to Missoula, especially midsummer when fishing guides and clients flock to the stream.

Avoiding the scene: Difficult to do in summer. Florence to Lolo has slightly less pressure because it is a long float and a logistically challenging shuttle. Launch early during summer to beat the guide hatch.

Inside tip: Nothing is more spectacular than a Bitterroot float trip with the leaves in full color—usually the first week of October.

Maps: USFS: Bitterroot; USGS: Hamilton, MT; Elk City, MT; Montana Afloat: #1 (The Bitterroot River); River Rat: Bitterroot.

Shuttle information: Angler's Roost, Hamilton, (406) 363-1268; Four Rivers Shuttle, Missoula, (406) 370-5845; Marty's Shuttle Service, Darby, (406) 274-6331.

River rules: Motors allowed only from May 1 to June 30 between Florence Bridge and the confluence with the Clark Fork at Kelly Island, and from October 1 to January 31 (15 horsepower or less) on the entire river. Complex fishing regulations—check with FWP.

For more information: Grizzly Hackle, Missoula; Missoulian Angler, Missoula; FWP, Missoula.

The Paddling

When famous mountain man Old Bill Williams found a river that pleased him, he would exclaim, "Thar my stick floats!" For many denizens of Missoula and Hamilton, their stick floats in the Bitterroot, an occasionally battered but still beautiful river. Even though this stream sometimes flows near civilization, it is an excellent spot for a daylong or multiday float trip.

Lined with cottonwoods and flanked to the west by the towering Bitterroot Mountains, the Bitterroot River's scenery is hard to beat.

Early trappers and explorers frequently spoke of the Bitterroot's beauty. The description Captain Lewis wrote in 1805 still works well: "It is a handsome stream about 100 yards wide and affords a considerable quantity of very clear water, the banks are low, and it's bed entirely gravel." The Corps first called the river the Flathead, then soon after Lewis dubbed the Bitterroot "Clark's River" to honor his esteemed co-leader. Some years later, the river reverted back to the Salish name that meant "place of the Bitterroot."

The proximity of the mountains makes Bitterroot River trips especially scenic. The saw-toothed Bitterroots flank the river on the west, while the more rolling and open Sapphires dominate the eastern horizon. The grass-covered Sapphires frequently glow spectacularly as the sun slides below the peaks of the Bitterroots.

Although the Bitterroot retains its clear and impressive vistas, civilization's heavy hand is often evident. Extensive riprapping done by the Northern Pacific Railway in the 1960s, using both crushed rock and car bodies, created eyesores. Thankfully, many landowners along the river have opted for natural erosion resistance techniques and most houses are located above the river's floodplain.

Irrigation places heavy demands on the Bitterroot's finite water supply. In dry years fish and wildlife suffer, and floating may not be possible or fishing may be closed because of high water temperatures. The problem is most acute near Victor, where the river branches into several small channels. State purchase of water from Painted Rocks Reservoir has helped alleviate this issue.

Despite its problems, the Bitterroot retains good wildlife populations. Deer, elk, mink, and muskrat are common, as are dippers and spotted sandpipers, which scurry along the shores. Canada geese nest in secluded areas and on islands, and beaver can be observed along most of the river. Great blue heron rookeries occur in several areas where the river winds away from civilization. During migration, waterfowl and migrating shorebirds such as the elusive avocet take advantage of the rich bug life. Near Stevensville the river flanks the Lee Metcalf National Wildlife Refuge for several miles.

The Bitterroot is a great place for the unusual. Once we spotted a yellow-bellied marmot sunning itself in a tree. Another time a young bull moose waded across the river in front of our canoe. Elk sometimes sneak down to the river bottom as well.

The Bitterroot can be floated for its entire distance, and intermediates can navigate its two forks if they can avoid logjams and maneuver through fast water. Most floaters start below the Highway 93 bridge between Conner and Darby at Hannon Memorial FAS. This upper section of the river generally has less development than below Hamilton. A catch-and-release fishing section between Darby and Como Bridge and Tucker Crossing to Florence Bridge receive heavy summertime float-fishing pressure from outfitters.

The Bitterroot upstream from Hamilton has more sharp bends, logjams, and fast water than the water downstream. It's all Class I water, but it's not the place for a maiden voyage. Logjams can be lethal, especially at high flows. Watch carefully for diversion dams between Darby and Hamilton. The Sleeping Child diversion (about 5 miles south of Hamilton) drops 20 feet and can be run during higher flows in rafts, but otherwise should be portaged.

Downstream from Hamilton the river gets progressively easier. River channels change remarkably from year to year, however, and new, dangerous logjams create hazards. Below Stevensville beginners can handle the Bitterroot if they watch out for snags and sharp turns. Logjams can often block entire channels and force floaters down narrow obstacle courses. Cutting wood out of the river, however, is illegal unless approved by the local conservation district.

While it's too late to preserve all the Bitterroot's natural attributes, some areas remain secluded and lightly developed. Large agricultural landowners who have refused to subdivide their land deserve the credit. It is remarkable and commendable that a large segment of the river close to Missoula—the stretch between Florence and Lolo—remains much as Lewis and Clark saw it. The explorers camped twice at a spot near where Lolo Creek meets the Bitterroot. In their journals they called it "Traveler's Rest." When traveling west to the Pacific, the Corps of Discovery used this campsite to make preparations for crossing the mountains. When returning east, Lewis and Clark camped here in preparation for splitting up and taking separate routes across Montana before meeting up at the juncture of the Yellowstone and Missouri Rivers.

The Bitterroot's proximity to Missoula and Hamilton makes it an extraordinary recreational and aesthetic resource. Private landowners need better incentives—conservation easements or perhaps even tax credits—for refraining from subdividing land with high public values. Significant parts of the Bitterroot River corridor deserve protection.

Float fishing: Fall may be the best time for fishing the Bitterroot. The streamside vegetation comes alive with color, water temps are cooler, and fish are feeding in preparation for winter. Since most ranchers stop irrigating about this time, flows level off and bug hatches are prolific. Those seeking an extended trip might want to take 5 or 6 days and float the river's entire 80-mile length. Dry-fly fishing seems to reach its peak about the same time the colors of the leaves achieve their most brilliant shade (usually the first week or two in October). It's possible to find public land for camping along most of the river, including below the high-water mark, but check maps to avoid private land. If camping within the river's high-water mark, do not camp within sight of occupied residences. Anglers from across the West descend on the Bitterroot in mid-March for the often-fabled skwala hatch. The Bitterroot is a dependable dry-fly river, and the mayfly hatches are unmatched.

Although the Bitterroot River remains a popular floating river, evening floats offer plenty of solitude.

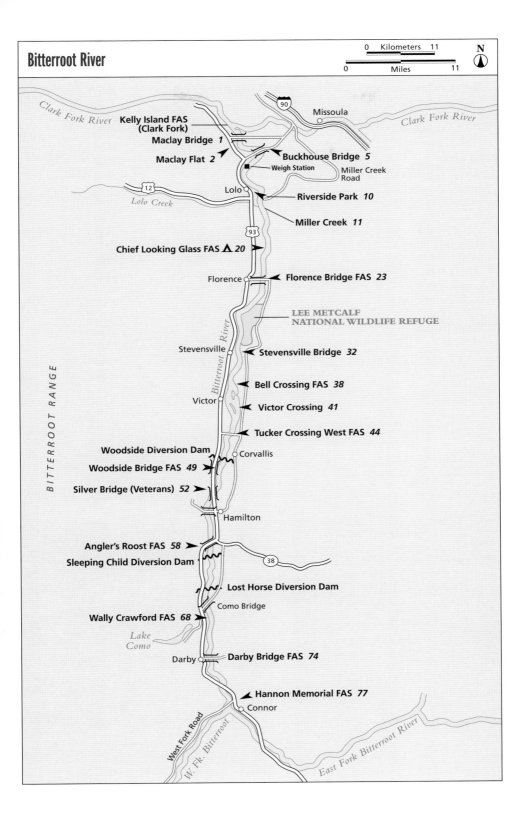

Key Access Points along the Bitterroot River

Access Point	Access Type	(River Mile)
Hannon Memorial FAS	Ramp	(77)
Darby Bridge FAS	Ramp	(74)
Wally Crawford FAS	Ramp	(68)
Angler's Roost Bridge	Ramp	(58)
Silver Bridge	Ramp	(52)
Woodside Bridge FAS	Ramp	(49)
Tucker Crossing West FAS	Ramp	(44)
Victor Crossing	Hand Launch	(41)
Bell Crossing FAS	Ramp	(38)
Stevensville Bridge	Ramp	(32)
Florence Bridge FAS	Ramp	(23)
Chief Looking Glass FAS	Walk-In	(20)
Miller Creek	Ramp	(11)
Riverside Park	Walk-In	(10)
Buckhouse Bridge	Walk-In	(5)
Maclay Flat	Walk-In	(2)
Maclay Bridge	Walk-In	(1)

5 Bitterroot River, West Fork

The West Fork is one of western Montana's few tailwater streams. Originating deep in the Bitterroot Mountains at Painted Rocks Reservoir, the West Fork flows over 20 miles of breathtaking scenery and crystal-clear pools before its confluence with the East Fork near Conner. The West Fork is similar in scenery to Rock Creek and shares many of its features: crystal-clear waters, stunning scenery, and an incredibly productive fishery. What it doesn't share is Rock Creek's dusty, teeth-chattering road thanks to a paved strip up to Painted Rocks Reservoir.

Vital statistics: 21.5 miles from Painted Rocks Reservoir to the confluence of the East Fork of the Bitterroot.

Level of difficulty: Class II for its entirety except for a couple of tricky Class III boulder gardens at higher flows. Expert canoeists only.

Flow: Annual mean flow: 200 cfs near Conner. Flows are consistent, but dependent upon water coming out of Painted Rocks Reservoir. Check the gauge before you float. Do not float when gauge reads below 250.

Recommended watercraft: Rafts.

Hazards: Numerous logjams, sharp turns, and narrow channels. Experienced paddlers only. Hazards are rarely signed, so be aware and cautious.

Where the crowd goes: Applebury to Job Corps; plenty of wade anglers throughout.

Avoiding the scene: Job Corps to Hannon Memorial on the main Bitterroot.

Inside tip: Fantastic stream for an overnight float with plenty of sandbars and swimming holes.

Maps: USFS: Bitterroot South; USGS: Burnt Ridge.

Shuttle information: Marty's Shuttle Service, Darby, (406) 274-6331.

River rules: Most of the West Fork is managed by the Forest Service. They maintain the numerous fishing access points along the upper stream. Due to the increase in float traffic in recent years, FWP has adopted a regime to reduce outfitting pressure. Each section of the stream has a designated noncommercial float day. July 1–September 15 closed to floating from Painted Rocks Dam to Applebury. Check with FWP or signage at put-ins for more information.

For more information: Bitterroot Fly Company, Darby; Missoulian Angler, Missoula; FWP, Missoula.

The Paddling

The West Fork is quickly becoming one of western Montana's most popular mountain streams. Historically this river saw little floating use due to inconsistent flows; however, recently flows out of Painted Rocks Reservoir have become much more consistent, allowing floaters an opportunity to paddle this secluded mountain stream without too much trouble.

In September 1805, the Lewis and Clark Expedition passed by the West Fork and mistakenly named it the "West Fork of Clark's River." The expedition camped near the confluence of the East and West Forks and remarked, "the greater Part of the Day

Flows are extremely variable in the West Fork and floaters should be prepared for log jams and tight rock gardens.

dark & Drisley we proceedd on down the river thro a Vallie passed Several Small Runs on the right & 3 creeks on the left The Vallie from 1 to 2 miles wide the Snow top mountains to our left, open hilley Countrey on the right."

The West Fork Road is popular among motorists and is paved all the way to Painted Rocks Reservoir where there is good camping. There are also several Forest Service campgrounds dotted along the creek and they are very popular in the summer months. For those up for some exploring, the Nez Perce Road continues for some 50 miles up Nez Perce Pass to the Idaho border and then flanks the Frank Church River of No Return Wilderness to the south and the Selway-Bitterroot Wilderness to the north, finally reaching Paradise Ranger Station along the Selway River. Alternatively, drive south past Painted Rocks and check out the undeveloped Horse Creek Hot Springs on your way over the mountains toward the Salmon River.

Floaters can begin floating just downstream of Painted Rocks Reservoir via an unmarked access road that darts down to the river at a school bus pullout. This section, downstream to the confluence of Nez Perce Creek, is beautiful, but floaters need to be aware that before Nez Perce Creek joins some 6 miles below, the uppermost section is only floatable when at least 300 cfs is spilling from the dam. The colorful lichens attached to the rocks in this section provide the namesake for the reservoir

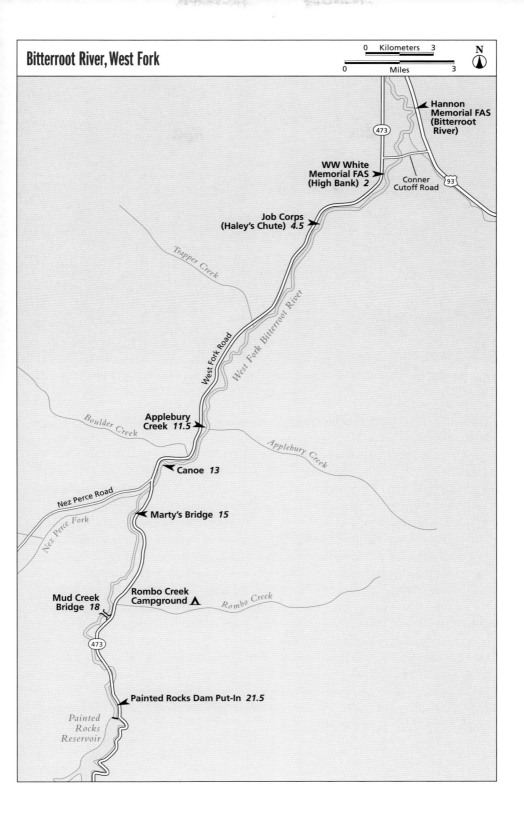

Bitterroot River, West Fork

0 Kilometers 3
0 Miles 3

N

Hannon Memorial FAS (Bitterroot River)

473

WW White Memorial FAS (High Bank) *2*

Conner Cutoff Road

93

Job Corps (Haley's Chute) *4.5*

Trapper Creek

West Fork Road

West Fork Bitterroot River

Boulder Creek

Applebury Creek *11.5*

Applebury Creek

Canoe *13*

Nez Perce Road

Nez Perce Fork

Marty's Bridge *15*

Mud Creek Bridge *18*

Rombo Creek Campground ⋀

Rombo Creek

473

Painted Rocks Dam Put-In *21.5*

Painted Rocks Reservoir

Boat access on the West Fork is quite good. Preparing to end a summer's day of floating near Job Corps.

upstream, built in 1939. Beware of tight corners, logjams, and sweepers. Above 1,000 cfs, this stream is extremely dangerous as new logjams can appear overnight and a low bridge on the upper river is a concern.

Below Nez Perce the character of the stream remains much the same as when early trappers explored this region 150 years ago. For the most part the stream is not visible from the road, and floaters can enjoy a somewhat solitary float, although floating traffic has significantly increased in recent years. The Forest Service maintains good access points throughout, and launching a raft is no problem at any of the several concrete ramps that have been installed. The Forest Service and FWP continue to monitor use to determine if their recreation rule is reducing the number of boats on the river. Many outfitters float the West Fork when the Bitterroot is too busy or when water temperatures make fishing challenging. While reducing commercial use is a difficult decision, it may help curb overuse and protect this valuable resource.

A tricky rock garden begins near Boulder Creek, and floaters should stay river left when approaching the private bridge that crosses the river. Drift boats are a no-go here unless you're willing to give your boat a serious beating. Only experienced canoeists should float the West Fork. Below Job Corps the river is somewhat more straightforward, and at lower flows intermediate canoeists should be able to navigate the tricky eddy lines and logjams.

Float fishing: The vast majority of boat traffic on the West Fork is fishing related. A number of outfitters guide clients on this stream, and anglers from Missoula don't think twice about running down the Bitterroot to fish the West Fork when flows allow. It's no mystery what draws the crowds to this stream: prolific bug hatches. Salmon flies begin hatching in early June, followed by golden stoneflies and then often a blanket spruce moth hatch in late July. Voracious cutthroats in the 14- to 18-inch range are plentiful, as well as browns and the occasional bull trout.

Key Access Points along the West Fork of the Bitterroot River

Access Point	Access Type	(River Mile)
Painted Rocks Reservoir	Hand Launch	(21.5)
Mud Creek Bridge	Ramp	(18)
Marty's Bridge	Ramp	(15)
Canoe	Ramp	(13)
Applebury Creek	Ramp	(11.5)
Job Corps	Ramp	(4.5)
WW White Memorial FAS	Ramp	(2)
Hannon Memorial FAS (Bitterroot River)	Ramp	(-1)

6 Blackfoot River

The Blackfoot is perhaps western Montana's most famous stream. Lined with large rocks, with swift water and running through deep canyons, the Blackfoot is a quintessential Montana trout stream. The dashingly beautiful stream provides outstanding whitewater excitement, incredible scenery, and dependable fishing. It's Missoula's favorite recreational river, and there's no better place on a hot summer day.

Vital statistics: 132 miles from Anaconda Creek near Rogers Pass to its junction with the Clark Fork River near Milltown.

Level of difficulty: Class I and II except at peak flows, when it's Class III+. The best whitewater lies between Russell Gates and Johnsrud Park.

Flow: Annual mean flow: 1,573 cfs near Bonner. Floatable all year below the North Fork of the Blackfoot. Flows above 1,000 cfs are optimum; 10,000 cfs is a maximum.

Recommended watercraft: Rafts are by far the most popular craft on the Blackfoot, but during lower flows intermediate canoeists can handle most of the river. Drift boats are suitable below Johnsrud or from Harry Morgan to Russell Gates when flows allow.

Hazards: Numerous logjams, sharp turns, and narrow channels in the upper river. Rapids in the middle section. Remain bear aware on the upper river.

Where the crowd goes: Roundup to Weigh Station; Harry Morgan to Russell Gates on the upper river sees tons of traffic midsummer.

Avoiding the scene: Few float between Lincoln and River Junction. In summer, go early in the morning before the river warms enough to attract inner-tubers and swimmers.

Inside tip: The designated float-in campsites are not to be missed.

Maps: USFS: Lolo, Flathead; USGS: Butte, MT; Choteau, MT; Montana Afloat: #2 (The Blackfoot River).

Shuttle information: Ovando River Shuttle, (406) 793-3717; Four Rivers Shuttle, Missoula, (406) 370-5845.

River rules: Special rules for river access, camping, and day-use along the mostly private 26-mile stretch of river from Russell Gates to Johnsrud Park. Generous property owners have made their property available for recreational use, and several designated float-in campsites have been developed to avoid landowner conflicts, so please respect these rules. Weigh Station to Milltown State Park is seasonally closed during high water periods (May 1 to June 30) because of safety issues with the old highway bridge pilings. Maps and river regulations can be found at most access points and at FWP in Missoula.

For more information: Grizzly Hackle, Missoula; Missoulian Angler, Missoula; FWP, Missoula.

The Paddling

The Blackfoot has earned a reputation as one of Montana's most popular whitewater and trout-fishing streams.

While most streams run swiftly in their upper reaches and then slow down in the lower parts, the Blackfoot River does just the opposite. A brushy meadow stream where it originates near Lincoln, the Blackfoot picks up steam and offers some inter-mediate whitewater between Sunset Hill and Johnsrud. During the heat of summer, it is one of the most heavily used rivers in the state, especially the lower sections near town.

The Indians knew the Blackfoot as *Cokalihishkit*, meaning "river of the road to the buffalo." Tribes followed the river for its entire length, crossed the Continental Divide near the place we now call Rogers Pass, and then traveled to the plains surrounding present-day Great Falls in search of bison. Fur trappers willing to risk encounters with Blackfeet Indians also worked the river in the early days, and later, timber companies floated logs down the river to a mill at Bonner. When floating near the Weigh Station FAS keep your eyes peeled for sunken logs that never quite made it to the mill site.

Many Montanans call this stream the "Big" Blackfoot River to avoid confusion with the Little Blackfoot River, which runs into the upper Clark Fork near Garrison Junction.

Although the Blackfoot doesn't have the huge whitewater of an Alberton Gorge or a Bear Trap Canyon, it can be quite challenging and very dangerous when flows are high and the water is cold. Because of possible hypothermic conditions in spring, only strong intermediates or better should try the river at this time. Keep in mind the 100-degree rule: If the air temperature and water temperature combined do not exceed 100 degrees Fahrenheit, there's a real danger of hypothermia. It's a smart policy to go with several boats to a party. Each boat should have experienced people who know the river.

While parts of the Blackfoot can be floated by beginning rafters, beginning canoeists should first practice on easier rivers like the lower Bitterroot and lower Clark Fork. Get some experience before challenging yourself too much. Kayakers will enjoy the long whitewater sections, play waves, and ledges when flows are over 5,000 cfs. When the river is over 10,000 cfs, floating 30 miles in a day is no problem.

Blackfoot floats can start as high in the drainage as a few miles east of Lincoln, where the Landers Fork meets the main river. Although some of the upper river is slow and flat, the numerous logjams, occasional sharp turns, and narrow channels cre-ate too many hazards for beginners. Because canoes are the easiest craft to portage over logjams, they're the boat of choice for the upper river, although a small, light raft is a possibility. Beginners can handle this section at low flows only. Be prepared to portage your boat repeatedly; however, you'll be rewarded with a stream all your own.

Above its confluence with the North Fork of the Blackfoot (about 25 miles west of Lincoln), the Blackfoot braids frequently, and floating may be impossible in dry years. Below the North Fork, floating is almost always possible.

The North Fork of the Blackfoot has floating potential for those willing to drag their crafts across logjams and occasional blocked channels. It frequently gets too low to float by late summer. Above MT 200, the North Fork is more popular with whitewater enthusiasts. In addition, many wilderness treks begin at the North Fork Trailhead.

There is a reason the Big Blackfoot River has received so much attention over the years—it's rugged canyons and cliffs offer floaters a unique experience. TIM PALMER

Between Lincoln and Russell Gates FAS, the main Blackfoot offers outstanding scenery as it meanders through undeveloped river bottoms, occasional farmland, and secluded canyons. It's an excellent area to see bald eagles and owls, as both like the river-bottom habitat. Look for white-tailed deer, elk, sandhill cranes, and waterfowl as well, and be advised that grizzly bears have recolonized this part of the upper Blackfoot Valley. It is smart to bring bear spray and make noise if you venture into the woods. Please be considerate of private landowners by staying within the river's high-water mark.

Between River Junction and Russell Gates lies a 5-mile section of river known as the Box Canyon. One of the most memorable scenes in Norman Maclean's excellent book *A River Runs Through It* takes place here (the movie was filmed on the Gallatin River). Steep cliffs rise from both sides of the river, and thick timber blankets surrounding hillsides. Cliff swallows construct mud nests on the cliff walls, and hawks and eagles often soar overhead. While the river has several rocky ledges and drop-downs, the canyon has only one moderately difficult rapid. It's at the lower end of the canyon, about 0.5 mile above Scotty Brown Bridge, and it will swamp the inexperienced or the unprepared. We once saw a canoe wrapped around the biggest rock in the rapid. Those not interested in earning whitewater merit badges can easily walk around it.

Some of the river's toughest rapids lie 3 miles downstream from Russell Gates FAS near the Bear Creek Bridge pilings. Between here and the Clearwater Bridge, watch for a couple of drops with big rocks and high waves. Most drops are followed by big pools, allowing time for recovery if problems occur. In high water, this water is best handled in a raft or by very experienced whitewater canoeists or kayakers.

Between Russell Gates and Roundup, it's all Class I and Class II water at normal flows, but the drops bump up to Class III during runoff. Immediately upstream from the Highway 200 bridge at Roundup lies a big rock garden that lasts for several hundred yards.

Whitewater continues for several miles below Roundup, with plenty of big rocks. At high flows the rapids can be fairly continuous, allowing little time for recovery if there's an upset. But you can catch your breath in the 6-mile stretch of quiet water between Ninemile Prairie and Whitaker Bridge. A mile after Whitaker look for the Blackfoot's best-known piece of whitewater—Thibodeau Rapids, named after a river boss from the Anaconda Company who floated logs down the Blackfoot. The rapids posed a significant challenge to early log drives. Floaters today should look for big rocks and a drop; the safest route is on the left. Watch for several other frisky rapids in the next few miles below Whitaker and Johnsrud Park. Most of the river between Roundup and Johnsrud is Class I or II except during high water, when the larger drops become Class III. By midsummer, however, experienced inner-tubers can tackle the entire river, as long as they don't mind a pinball-style ride through the rock gardens.

At high flows, even the 10-mile section between Johnsrud Park and the weigh station at Bonner can be exciting. It's mostly Class II or less, but high waves can develop, and the current is very fast.

Access to the lower Blackfoot (below Russell Gates) is quite good, thanks mainly to private landowners, who, along with federal, state, and local agencies, have formed a cooperative river management zone that protects the river and makes it accessible to the public. Along this 26-mile corridor (from Russell Gates to Johnsrud Park), various sites have been designated for boat launching, day use, overnight camping, and other uses. A pamphlet that details regulations and provides a floating map is available from the FWP Missoula office. Be sure to follow regulations—it's only through the goodwill of the various landowners that this outstanding section of the river has been protected and made available to floaters. Many experts point to the Blackfoot's innovative management as a national example of how cooperation can protect a river.

The Blackfoot between Roundup and the Bonner weigh station receives more use than any other portion of the river. From Ninemile Prairie to Whitaker Bridge, floating is easy, suitable for beginners.

Beginners should pull out at a day-use launch at Whitaker Bridge, as Thibodeau Rapids lies less than a mile below. Watch out for the big rock on the right side of the river as you enter the rapid; it's been known to wrap boats.

Next comes Johnsrud Park, the most common starting point for a Blackfoot float. The standard trip starts here and ends 10 miles downstream at Bonner. At normal flows it takes around 5 hours. The site is so popular it has two different boat launch sites, one at the beach and another 200 yards downstream near a pavilion. At low flows this section is suitable for beginning rafters and canoeists, but watch carefully for rocks and snags. Many people use inner tubes during the heat of summer. Be prepared for heavy use, and take along a bag to pick up trash left by our unthinking beer-drinking brethren.

Since the 2005 removal of a run-of-the-mill dam behind Stimson Lumber Company, the Blackfoot flows freely into the Clark Fork River at Bonner. Floaters can now explore the waters below Weigh Station FAS to the confluence of the Clark Fork and the newly constructed Milltown State Park. During high flows, however, FWP has put a seasonal floating closure (May 1 to June 30) below Weigh Station because of the I-90 bridge abutments that pose a significant safety threat.

Despite the cooperative management plan, the Blackfoot has problems. Private housing developments, subdivisions, and rampant commercialization of the stream are the biggest threats. Fortunately, recent initiatives have blocked mining on the upper Blackfoot, but it is unknown how long this beautiful river will remain undisturbed. While a mine on the Blackfoot seems unthinkable, it could happen if river lovers fail to remind decision-makers that this river is far more precious than gold.

Float fishing: Fishing is good on the Blackfoot. Insect carapaces on the cliff walls tell the story of significant salmon fly hatches that generally occur in mid-June. In most years this hatch coincides with high water, making fishing difficult. The upper

The Blackfoot River is a famed western Montana fishery for good reason. The upper river experiences high angling pressure in the spring and summer. A fall float offers much more solitude.

Blackfoot River

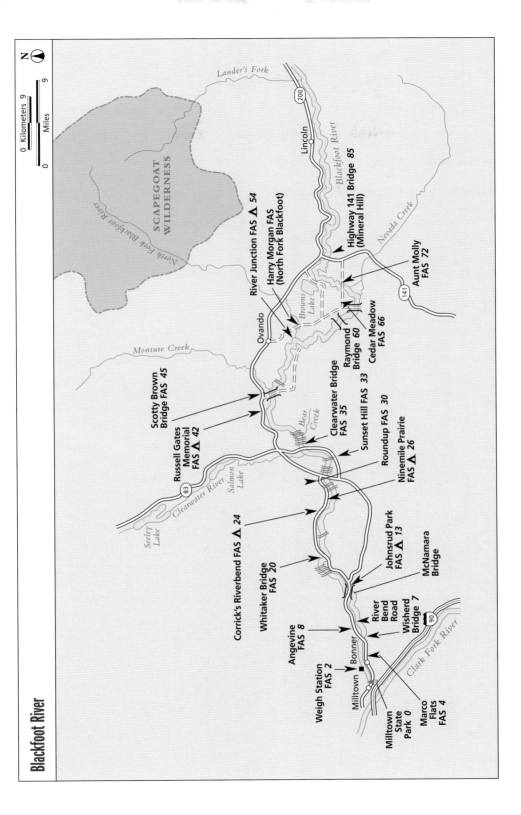

N

0 Kilometers 9
0 Miles 9

SCAPEGOAT
WILDERNESS

North Fork Blackfoot River

Lander's Fork

200

Lincoln

Blackfoot River

River Junction FAS △ 54

Harry Morgan FAS
(North Fork Blackfoot)

Highway 141 Bridge 85
(Mineral Hill)

Nevada Creek

141

Aunt Molly
FAS 72

Ovando

Browns
Lake

Raymond
Bridge 60

Cedar Meadow
FAS 66

Monture Creek

Scotty Brown
Bridge FAS 45

Russell Gates
Memorial
FAS △ 42

Bear
Creek

Clearwater Bridge
FAS 35

Sunset Hill FAS 33

Roundup FAS 30

83

Clearwater River

Salmon
Lake

Ninemile Prairie
FAS △ 26

Seeley
Lake

Corrick's Riverbend FAS △ 24

Johnsrud Park
FAS △ 13

Whitaker Bridge
FAS 20

McNamara
Bridge

Angevine
FAS 8

River Bend
Road

Wisherd
Bridge 7

90

Clark Fork River

Weigh Station
FAS 2

Bonner

Milltown

Milltown
State
Park 0

Marco
Flats
FAS 4

Blackfoot contains a mix of brown trout, rainbows, cutthroats, and bull trout (which must be released). Streamer fishing at high water can be productive as large browns are tucked closer to the banks.

Key Access Points along the Blackfoot River

Access Point	Access Type	(River Mile)
Mineral Hill	Hand Launch	(85)
Aunt Molly FAS	Hand Launch	(72)
Cedar Meadow FAS	Ramp	(66)
River Junction FAS	Ramp	(54)
Scotty Brown Bridge	Hand Launch 50 Yards	(45)
Russell Gates Memorial FAS	Gravel Bar	(42)
Clearwater Bridge FAS	Walk-In	(35)
Sunset Hill FAS	Steep Hand Launch	(33)
Roundup FAS	Slide-In Ramp	(30)
Corrick's Riverbend FAS	Ramp	(24)
Whitaker Bridge	Ramp	(20)
Johnsrud Park FAS	Ramp	(13)
Angevine FAS	Walk-In	(8)
Wisherd Bridge	Gravel Bar	(7)
Marco Flats FAS	Walk-In	(4)
Weigh Station FAS	Ramp	(2)
Milltown State Park	Hand Launch 50 Yards	(0)

7 Boulder River

The Boulder rushes through spectacular cottonwood bottoms before joining the mighty Yellowstone near Big Timber.

Vital statistics: 65 miles from its headwaters at the confluence of the South Fork of the Boulder and Basin Creek to the confluence of the Yellowstone River. Floating begins downstream of Natural Bridge Falls. Not to be confused with the Boulder River that joins the Jefferson near Cardwell.

Level of difficulty: Mostly Class I and II.

Flow: Average annual flow: 582 cfs at the Big Timber gauge station. Stay away when it's over 2,000 cfs. Optimal flow is 500 cfs; below 250 it is difficult to float in a raft.

Recommended watercraft: Canoes for experts, rafts.

Hazards: Logjams, diversions, and endless boulder dodging.

Where the crowd goes: Downstream from Big Rock FAS.

Avoiding the scene: Lug your boat down to the falls at Natural Bridge and take out at the East Fork Bridge.

Inside tip: Excellent water for experienced canoeists at lower flows.

Maps: USFS: Gallatin, Custer; USGS: Bozeman, Billings.

Shuttle information: B&G River Shuttle, Livingston, (406) 222-3174; Sweetcast Angler, Big Timber, (406) 932-4469.

River rules: None.

For more information: FWP, Bozeman; Sweetwater Fly Shop, Livingston.

The Paddling

From its headwaters deep in the Absaroka-Beartooth Mountains to its confluence with the Yellowstone near Big Timber, the Boulder provides an adventurous escape from the hordes of floaters on the Yellowstone. It doesn't take a geologist to figure out how the Boulder earned its name. Rocks, rocks, and more rocks. This translates into some tricky paddling, and only intermediate and experienced floaters should attempt this river. At higher flows, the Boulder is a torrent of whitewater. At lower flows, the Boulder is an exhausting run of rock dodging.

Paddling can begin as high as Hells Canyon Campground, but only for experienced kayakers, as this section boasts impressive Class IV and V whitewater until the unrunnable falls at Natural Bridge. For the sane, floating begins just below the falls where a winding, steep trail leads to the water. Larger crafts or those unwilling to carry their boats a significant distance down into the canyon can launch from the East Fork Bridge 10 miles downstream. Don't miss a visit to the Natural Bridge Falls viewing area. Before its collapse in 1998, the limestone rock canyon formed a natural bridge where the water would disappear underground and reemerge as a torrent gushing from the cliff wall below. Today the 105-foot falls is still impressive, and has been run by a couple of hare-brained kayakers in recent years.

Think twice about floating the upper Boulder unless you're looking for a wild ride. Most floating begins about 10 miles below Natural Bridge at Boulder Forks Fishing Access Site.

The Boulder River valley has long been recognized for its beauty, and as a consequence has largely been developed both for agricultural purposes and recreational homesites. The valley has several ranches owned by the likes of Tom Brokaw, Tom McGuane, and others. Very little public land exists on the lower Boulder, and as a consequence, access remains a challenge. The Boulder valley was first settled in the 1880s by W. F. McLeod, who trailed 100 cattle and 200 horses from Oregon and established the first town (present-day McLeod). Early gold discoveries in the upper valley attracted even more settlers, and by 1900 some 500 residents called the Boulder valley home. As a result of the mineral discoveries, the US government took the land back from the Crow Indian tribe, which had been ceded the land with the signing of the Fort Laramie Treaty in 1851. Since then, most of the mining activity has died down; unfortunately many of the scars remain on the landscape. A platinum mine is still in operation at the headwaters of the East Boulder—seemingly a ticking time bomb.

Most floating begins at the East Fork Bridge at river mile 22. None of the put-ins on the Boulder are easy ramps, but county bridge right-of-ways do provide decent access points every 4 or 5 miles down to Big Timber. Some require a fair amount of bushwhacking. Small rafts, pontoons, and canoes are the easiest crafts to launch on the Boulder. At higher flows the water is fairly easy to navigate, but at lower flows exposed rock gardens can spell trouble for even expert canoeists. The Boulder meanders through agricultural fields and dense cottonwood bottoms abundant with wildlife. Bald eagles, sandhill cranes, and great blue herons are frequent visitors to this valley along with big-game animals that migrate north from the Beartooths.

The floating season is somewhat short on the Boulder, with most of it occurring in July. By mid-August the Boulder is often heavily dewatered for agricultural uses, and floating is impossible. More water enters near Boulder Forks and is often a safer bet at lower flows; however, a couple of irrigation ditches take significant amounts of water from the lower river. A popular take-out is the Big Rock FAS, or boaters can continue down to Big Timber. When Captain Clark traveled through this area in 1806, he referred to it in his journal as "rivers across." If you're able to hit this stream when the flows are right, it is a float you will not forget.

Float fishing: Most anglers in this region focus their efforts on the mighty Yellowstone. But for those looking to get away from the crowds and experience a more intimate fishing and floating experience, the Boulder is a great option. Large browns, rainbows, and Yellowstone cutthroats escape up the Boulder to spawn and feast on the plentiful bug life. The hopper fishing starts to pick up in mid-July, putting big fish on the feed. The Boulder receives only light angling pressure, and the majority of that is

The Boulder River flows north out of the Absaroka-Beartooth Wilderness towards Big Timber where it meets the Yellowstone River.

Boulder River

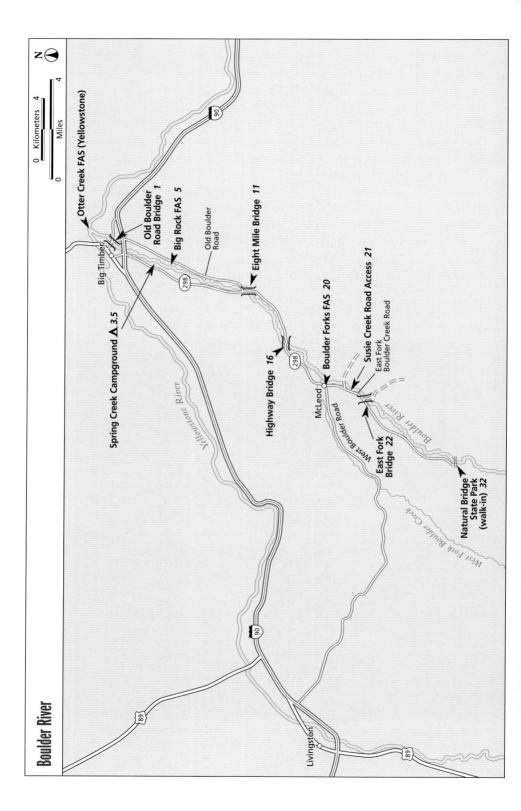

Otter Creek FAS (Yellowstone)

Old Boulder Road Bridge *1*

Big Rock FAS *5*

Spring Creek Campground Δ *3.5*

Big Timber

Old Boulder Road

298

Eight Mile Bridge *11*

Yellowstone River

Highway Bridge *16*

298

Boulder Forks FAS *20*

Susie Creek Road Access *21*

East Fork Boulder Creek Road

McLeod

Boulder River

West Boulder Road

East Fork Bridge *22*

Natural Bridge State Park (walk-in) *32*

West Fork Boulder Creek

Livingston

90

89

89

90

N

0   Kilometers   4

0   Miles   4

from wade fishers staying at one of the many posh dude ranches in the valley. Several scenes from *A River Runs Through It* were filmed on the Boulder. For novice anglers, "shadow-casting" is a surefire way to bring big fish to the surface.

Key Access Points along the Boulder River

Access Point	Access Type	(River Mile)
Natural Bridge Falls	Walk-In	(32)
East Fork Bridge	Hand Launch	(22)
Susie Creek Road Access	Hand Launch	(21)
Boulder Forks FAS	Hand Launch	(20)
Highway 298 bridge	Hand Launch	(16)
Eight Mile Bridge (Hwy 298)	Hand Launch	(11)
Big Rock FAS	Hand Launch	(5)
Spring Creek Campground	Ramp	(3.5)
Old Boulder Road Bridge	Hand Launch	(1)
Otter Creek FAS (Yellowstone River)	Ramp	(0)

8 Bull River

The Bull gently meanders through lush grasslands and timbered bottoms before reaching the Cabinet Gorge Reservoir in northwest Montana. It is perhaps one of the most idyllic, undeveloped river bottoms in western Montana.

Vital statistics: 25 miles from the confluence of the South Fork of the Bull.

Level of difficulty: Mostly Class I except a 3-mile Class III+ whitewater section as the Bull spills down the canyon into the reservoir.

Flow: Average annual flow: 375 cfs. No USGS gauge station. In dry years it may be too low to float by August.

Recommended watercraft: Canoes, small rafts.

Hazards: Logjams, low-hanging branches, brief Class III whitewater section the last 3 miles.

Where the crowd goes: No crowd here.

Avoiding the scene: Downstream from the Bull River Guard Station.

Inside tip: Although distances seem short on the map, flows are very slow; allow extra time to explore this sinuous stream.

Maps: USFS Kootenai; kroutfitters.com.

Shuttle information: Pack a bike or use your thumb.

River rules: None.

For more information: FWP, Kalispell; Kootenai River Outfitters, Troy.

The Paddling

What the Bull River lacks in length (a measly 25 river miles), it gains in beauty. Tucked against the Cabinet Mountains, the Bull slowly meanders through lowland grassy meadows and lush cedar forests. The Bull River earned its name purportedly because of bull moose antlers that were found near the mouth of the river in the early 1800s. Bull Lake is often mistaken as the headwaters of the Bull. The true headwaters are found nearby to the southeast, at the confluence of the North and Middle Forks. Floating begins at the confluence of the South Fork and the main Bull at river mile 25. The upper reaches of the stream are often too low to float by midsummer unless you're willing to drag your canoe over rocks and logs. Most floating begins at a road-side put-in at river mile 22.

The remote Bull River valley has a storied history of trapping, logging, and resource development. By the late 1890s timber companies began to take notice of the massive trees in the Cabinet Mountains. This is the wettest area in the state with 50 to 100 inches of rain annually. The Bull River Road was first opened as a county road (Missoula) in 1890, but failed to adequately provide access between the Clark Fork and Kootenai valleys until 1915 when the first automobile made the journey in a cool 15 hours. The same scenic section of highway today takes motorists a little over an hour.

Until recently the Bull River has been an often overlooked and neglected stream. Logging and mineral development greatly impacted the upper reaches of the stream. Luckily, because of recent concerted restoration projects, the Bull is shaping up to be

The Bull River sees very little boat traffic and most of the river is well suited for beginner canoeists. CAROL FISCHER

a high-quality fishery and floating stream. In recent years it has become more popular with anglers from northern Idaho and the Spokane area as it is a convenient drive.

Near the Eight Mile Bridge floaters get a first glimpse of the beautiful Bull River valley. Much of the valley is private property, and access points are primarily limited to highway bridges and several wide pullouts where floaters can bushwhack a short distance with a light raft or canoe down to the river. Some of the land along the river is owned by Avista, the owner of the Cabinet Gorge and Noxon Dams. They have also funded restoration work and access points along the Bull River.

An easy half-day float can be done between the highway pullout at river mile 16 down to the Eight Mile Bridge at river mile 12. Although this section is only 4 miles in length, the Bull slowly creeps along in a deep, sinuous fashion perfect for beginner canoeists. The Eight Mile Bridge access is wonderful and is the best spot to launch

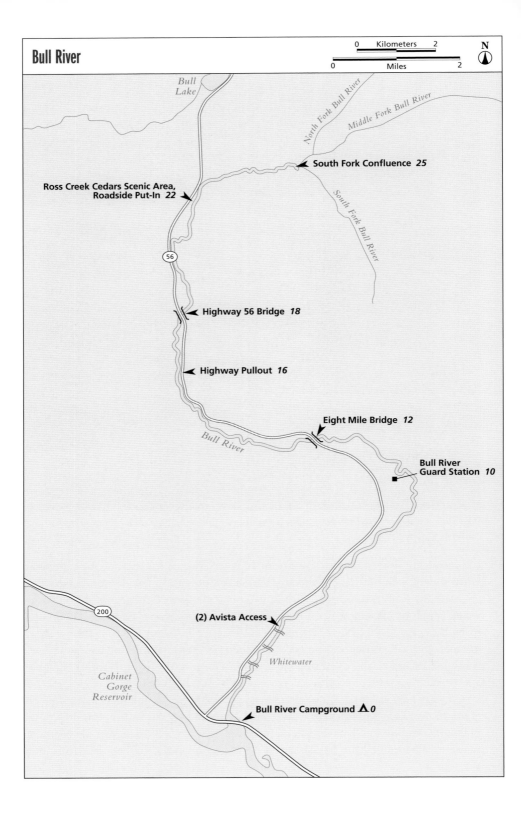

Bull River

0   Kilometers   2

0   Miles   2

N

Bull Lake

North Fork Bull River

Middle Fork Bull River

South Fork Confluence *25*

Ross Creek Cedars Scenic Area, Roadside Put-In *22*

South Fork Bull River

56

Highway 56 Bridge *18*

Highway Pullout *16*

Eight Mile Bridge *12*

Bull River

Bull River Guard Station *10*

200

(2) Avista Access

Whitewater

Cabinet Gorge Reservoir

Bull River Campground ▲ *0*

a raft or drift boat. In this section, the water is moving so slowly, it's possible for an enterprising canoeist or kayaker to make their way upstream from the bridge.

Although the width of the stream averages only 50 feet, its depth ranges from 0.5 feet to over 40 feet. High grassy banks provide little shade, however, and the fishery suffers from warm water temperatures in the summer months. Recent streamside restoration has included vegetative planting to displace the highly invasive reed canary grass that has infested much of the river bottom. The bottomland abounds with wildlife. Moose, deer, bears, waterfowl, and abundant songbirds take advantage of the rich bottomland. Grizzly bears have been sighted in this area, and floaters should remain aware when on the river.

Just downstream of the Eight Mile Bridge, floaters can access the river at the historic Bull River Guard Station. Surviving the great burn of 1910, this guard station was constructed by Granville "Granny" Gordon; she hosted notables such as Theodore Roosevelt in the early 1900s as the Forest Service fought the "cedar savages" and closed much of the timber harvest in the Cabinets. Timber harvest is still a point of consternation in this region. The guard station is available for rent via online reservation on the USDA Forest Service recreation website and is a great location for a river exploration and hiking basecamp.

The lower reach of the Bull below the guard station is more difficult access except for a new launch recently established 2 miles up from the mouth, immediately before the whitewater section. Below this last take-out, floaters should be aware of a fairly tricky whitewater section the last 2 or 3 miles. At higher flows it is fairly continuous Class III whitewater and should only be attempted by experienced paddlers. When water allows, fall floating is spectacular, as western larch cast a golden hue across the valley.

Float fishing: The Bull is largely undiscovered by anglers. Besides some local worm dunkers and tourists passing through tossing a line, the river sees very little angling pressure. Brown, bull, and cutthroat trout all inhabit this stream, and anglers can expect fish in the 14-inch range. Because of its low elevation, the Bull is an excellent spring fishery and can be productive when other streams are buried in ice and snow. It boasts an excellent brown drake hatch in April that can bring big, healthy fish to the surface. Golden stoneflies make an appearance in late June. Hoppers are a sure bet later in the summer.

Key Access Points along the Bull River

Access Point	Access Type	(River Mile)
South Fork confluence	Walk-In	(25)
Roadside put-in	Walk-In	(22)
Highway 56 bridge	Hand Launch	(18)
Highway pullout	Hand Launch	(16)
Eight Mile Bridge	Ramp	(12)
Bull River Guard Station	Walk-In	(10)
Avista Access	Ramp	(2)
Bull River Campground	Ramp	(0)

⑨ Clark Fork River

The Clark Fork starts out small, but exits the state as Montana's largest river. It meanders through pastures and woodlands with I-90 paralleling much of its route.

Vital statistics: 334 miles from Warm Springs Creek to the Montana-Idaho border.

Level of difficulty: Mostly Class I water except for a difficult whitewater section through the Alberton Gorge that has Class III and IV rapids. Other than the gorge, practiced beginners can handle much of the Clark Fork.

Flow: Annual mean flow: 7,128 cfs at St. Regis. Floatable all year long below Rock Creek. May get too low above Rock Creek by late summer in dry years (1,200 cfs minimum). Maximum flow for floating Alberton Gorge in less than 16-foot rafts is 18,000 cfs (St. Regis gauge).

Recommended watercraft: All crafts are suitable by intermediate river runners; special caution should be taken during high flows and through the Alberton Gorge.

Hazards: Continuous meanders, swift currents, logjams, and snags above Milltown. Additional logjams between Silver Park and Kelly Island make this section usually impassable for rafts and drift boats. Numerous dams and diversions below Milltown. Large standing waves in the lower river.

Where the crowd goes: Rock Creek to Turah and Kelly Island to Kona Bridge. Alberton Gorge in summer.

Avoiding the scene: Get outside the Missoula zone of influence; upstream from Rock Creek and downstream from Forest Grove.

Inside tip: Excellent waterfowl hunting between old Harper's Bridge and Petty Creek. Good fall fishing below Forest Grove.

Maps: USFS: Deerlodge, Lolo, Kootenai; USGS: Butte, MT; Hamilton, MT; Wallace, ID; Kalispell, MT; River Rat Maps: Clark Fork; Montana Afloat: #4 (The Clark Fork River).

Shuttle information: Upper river: Four Rivers Shuttle, Missoula, (406) 370-5845; Lower river: Sonja's, (406) 822-4358.

River rules: Seasonal and permanent motor restrictions between Kelly Island FAS and the mouth of Fish Creek. Contact FWP for more information.

For more information: FWP, Missoula; Grizzly Hackle, Missoula; Missoulian Angler, Missoula; Lewis & Clark Trail Adventures, Missoula; 10,000 Waves-Raft & Kayak Adventures, Missoula; Montana River Guides, Missoula.

The Paddling

As recently as 1972 the Clark Fork River ran red with pollution, and even the most daring river runners didn't risk their necks on the placid-but-acid upper river. Thanks to the Anaconda Company, all forms of aquatic life were wiped out in parts of the upper river; nearly 100 miles of stream were affected. The Environmental Protection Agency eventually designated the entire upper Clark Fork drainage as a Superfund site. Stretching from Butte all the way to the now-removed Milltown Dam, it was the nation's largest toxic waste problem area.

But this unfortunate situation has improved. Responding to public pressure, the Anaconda Company began to clean up its act. Initial results were encouraging. A section of river below the Warm Springs ponds that had an average of four trout per mile in 1972 increased its yield to an average of 984 catchable (over 6 inches) trout per mile by 1978. Aquatic insects returned in some areas, as did beaver and waterfowl. Active restoration is still occurring in sections of the upper river, and floaters should expect intermittent closures as large machinery is physically removing the heavy metals from the streambed.

While much of the river has recovered significantly, with vegetation and fish numbers improving, the bad news is that trout populations remain low between Garrison and Rock Creek, and fish kills still occurred with some regularity during the 90s and 2000s. Biologists believe that high-water episodes associated with spring runoff or heavy storms wash toxic materials that have accumulated along streambanks into the river.

While the upper Clark Fork's water quality problems can be deadly for fish, they don't impede floating. This river remains one of western Montana's popular float streams. The Clark Fork (this is the Clark Fork of the Columbia, not to be confused with the Clarks Fork of the Yellowstone) begins its 333-mile trek across the state near Warm Springs and can be floated its entire distance in Montana. The upper sections are challenging floating, with brush lining the winding banks, while the lower sections are broad and deep.

The Clark Fork grows from a medium-size river (about 3,000 cfs) to a large river (about 10,000 cfs) just above its confluence with the Flathead River, bolstered by the influx of both the Bitterroot and Blackfoot Rivers. By the time it departs Montana on its way to meet the Columbia River, the Clark Fork carries more water than any other river in Montana, with a flow nearly equal to the Missouri and Yellowstone Rivers combined.

The confluence of the Blackfoot and Clark Fork Rivers at the now defunct Milltown Dam, about 5 miles east of Missoula, creates the artificial distinction between the upper and lower river. The dam was removed completely in 2009, along with over 150,000 truckloads of arsenic-laden soil that had been deposited at the head of the dam. This river has proven to be an amazing environmental success story. Milltown State Park was constructed at the old dam site, complete with interpretive trails, walk-in boating access, and picnic shelters.

The Blackfoot and Clark Fork Rivers join at the head of Hellgate Canyon, an area named by French trappers. In early times the canyon was an ideal spot for ambushes and horse stealing. Since enemies didn't worry too much about funeral arrangements, the place became so cluttered with bones and skulls that the Frenchmen named it "the Gates of Hell." If the origin of this name depresses you, keep in mind that Paradise—a small town near where the Clark Fork joins the Flathead—is a mere 121 miles downstream.

I-90 parallels the Clark Fork for most of its distance in Montana. Fortunately it's usually far enough from the river that one has a sense of solitude. Surprisingly, even with an interstate nearby, access isn't always easy. County road bridges, along with a few FWP fishing access sites, provide most of the access.

On the upper river, floating can start right below the settling ponds at Warm Springs. The river is small and windy for its first 15 miles between Warm Springs and Deer Lodge. In dry years count on scraping and carrying your craft across riffles. Canoes are best at negotiating the sharp turns and avoiding the overhanging brush in this section. It's a great section for solo boating with a small craft. This section is also renowned for the large fish that migrate upstream near the spillway at the Warm Springs Ponds.

The scenery of the upper river is exceptional as the river wanders by the Flint Range, and sunsets can be spectacular. Beginners can handle this section when the weather is favorable and the water is low. From Deer Lodge to Garrison, the river broadens and gets shallower, and it may get too low to float in dry years. There's little floating pressure anywhere in the upper river. The Native Americans of the area knew the upper Clark Fork as the Arrowstone River because of a semitransparent stone found near the river that they used to make arrowheads.

At Garrison the Little Blackfoot River flows into the Clark Fork, improving both water quality and quantity from Garrison to Drummond. The river gradually winds away from civilization as it flows through thick cottonwood bottoms alive with white-tailed deer, elk, and beaver. This section has a fair brown trout fishery, and anglers occasionally reel in cutthroat trout. In fall and winter, waterfowl use the river heavily. Between Drummond and Rock Creek the river flows closer to I-90, fish populations are low, and the interstate's constant hum deters most floaters.

The repeated bends, occasional diversion dams, and possible barbed-wire fences make the Garrison-to-Drummond stretch a little too difficult for beginners except when the water is low. Much of this section flows through private land where landowners are very sensitive about trespassing, so stay within the high-water mark.

The Clark Fork from Clinton to Turah is by far the most heavily used portion of the upper river. Rock Creek provides a slug of high-quality water, and the fishing improves. Numerous downed trees, logjams, and tricky channels make the Clinton (Schwartz Creek FAS) to Turah run challenging, especially when the river is high. Beginners should avoid this section.

The Clark Fork changes complexion and becomes a large, broad river after being joined by the Blackfoot and Bitterroot Rivers near Missoula. The lower river flows mainly through cottonwood bottoms, although in some areas steep, pine-covered hillsides come down to the river's edge.

Although access to the lower Clark Fork is generally good, floating pressure is much heavier near Missoula. The section between Milltown and Missoula is quite popular, particularly in the heat of summer as tubers take over the river. The lower Clark Fork probably offers the easiest floating close to Missoula, but beginners should stay away until after spring runoff. Man-made hazards such as diversion dams and weirs pose the biggest threat.

Those floating through Missoula should watch for a diversion just upstream from the Eastgate Shopping Center, and the man-made whitewater park known as

Brennan's Wave immediately downstream from the Higgins Street bridge. The last major access in town is at Silver Park with a boat ramp near the Missoula Paddle-Heads' baseball field. For the adventuresome urban floaters continuing through town, take the left channel that goes by the Kelly Island FAS access. The right channel has a diversion dam just above the confluence of the Bitterroot and Clark Fork Rivers that must be portaged. Pinch your nose as you float past the Missoula sewage treatment plant. Most years this section is impassable because of numerous logjams and braided channels. Another popular close-to-town float starts on the Bitterroot River at Buckhouse Bridge (Highway 93 bridge near Missoula) and ends 9 miles downstream at Kona Bridge on the Clark Fork. It's suitable for beginners and has decent fishing. Experienced floaters may want to try it in winter, when goldeneyes, mergansers, Canada geese, and bald eagles concentrate along the river. It's possible to see a half dozen or more mature baldies along this stretch on a bright winter day.

Below Harper's Bridge (which largely burned down in the 1990s), the Clark Fork winds past the shuttered Frenchtown pulp mill and flows placidly until it

Above Harper's Bridge, the Clark Fork runs wide and slow and provides lazy floating opportunities.

Clark Fork River (Upper)

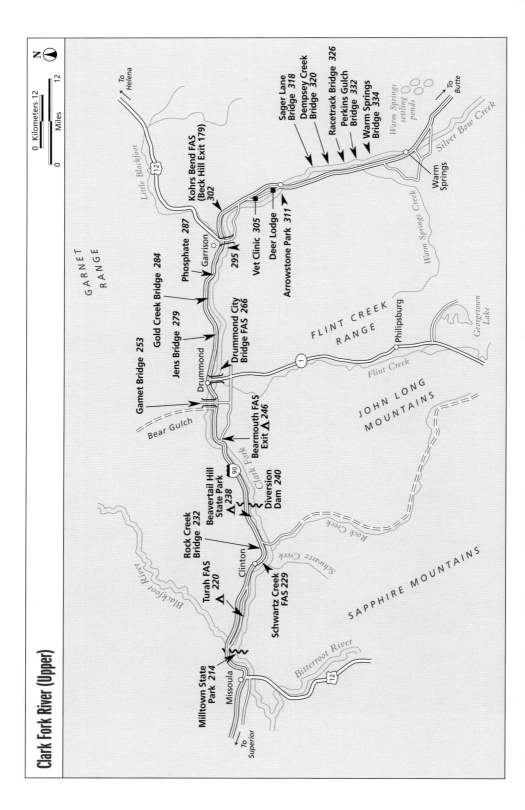

Key Access Points along the Clark Fork River (Upper)

Access Point	Access Type	(River Mile)
Warm Springs Bridge	Walk-In	(334)
Perkins Gulch Bridge	Walk-In	(332)
Racetrack Bridge	Walk-In	(326)
Dempsey Creek Bridge	Walk-In	(320)
Sager Lane Bridge	Hand Launch	(318)
Arrowstone Park	Ramp	(311)
Kohrs Bend FAS	Walk-In	(302)
Garrison	Ramp	(295)
Phosphate	Ramp	(287)
Gold Creek Bridge	Ramp	(284)
Jens Bridge	Ramp	(279)
Drummond City Bridge FAS	Ramp	(266)
Garnet Bridge	Ramp	(253)
Bearmouth Exit	Ramp	(246)
Beavertail Hill State Park	Ramp	(238)
Rock Creek Bridge	Hand Launch	(232)
Schwartz Creek FAS	Ramp	(229)
Turah FAS	Ramp	(220)
Milltown State Park	Walk-In	(214)

reaches Alberton. Although the paper plant's scar on the landscape may discourage you, the river here is quite isolated, and fishing can be good. Sadly, although the pulp mill is now closed, toxic sediments continue to leach into the river system. In 2013 FWP issued a notice to anglers to avoid eating northern pike caught in the area. Local groups continue to advocate for the area to be designated a Superfund cleanup site.

Not far below Alberton the river enters the Alberton Gorge, also known as Cyr Canyon. Experts with large rafts or kayaks will have a ball, but inexperienced floaters with canoes or small rafts don't have a chance. Several commercial outfitters take groups or individuals through the gorge. (Paddling details are provided in a separate section below.)

Safe floating starts again near Tarkio and continues to Thompson Falls with only minor rapids. Beginners should portage Cascade Rapids, 200 yards of difficult water between St. Regis and Paradise. The other tough spot occurs about 5 river miles after the Plains Bridge access. Beginners may want to use the shoreline and portage river left. Floating ends near Thompson Falls, where dams form continuous reservoirs to the Idaho border.

Much of the lower Clark Fork still has undisturbed shoreline, with mountains rising up from both sides of the river. The river has excellent rainbow trout populations. In fall copious mayfly hatches bring the trout to the surface, where they feed with abandon. The cold nights and warm afternoons create some of the most consistently good fishing conditions of the year.

ALBERTON GORGE

When anyone talks about whitewater on the Clark Fork, you can be sure they're talking about Alberton Gorge, sometimes known as Cyr Canyon. This 20-mile whitewater section, which begins just west of Alberton, has some outstanding rapids in a beautiful, isolated setting. Although I-90 parallels the river, it's only noticeable in a few places where bridges span the river. For the most part the gorge provides a primitive experience, with little development or other signs of human use.

Access to the gorge is limited. The standard Alberton Gorge trip starts at Cyr Bridge and ends at Tarkio (although those who want a longer float often go to Forest Grove). The Cyr Bridge access is via a steep raft slide down into the gorge. Most of the heavy whitewater action comes in the first part of the trip. After Fish Creek the rapids aren't nearly as difficult.

Those starting at Cyr will miss the Rest Stop Rapids (creatively named for an adjacent I-90 pullout). At high flows it's a Class IV (for experts only) with big waves and a huge hole. To hit the Rest Stop Rapids, put in at St. John's FAS. The rapids lie immediately below the put-in, leaving little time to get acclimated to the river before the action starts. Rest Stop is skipped by most floaters as it's a bit of flatwater to the first set of rapids below Cyr. At normal flows, Rest Stop is a routine Class II.

For the first couple of miles below Cyr, expect only minor Class II rapids. Steep cliffs and a dull roar will let you know you are approaching the Ledge Rapids. Expect big waves and some jagged sleeper rocks that create a narrow passage in a rock shelf extending across the entire river. The rocks that form this Class III run have shredded the rafts of unwary rafters at low flows. After the Ledge look for Cliffside 1 and Cliffside 2, two Class III rapids that get bigger and steeper with lower flows. At higher flows they have significant hydraulics that can cause problems for novice kayakers and canoeists.

The most difficult rapids in the gorge come right after the Triple Bridges. The canyon narrows significantly, and at high flows the rapids are continuous and the current extremely swift. The gorge's toughest rapid, Tumbleweed, lies in this 2-mile section. It's easy to spot because the river gets very narrow and there's a huge rock mid-river (submerged at high water). Scout Tumbleweed by pulling out on the left. At low flows it's a Class III, but at high flows it's a Class IV. A flip at high water can mean a long swim with little immediate opportunity to swim to shore as cliffs straddle both sides of the river. It's best to stay left; watch out for a big hole behind the rock.

Not far downstream from Tumbleweed come three more of the gorge's toughest rapids: Boat Flipper, Boateater, and Fang. At high flows they have tremendously big waves that can flip even large boats. Exciting but not technically difficult, they are strong Class III rapids at high flows; at low water Boat Flipper doesn't exist. After Fang it's only a short run to where Fish Creek enters the river; from Fish Creek on, it's Class I and II water.

The two standard take-out points for gorge trips are Tarkio and Ralph's Take-Out. While not recommended as a normal access point, in case of emergencies there's a steep, narrow trail where Fish Creek enters the river. The mouth of Fish Creek is a popular stopping point for outfitters and is usually quite busy.

Alberton Gorge changes dramatically based on the water flows. Places like Rest Stop Rapids and Boat Flipper become formidable in high water, while other rapids, like Cliffside, may wash out. Conversely, some rapids become more technical at low flows.

Average whitewater conditions can be found at flows between 2,000 and 10,000 cfs. These flows are measured at a gauge station at St. Regis. Between 10,000 and 20,000 cfs, the river gets much more difficult and dangerous. The normal peak flow generally is between 18,000 and 22,000 cfs. Above 20,000 cfs the current and high waves make the river extremely treacherous. At maximum flows, which may approach 40,000 cfs, the flows are so fast and the water so turbulent that a long swim is likely if your boat flips. Given the cold water temperatures and the likelihood of debris in the river, this creates a dangerous situation.

At higher flows the gorge is for advanced intermediates and experts. Be sure to have more than one raft in your party in case of trouble, and wear a high-quality life jacket. Big self-bailing rafts with rowing frames (16 feet and up with 20-inch tubes) are the standard equipment for runs from mid-May through June.

Less adventuresome people should try the gorge when the water drops and the temperatures rise. In a normal year, paddle rafts are a possibility after early July; smaller boats get to be more fun as the water drops more. At very low flows you may even see thrill-seekers on stand-up paddleboards. Do not mix alcohol with an Alberton Gorge trip; the rapids are difficult, and it's best to have your wits about you if you end up out of the boat.

KAYAKING THE GORGE

The gorge offers exceptional kayaking year-round and is highly esteemed in the kayak community as a playboater-friendly river. Most kayakers put in just above the place where three bridges cross the Clark Fork (take the Fish Creek exit off I-90) and carry their boats a short distance down to the river. The first rapid is located hundreds of feet beneath the interstate bridges and is aptly named "Triple Bridges." At most water levels the wave train is eddy accessible, and several features come and go during the season. The first wave is the most desirable and becomes a green wave with a small pile at 3,000 cfs. A larger hole is often present at high water, located upstream on river right, but should only be attempted by experts.

The next 1.5 miles of the river have great whitewater, but no easily accessed play spots. Surfer Joe is great for beginners, and often Boateater has a surging hole toward the bottom of the run that can be accessed via an eddy on river left.

The last and arguably most exciting rapid is Fang—an experienced playboater's paradise. The upper section of the rapid has several large play holes, and the first wave on the lower wave train is a surging monster above 4,000 cfs. The wave is eddy accessible—if you call a surging whirlpool an eddy! The rapid seems to change year to year as the streambed is slowly transformed, but there is always at least one feature that will leave you gasping for air.

Most kayakers (and some beefy rafters) pull off the river at Ralph's Take-Out, about 1 mile below Fang on river right. The take-out isn't marked, so look for a wooden staircase leading up the side of a steep embankment just after a small set of rapids. The parking area is about 200 yards up the trail. To drive to Ralph's, exit I-90 at Crystal Springs, turn left at the stop sign, and head west down the frontage road crossing under the interstate. The road soon turns to dirt; keep driving (about 3 miles) until there is an obvious left turn. The road deteriorates quickly for 1 more mile on an old railroad grade (four-wheel drive is recommended) as it leads closer to the river.

Alberton Gorge is for seasoned boaters. If you don't have friends with experience, there are at least two alternatives. A number of outfitters take people down the gorge. Another choice is the University of Montana's Campus Recreation Outdoor Program. See appendix A for the phone number.

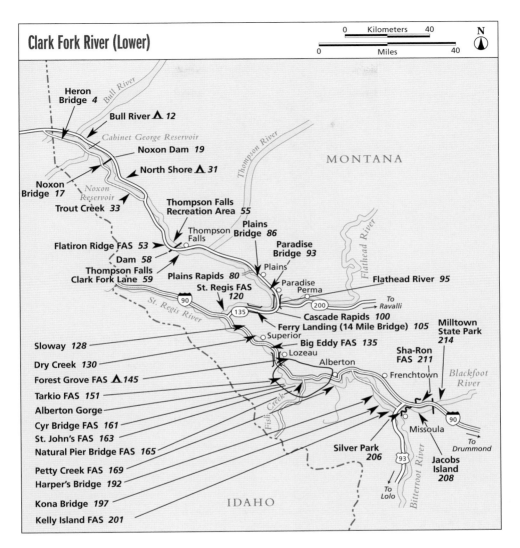

Motorboats and jet boats have long threatened to become a nuisance on the Clark Fork. Luckily, in 2011 FWP responded to a high level of concern about the use of powerboats in the Clark Fork around Missoula. Seasonal and horsepower restrictions now exist on both the Bitterroot and Clark Fork Rivers near Missoula, limiting the amount of motorized use near town. In addition, the Alberton Gorge section is permanently closed to motorboats. In 1984 a citizens' group called the Clark Fork Coalition formed to protect the Clark Fork River watershed. They do a commendable job. To join, write to the coalition at the address in appendix B.

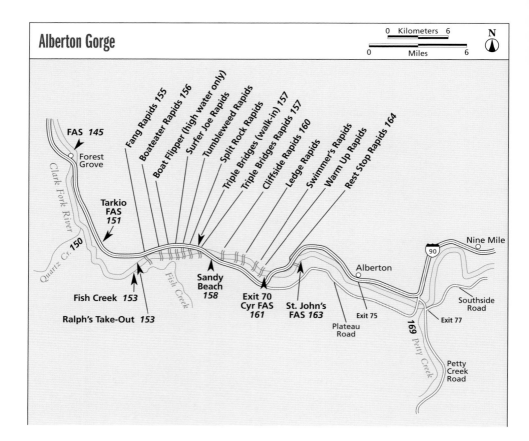

0 Kilometers 6

0 Miles 6

N

Fang Rapids 155
Boateater Rapids 156
Boat Flipper (high water only)
Surfer Joe Rapids
Tumbleweed Rapids
Split Rock Rapids
Triple Bridges (walk-in) 157
Triple Bridges Rapids 157
Cliffside Rapids 160
Ledge Rapids
Swimmer's Rapids
Warm Up Rapids
Rest Stop Rapids 164

FAS 145
Forest
Grove

Clark Fork River

Tarkio
FAS
151

Quartz Ct. 150

Nine Mile

90

Alberton

Fish Creek

Sandy
Beach
158

Exit 70
Cyr FAS
161

St. John's
FAS 163

Southside
Road

Fish Creek 153

Ralph's Take-Out 153

Exit 75

Exit 77

Plateau
Road

169

Petty Creek

Petty
Creek
Road

Float fishing: Although trout numbers vary greatly from the headwaters to the confluence of the Flathead near Paradise, the Clark Fork remains a dependable trout stream. Near Rock Creek the Clark Fork comes into form, and the water quality and, concurrently, bug life are boosted significantly. Below Missoula, late-night caddis hatches keep the big rainbows happy. If the bugs aren't hatching, try crawdad patterns to catch brown trout lurking in colder, deep pockets of water. Nonnative pike also grow large in the section near the old Smurfit Stone Paper Mill; just don't be tempted to serve them for dinner as toxicity levels are high. The removal of Milltown Dam reportedly had a negative effect on the downstream fishery for several years, but by all accounts taken from recent test outings, the fishery is clearly on its way back.

Key Access Points along the Clark Fork River (Lower)

Access Point	Access Type	(River Mile)
Milltown State Park	Walk-In	(214)
Sha-Ron FAS	Ramp	(211)
Jacobs Island	Walk-In	(208)
Silver Park	Ramp	(206)
Kelly Island FAS	Ramp	(201)
Kona Bridge	Ramp	(197)
Harper's Bridge	Ramp	(192)
Petty Creek FAS	Ramp	(169)
Natural Pier Bridge FAS	Walk-In	(165)
St. John's FAS	Ramp	(163)
Cyr Bridge FAS	Slide-In Ramp	(161)
Triple Bridges	Walk-In	(157)
Ralph's Take-Out	Walk-In 500 Yards	(153)
Tarkio FAS	Ramp	(151)
Forest Grove FAS	Ramp	(145)
Big Eddy	FAS Ramp	(135)
Dry Creek	Ramp	(130)
Sloway	Ramp	(128)
St. Regis FAS	Ramp	(120)
Ferry Landing	Ramp	(105)
Paradise Bridge	Ramp	(93)
Plains Bridge	Ramp	(86)
Thompson Falls Clark Fork Ln.	Ramp	(59)
Thompson Falls Recreation Area	Ramp	(55)
Flatiron Ridge FAS	Ramp	(53)
Trout Creek	Ramp	(33)
North Shore	Ramp	(31)
Noxon Bridge	Ramp	(17)
Bull River	Ramp	(12)
Heron Bridge	Ramp 500 Yards Downstream	(4)

10 Clarks Fork of the Yellowstone

East of Yellowstone National Park in the shadow of the Beartooth Mountains, the Clarks Fork meanders through isolated cottonwood groves and beautiful prairie country.

Vital statistics: 73 miles from the Montana border near Belfry to its junction with the Yellowstone River near Laurel. On the Wyoming side it is Wyoming's only designated Wild and Scenic river.

Level of difficulty: Class I for its entire length in Montana (the whitewater is in Wyoming). Suitable for practiced beginners at normal flows.

Flow: Annual mean flow: 929 cfs near Belfry. Can be too low for floating in September between Bridger and Fromberg. Minimum flow for floating is 100 cfs; maximum is 4,000 cfs.

Recommended watercraft: Due to a high number of diversion dams, canoes and lighter crafts are recommended.

Hazards: Seventeen diversion dams. Lind (Golden) diversion just north of Belfry and Orchard diversion south of Bridger are portages.

Where the crowd goes: Nowhere.

Avoiding the scene: Just show up.

Inside tip: This is the perfect trip for those seeking solitude and good wildlife viewing. It's what most Montana rivers were like 30 years ago.

Maps: USFS: Custer (Beartooth); USGS: Billings, MT.

Shuttle information: Do it yourself; not much for fly shops or people in this area.

River rules: Mostly private land; stay within the high-water mark.

For more information: FWP, Billings.

The Paddling

When Captain Clark floated down the Yellowstone on his 1806 return trip across Montana (he met Captain Lewis at the juncture of the Yellowstone and the Missouri), he mistook the Clarks Fork for the Bighorn River. He realized his mistake when he hit the actual Bighorn a few days downstream—and compensated for his error by naming this mistaken river for himself. The captain describes the Clarks Fork in his journal as "a bold river, 150 yards wide at the entrance, but a short distance above is contracted to 100 yards. The water is of a light muddy color and much colder than that of the Yellowstone; its general course is south and east of the Rocky mountains." Although the River bears Captain Clark's name, Jim Bridger, a local mountain man, was one of the first white men to investigate the drainage decades later.

The Clarks Fork remains the same color at its mouth that Clark observed: light coffee to medium chocolate. What the captain didn't know is that the Clarks Fork starts clear and pure as a mountain stream. It originates 3 miles east of Cooke City, enters Wyoming, and then reenters Montana 67 miles later as a prairie stream with little sign of its mountainous origin.

The best-known sections of the Clarks Fork are in Wyoming and possess challenging whitewater. In Montana floating can start right at the state line. The 31 miles

The Clarks Fork of the Yellowstone is known for it's challenging whitewater in Wyoming; however, as it enters Montana it mellows significantly. SCOTT HEYWOOD

of river between the border and Bridger contain the best water quality and easiest access. County roads and highway bridges provide nearly all the access. Upstream from Bridger, access points are well defined. Below Bridger, most accesses lack vehicle pullouts, and routes to the river may be blocked by barbed wire. Fromberg and Silesia Bridges both provide access to the lower river.

Diversion dams and irrigation jetties provide the greatest obstacles to a pleasant float. This river may have more diversions per mile than any river in Montana. Some require portaging (Lind and Orchard), and some you can scrape over, based on flows. Abundant diversion dams are a sure sign of a river with high irrigation demands. Serious dewatering, especially between Bridger and Fromberg, often occurs on the Clarks Fork, so expect a scratchy float in late summer, except in wet years, and expect some serious drops in the spring when flows are high.

Below Bridger the river gets murkier and loses more water to irrigation. From Edgar to the Yellowstone River, the river is more isolated, rarely coming near the highway. Rock Creek flows in above Silesia and provides a blast of cold, clear water.

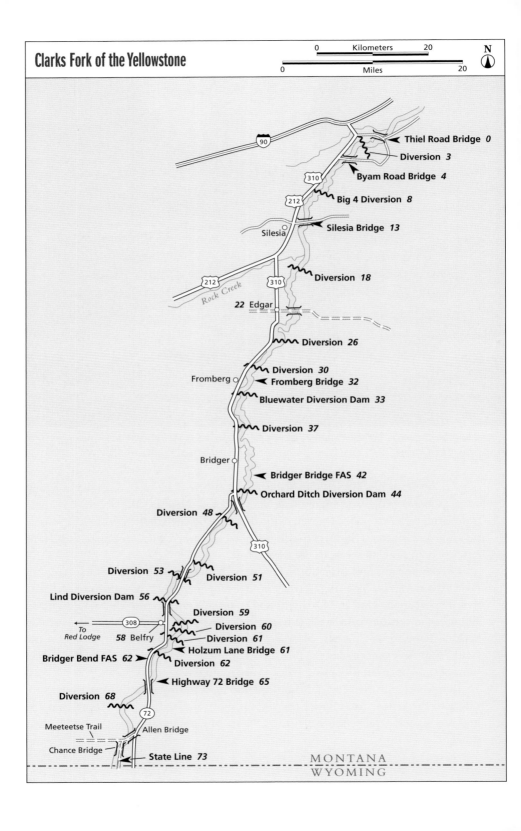

Clarks Fork of the Yellowstone

0   Kilometers   20

0   Miles   20

N

90

Thiel Road Bridge 0

Diversion 3

310

Byam Road Bridge 4

212

Big 4 Diversion 8

Silesia

Silesia Bridge 13

212

Rock Creek

310

Diversion 18

22 Edgar

Diversion 26

Diversion 30

Fromberg

Fromberg Bridge 32

Bluewater Diversion Dam 33

Diversion 37

Bridger

Bridger Bridge FAS 42

Orchard Ditch Diversion Dam 44

Diversion 48

310

Diversion 53

Diversion 51

Lind Diversion Dam 56

Diversion 59

To
Red Lodge

308

Diversion 60

58 Belfry

Diversion 61

Holzum Lane Bridge 61

Bridger Bend FAS 62

Diversion 62

Highway 72 Bridge 65

Diversion 68

72

Meeteetse Trail

Allen Bridge

Chance Bridge

State Line 73

MONTANA

WYOMING

Practiced beginners can handle the entire Clarks Fork in Montana. Watch for downed cottonwoods, diversions, and almost invisible sandbars. The river's milky color makes it difficult to read the water. It's easy to miss the shallow spots and get hung up.

Float fishing: Even though the Clarks Fork isn't far from Billings, it receives light use. While not a great fishing stream, it offers beautiful scenery, wildlife, and isolation. The river does not fish especially well in summer months due to high water temperatures and muddier flows due to irrigation returns. Most fishing takes place upstream from Bridger, where the river is clearer. Although the trout populations aren't outstanding, persistent anglers catch rainbows, browns, cutthroats, and whitefish up to 15 inches or more. The Clarks Fork in Montana isn't on anyone's list of famous trout rivers, so you'll probably have the river to yourself if float fishing.

Your best bet is to hit this stream pre-runoff and throw streamers and nymphs in deep, slow pockets. On warmer winter days midges may entice a few fish to the surface. What this stream lacks in numbers (100 to 400 fish per mile), it makes up for in size, with many fish in the 16- to 18-inch range. For those who seek rivers far from the madding crowd, this may be a spot for you.

Key Access Points along the Clarks Fork of the Yellowstone

Access Point	Access Type	(River Mile)
State Line	Hand Launch	(73)
Highway 72 bridge	Hand Launch	(65)
Bridger Bend FAS	Ramp	(62)
Holzum Lane Bridge	Hand Launch	(61)
Bridger Bridge FAS	Ramp	(42)
Fromberg Bridge	Hand Launch	(32)
Silesia Bridge	Hand Launch	(13)
Byam Road Bridge	Hand Launch	(4)
Thiel Road Bridge	Hand Launch	(0)

11 Clearwater River

This aptly named river flows through pine forests, lakes, and mountain meadows with the famous Bob Marshall Wilderness to the east and the towering Mission Mountains to the west.

Vital statistics: 42 miles from Clearwater Lake to its juncture with the Blackfoot River.

Level of difficulty: Mostly Class I water, suitable for practiced beginners. A 2-mile section of Class II and III whitewater starts in a canyon 1 mile downstream from Salmon Lake.

Flow: Annual mean flow: 287 cfs near Clearwater. Adequate all year except in the driest years.

Recommended watercraft: Canoes are the boat of choice above Salmon Lake; below Salmon, rafts are necessary to negotiate the short whitewater section.

Hazards: Logjams and beaver dams, and on the short whitewater stretch below Salmon Lake, three diversion dams. Lake Alva to Seeley has numerous logjams and portages and is not recommended for floating.

Where the crowd goes: The Clearwater Canoe Trail (3 miles north of Seeley Lake).

Avoiding the scene: Between Seeley and Salmon Lakes.

Inside tip: Watch migrating songbirds along the Clearwater Canoe Trail in spring.

Maps: USFS: Flathead; USGS: Choteau, MT; Butte, MT.

Shuttle information: An easy walk for the canoe trail. Longer river shuttles may be arranged through Four Rivers Shuttle, Missoula, (406) 370-5845.

River rules: No wake on the Clearwater Canoe Trail.

For more information: Lolo National Forest, Seeley Lake; FWP, Missoula.

The Paddling

To any person driving around western Montana in May and June, the Clearwater seems appropriately named. While other rivers gush brown with runoff, the Clearwater runs strikingly clear. The reason? It flows through a heavily forested landscape and gets filtered through a chain of lakes that include Rainy, Alva, Inez, Seeley, and Salmon Lakes.

Although the source of the 42-mile-long Clearwater River is Clearwater Lake (upstream from Rainy Lake), there isn't any decent floating until below Lake Inez. Don't miss the Clearwater Canoe Trail, a truly exceptional canoe trip with an ingenious design. First you float about 4 miles down the river (about 1 to 2 hours), and then you walk about 1.5 miles back on a groomed trail to get your car (about 30 minutes). Both the water and the walk lead through a dense willow marsh on an isolated portion of the Clearwater. It's a great opportunity to see warblers, loons, bitterns, catbirds, snipe, kingfishers, and wood ducks. You'll likely see turtles, fish, and muskrat as well.

This is a great trip for beginners. Even kids can handle the placid flows here. The last part of the trip crosses the top of Seeley Lake, so skirt the shore if the wind is strong.

There's also good floating and easy access between Seeley and Salmon Lakes, though there can be minor obstructions as this section is rarely floated. Below Salmon Lake lies a difficult 2-mile-long whitewater canyon that's only for experienced boaters. At lower flows this section is impassible in a raft, so aim to float before July. The whitewater ends at Elbow Lake, and a small dam creates a large marsh that's an excellent place for bird-watchers to paddle their canoes. Below Elbow the river winds through an old-growth juniper and Douglas fir forest until it enters Clearwater Lake. In fact, some people pull off at the picnic area right at MT 200 and paddle upstream in the lazy current. It's an excellent spot for beginners. An easier launch is located on the west side of the river opposite the fishing access site.

The last 3.5 miles of the Clearwater below the Highway 200 bridge aren't difficult, but be aware that the Blackfoot contains several difficult rapids in the section immediately below where the Clearwater enters. Beginners should get out at the access point where the Blackfoot meets the Clearwater.

Above Salmon Lake, the Clearwater slowly meanders through lush willows and old growth forest. TIM PALMER

Arguably some of the best early season water, putting in at Salmon Lake is a good bet. Just beware of losing your boat in the lake at the put-in.

Float fishing: The Clearwater offers decent fishing as it winds between the chain of lakes in the valley. The lower section offers the best fishing, as fish from the Blackfoot are looking for warmer, clearer water in the spring months. The inlets and outlets of the lakes are great spots to target pike. Unfortunately, FWP has received recent reports of smallmouth bass illegally stocked into Seeley Lake. Bucket biology threatens the long-term survival of many western Montana lakes and streams. Call (800) TIP-MONT (847-6668) to report illegal activities and preserve our valuable fisheries.

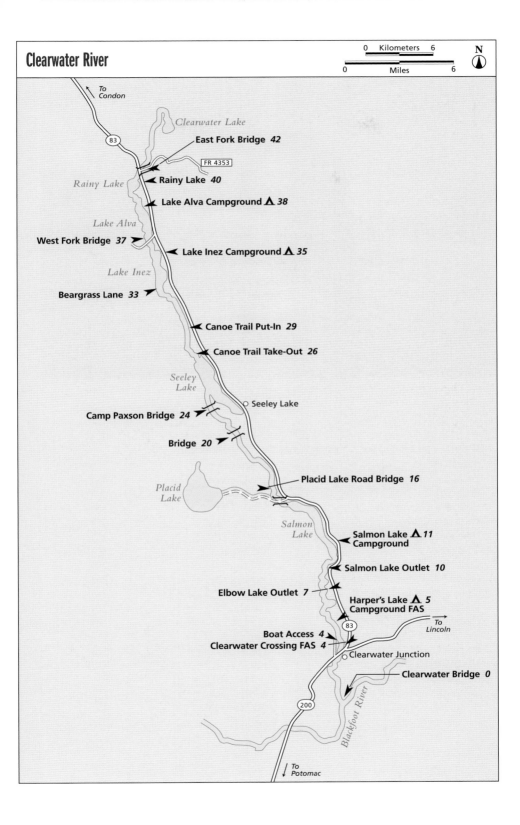

Clearwater River

0 Kilometers 6
0 Miles 6

N

To Condon

83

Clearwater Lake

East Fork Bridge *42*

FR 4353

Rainy Lake *40*

Rainy Lake

Lake Alva Campground △ *38*

Lake Alva

West Fork Bridge *37*

Lake Inez Campground △ *35*

Lake Inez

Beargrass Lane *33*

Canoe Trail Put-In *29*

Canoe Trail Take-Out *26*

Seeley Lake

○ Seeley Lake

Camp Paxson Bridge *24*

Bridge *20*

Placid Lake

Placid Lake Road Bridge *16*

Salmon Lake

Salmon Lake △ *11*
Campground

Salmon Lake Outlet *10*

Elbow Lake Outlet *7*

Harper's Lake △ *5*
Campground FAS

83

To Lincoln

Boat Access *4*
Clearwater Crossing FAS *4*

○ Clearwater Junction

Clearwater Bridge *0*

200

Blackfoot River

To Potomac

During spring runoff, the Clearwater lives up to its name and is a great alternative to the Blackfoot River.

Key Access Points along the Clearwater River

Access Point	Access Type	(River Mile)
East Fork Bridge	Hand Launch	(42)
Rainy Lake	Walk-In	(40)
Lake Alva Campground	Ramp	(38)
West Fork Bridge	Gravel Ramp	(37)
Lake Inez Campground	Ramp	(35)
Beargrass Lane	Hand Launch	(33)
Canoe Trail Put-In	Hand Launch	(29)
Canoe Trail Take-Out (Ranger Station)	Hand Launch	(26)
Camp Paxson Bridge	Hand Launch	(24)
Bridge	Hand Launch	(20)
Placid Lake Road Bridge	Hand Launch	(16)
Salmon Lake Campground	Ramp	(11)
Salmon Lake outlet	Hand Launch	(10)
Elbow Lake outlet	Hand Launch	(7)
Harper's Lake Campground FAS	Hand Launch	(5)
Clearwater Lake boat access	Gravel Launch	(4)
Clearwater Crossing FAS	Gravel Launch	(4)
Clearwater Bridge	Walk-In	(0)

12 Dearborn River

Crystal-clear waters rush through narrow canyons with sheer walls and spectacular rock formations on this highly scenic small stream.

Vital statistics: 67 miles from Scapegoat Mountain east of Lincoln to its juncture with the Missouri River.

Level of difficulty: Class I and II water with rock gardens, rapids, and sharp drops. Not for beginners.

Flow: Annual mean flow: 220 cfs near Craig. Typically too low to float by late July. Minimum flow is 250 cfs. Ideal flows are around 400 cfs. Flows over 1,000 cfs should be avoided by those in canoes. Watch the gauge carefully as this stream can rise very quickly during runoff.

Recommended watercraft: Rafts and canoes are your best bet until the river dries up in August.

Hazards: A small cascade at mile 34, 10 miles downstream from the Dearborn Canyon Road put-in, is often portaged. Fences, rock gardens, rapids, and shallow waters.

Where the crowd goes: Highway 287 bridge to the Missouri River.

Avoiding the scene: Dearborn Canyon Road Bridge to Highway 287 bridge.

Inside tip: Extend your Dearborn trip and continue down the Missouri. Excellent fishing and scenery.

Maps: USFS: Lewis and Clark (Rocky Mountain Division); USGS: Great Falls, MT; Choteau, MT.

Shuttle information: Missouri River Trout Shop, Craig, (406) 235-4474.

River rules: Be sure to stay within the high-water mark, as almost all the land along the Dearborn is privately owned.

For more information: Montana Fly Goods, Helena; FWP, Great Falls.

The Paddling

Anyone who floats the Dearborn River at low flows can't help but be mesmerized by the extreme clarity of this small stream. Even in the deep pools, it's almost always possible to see the brightly colored rocks that dot the streambed. Thanks to the clarity, the last float we took down the upper section resulted in three massive elk sheds found in the bottom of the river.

The Dearborn's clarity impressed Meriwether Lewis, and he made this observation after a brief exploratory trip on July 18, 1805:

> At the distance to 2.5 miles we passed the entrance of a considerable river on the Stard. side; about 80 yds. wide being nearly as wide as the Missouri at that place. it's current is rapid and water extreamly transparent; the bed is formed of small smooth stones of flat rounded or other figures. it's bottoms are narrow but possess as much timber as the Missouri. the country is mountainous and broken through which it passes. it appears as if it might be navigated but to what extent must be conjectural. this handsome bold and clear stream we named in honor of the Secretary of war calling it Dearborn's river.

Above Highway 200, the Dearborn sees far fewer floaters than the popular section downstream from Highway 200 to the Missouri.

The highly picturesque Dearborn gets its start high on Scapegoat Mountain near the Bob Marshall Wilderness, and it carves a deep and beautiful path as it winds its way out of the mountains and onto the open country that once was the buffalo hunting grounds of the Blackfeet Indians. Although the Dearborn is rather small, it's a high-quality stream with a floatable distance of 45 miles.

The Dearborn can be logically divided into three sections, each floatable in a day during late spring when days are long. The uppermost section begins at the Dearborn Canyon Road Bridge (also known as Clemons Creek Bridge) and flows for about 16 river miles to the Highway 200 bridge. The Highway 434 bridge, also known as "High Bridge," about 4 miles downstream from the Dearborn Canyon Road Bridge, offers another decent access point, but the banks are rather steep, making access more difficult.

The river in this section is quite small and shallow, so it's primarily an early season trip. It's a popular run for advanced canoeists. The river passes through a narrow canyon with many rocks and sharp turns. Watch out for fences, and beware of a waterfall about 10 miles downstream from the Dearborn Canyon Road put-in. It's a mandatory portage for canoeists. The shortest portage is on river right over bedrock, but if the river is up, you may have to use the trail on river left. Pieces of canoe were seen on a recent float down this stream and are a reminder that the upper Dearborn is not for intermediate paddlers. Rafts can navigate this section when flows are above 500 cfs and are a safer bet.

The middle section, from the Highway 200 bridge (another steep put-in spot) to the Highway 287 bridge, flows for about 10 miles. It's another popular canoe stretch, though not as difficult as upstream. The only real hazard other than fences, fallen trees, and swift water is a 3-foot drop about 3 miles below the Highway 200 bridge. The river generally runs through open country with occasional bluffs. This section is still too tough for beginners except at low flows.

The most popular and scenic Dearborn float is the 19-mile section that runs from the Highway 287 bridge to the Missouri River. Although the distance is less than 12 miles as the crow flies, the river twists and turns through a narrow canyon. The river cuts through this highly scenic gorge, replete with sheer walls that rise hundreds of feet with unusual rock formations. Most people either take out right where the Dearborn meets the Missouri (a difficult take-out on the southeast shore) or float a few miles down the river to the Mid-Canon access and take in the good fishing and scenery there.

This lower section of the Dearborn is suitable for small rafts or canoes. Several tricky rock gardens and a few rapids occur below where Flat Creek enters the Dearborn, about 6 miles downstream from the Highway 287 bridge. These rapids pose a serious hazard to beginning canoeists and an exciting challenge to intermediates. They aren't so hard in a raft. The rock gardens require quick boat handling and become more challenging as the water level drops below 400 cfs.

While many people do this lower section in one day, if you take much time for photography, fishing, or swimming, you won't make it. The Dearborn Canyon is so spectacular that you will want to take your time, but public land camping opportunities are extremely limited, which makes it difficult to stay overnight on the river. Montana law does allow camping within the high-water mark of the river (defined as the place where the presence of water upon the land changes its characteristics below the line), as long as the camping is not within sight, or within 500 yards, of an occupied dwelling. Islands and gravel bars are the best bets, and a good one is located on river right just as you enter the canyon a couple miles below the Highway 287 access. Respect private property and do not trespass. This river has some very sensitive landowners.

Beaver, deer, and raptors abound along the Dearborn, and you may spot one of Montana's less common streamside denizens, the river otter. This is a predator that everyone can like: They don't eat sheep, grass, or people. Although Lewis and Clark regularly encountered river otters in Montana, count yourself fortunate to see one today.

For most of its floatable distance, the Dearborn offers a semi-wilderness float. Much of the canyon is relatively pristine and very scenic. Along parts of the lower river, however, subdivisions and other signs of human activities scar the river. Management of the river corridor is sorely needed if this spectacular river is going to keep

Dearborn River

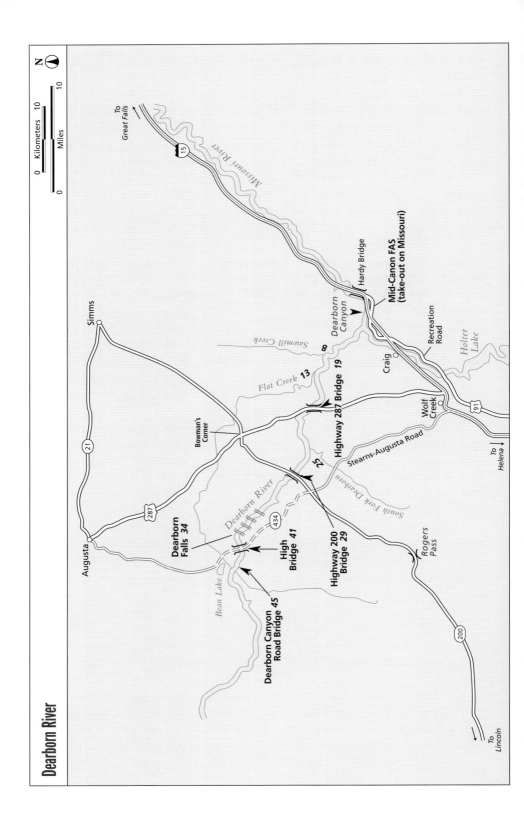

its outstanding natural attributes. A cooperative management effort, like that on the Blackfoot River, would be a big step forward as increased floating pressure continues to mount.

Float fishing: The typical Dearborn River fishing season is quite short. The water is often high and dirty into early June, and it often gets too low to float by mid-July. The river offers excellent fly fishing for small rainbows and some cutthroats. A few large brown trout reside in the deep pools. During higher flows and the fall brown trout spawn, big Missouri fish can move up the river and provide exceptional fishing when flows allow for floating; just don't try it in a raft after water levels drop.

Key Access Points along the Dearborn River

Access Point	Access Type	(River Mile)
Dearborn Canyon Road Bridge	Hand Launch	(45)
Highway 434 bridge (High Bridge)	Hand Launch	(41)
Highway 200 bridge	Hand Launch	(29)
Highway 287 bridge	Hand Launch	(19)
Mid-Canon FAS	Ramp	(take-out on the Missouri River)

13 Flathead River, Main Stem

This wide river with aquamarine glacial waters flows tranquilly past the spectacular Mission Mountains.

Vital statistics: 158 miles from the confluence of the Middle and North Forks to its juncture with the Clark Fork River near Paradise.

Level of difficulty: Almost all Class I water except for a whitewater section (Buffalo Rapids) with Class III and IV rapids immediately below the former Kerr Dam, now named Seli'š Ksanka Qlispe' Dam.

Flow: Annual mean flow: 11,070 cfs at Perma. Plenty of water all year. Optimum flows for Buffalo Rapids: 10,000 to 13,000 cfs. Maximum flows for floating are 30,000 cfs.

Recommended watercraft: Besides at Buffalo Rapids, any type of craft is suitable.

Hazards: Fluctuating water levels caused by dam releases. Occasional big standing waves.

Where the crowd goes: Upper river: Pressentine to Old Steel Bridge. Lower river: Buffalo Rapids.

Avoiding the scene: Upper river: Old Steel Bridge to Sportsmans Bridge. Lower river: Dixon to Paradise.

Inside tip: Buffalo Bridge to Sloan Bridge is an excellent overnight trip.

Maps: USFS: Flathead, Lolo; USGS: Kalispell, MT; Wallace, ID.

Shuttle information: Glacier Raft Company, West Glacier, (406) 888-5454; Flathead River Shuttle, Dixon, (406) 752-5331.

River rules: Most of the river flows through the Flathead Indian Reservation; floaters age 12 and older need a tribal recreational use permit on the section of river within the reservation. No motors on the reservation (Seli'š Ksanka Qlispe' Dam to 7 miles downstream from Perma Bridge) March 15 to June 30. Motors over 15 horsepower prohibited at all times. No camping on islands within the Flathead Reservation. Motors over 10 horsepower prohibited above South Fork confluence. Catch-and-release cutthroat regulations for the entire river. Bull trout fishing is closed on entire river.

For more information: Flathead Raft Company, Polson; FWP, Kalispell; Confederated Salish and Kootenai Tribes, Pablo.

The Paddling

If Huck Finn had run away to Montana, he might have made the main branch of the Flathead his home. It's a big, broad, peaceful river—the perfect spot to lie back in a raft or canoe and dream away a summer afternoon. Although its three magnificent forks often get more attention, the main Flathead offers scenic floats with good access that are suitable for beginners.

Floating on the main stem of the Flathead begins near Blankenship Bridge, where the North and Middle Forks join. Watch for a rapid known as the Devil's Elbow just downstream from here. The South Fork enters a few miles downstream, just east of Columbia Falls, and there are also a few small rapids in this area.

Fluctuations in water levels caused by releases from Hungry Horse Dam (on the South Fork a few miles upriver from the mouth) create one of the main river's hazards. The water can rise 2 to 3 feet in a short period of time, which speeds up the current significantly. Otherwise the river can be floated easily all the way to Flathead Lake.

Below where the South Fork enters, the main stem of the Flathead can be navigated by practiced beginners in a canoe or raft. It's popular with local residents. The river is particularly intriguing east of Kalispell, where it meanders through swampy lowlands. Here the river channels repeatedly and creates many islands. Old river channels have formed backwaters and oxbows that can teem with waterfowl and beaver. Watch for osprey nests and great blue heron rookeries on secluded islands.

The section of river from Pressentine to Old Steel Bridge is popular with anglers and floaters. Cutthroats and lake whitefish are the primary catch. Immediately upstream from Flathead Lake, the river gets used by floaters, anglers, motorboaters, and even water-skiers.

Below Flathead Lake, easy floating resumes at Buffalo Bridge, which spans the river about 7 miles downstream from Seli'š Ksanka Qlispe' Dam. Most casual floaters

The Flathead River provides secluded camping opportunities and receives little floating pressure below Buffalo Rapids.

BUFFALO RAPIDS—SELIˇ`S` KSANKA QLISPE' DAM TO BUFFALO BRIDGE

While most of the main stem Flathead flows calm and flat, the 6-mile section south of Polson, known as Buffalo Rapids, is a definite exception.

The starting point for a Buffalo Rapids trip is immediately below Kerr Dam Road, only a short distance from where the river exits Flathead Lake. This section lies completely within the Flathead Indian Reservation, and tribal recreational permits are required. (Call the Confederated Salish and Kootenai Tribes at the number listed in appendix A.) The take-out is 7 miles downstream at Buffalo Bridge.

Fluctuating water levels from Seliˇ`s` Ksanka Qlispe' Dam can complicate a Buffalo Rapids outing. While summer flows average about 10,000 to 13,000 cfs, they sometimes get as low as 3,200 cfs or as high as 25,000 cfs. Peak flows during spring runoff can reach 60,000 cfs.

Surprisingly enough, the most difficult conditions do not occur at peak flows. In fact, at flows over 20,000 cfs many of the rapids wash out; at 30,000 cfs most of the big waves disappear and are replaced by wicked currents and whirlpools. A flip at high flows, even with a life jacket, can be a dangerous experience. The best whitewater conditions occur at flows between about 10,000 and 18,000 cfs, although some of the rapids get more difficult as the flow drops below 10,000.

The whitewater between Seliˇ`s` Ksanka Qlispe' Dam and Buffalo Bridge consists of four minor rapids separated by stretches of minor whitewater. The first rapid, known as the Ledge, occurs about 1 mile downstream where the river takes a big bend. A horizontal band of rock crosses the river and creates a small drop with some holes and waves. While the Ledge washes out at flows much over 15,000 cfs, at low flows (3,000 to 6,000 cfs) it can be the most difficult rapid.

Next, about 0.5 mile downstream, comes Pinball, where numerous large rocks create a hazard. At very low flows it's a rock-dodging course, and you may find yourself careening from one rock to another. At more normal flows the rocks disappear and some big waves develop, as well as at least one tricky hole. This rapid can wash out at high flows.

avoid the section between Seliˇ`s` Ksanka Qlispe' Dam and Buffalo Bridge because of the formidable Buffalo Rapids, which has some big-time whitewater that's suitable for good intermediates and experts only. Downstream from Dixon the Flathead braids significantly and has many good camping areas and sees very little floater traffic.

Below Buffalo Bridge the Flathead flows tranquilly for 65 miles before joining the Clark Fork River near Paradise. This extremely scenic section of river rolls by steep cliffs and unusual badlands. Abundant wildflowers and occasional abandoned

Another 0.25 mile downstream comes Eagle Wave Rapid, the longest continuous whitewater in the entire run and arguably the most interesting. At low flows it's a technical rapid with lots of rocks and fast channels. At higher flows a long set of standing waves creates great roller-coaster fun.

The last of the four minor rapids is Buffalo Rapids itself, generally considered the most difficult. It's a long S turn, with the water first sweeping left and then right. Buffalo Rapids is easily recognized because the river narrows markedly and the cliffs get higher. Be sure to scout if it's your first trip through. Look for an easy eddy where you can pull in on the left side of the river immediately above the rapid. You'll find a good path up to the cliffs for an excellent view of the river.

Watch for two major obstacles—a diagonal wave and a big rock in a narrow spot. Buffalo Rapids is ideal at about 15,000 cfs. At this flow a huge wave forms in the bottom part of the run. Many rafters make the big climb up this wall of water, stall out in the vertical position, and flip over. The obvious line through Buffalo runs down the left channel, and almost everyone runs it that way. It's much more hazardous on the right. After Buffalo it's mostly flatwater before hitting the take-out at Buffalo Bridge.

While Buffalo Rapids isn't particularly difficult (strong intermediates will do fine), they can be hazardous because of the high water volume and strong currents. The rapids are Class II and III, with Buffalo a difficult Class III at flows over 9,000 cfs. You can get information on water levels by calling the office at Seli's Ksanka Qlispe' Dam. Be aware that these are current flows, not forecasts, and actual levels can vary significantly between morning and evening.

Floater use of Buffalo Rapids has increased markedly during the past two decades. According to recreation officials with the Confederated Salish and Kootenai Tribes, peak days may see more than 200 people on the river with many outfitted trips. For those interested in commercial trips, the Flathead Raft Company generally runs two trips per day, June through Labor Day (see appendix A for the company's phone number).

homesteads accentuate the broad vistas along this isolated and undisturbed portion. The clear, aquamarine waters add a dimension to a trip quite unlike any other in western Montana.

Bird-watchers enjoy the great variety of avian life that darts and hops along the river; one group of floaters spotted more than seventy species during a 2-day trip. During migration it's possible to see more than one hundred species. Raptors are particularly prevalent, as the high cliffs provide excellent habitat. At least three breeding

Nearly the entirety of the Flathead River is within the Confederated Salish and Kootenai Tribe's Reservation.

pairs of bald eagles nest along the lower river. Many species of waterfowl nest along the river, including trumpeter swans that are closely monitored in the area. In addition, concentrations of several thousand geese are not uncommon in early winter.

Motorboats are prohibited on the entire lower Flathead during the waterfowl-nesting season (March 15 through June 30). Motors larger than 15 horsepower are prohibited at all times.

The lower Flathead has four major access points: Buffalo Bridge, Sloan Bridge, Dixon, and Perma. The 20-mile section between Buffalo Bridge and Sloan Bridge is one of the nicest. While this trip can be made in a day with an early start, some people prefer to stay overnight and continue to Dixon, the next access point. A Flathead Indian Reservation camping stamp can be purchased online and at sporting goods stores in Missoula.

The section of the river between Dixon and Perma receives little pressure from floaters but receives some use by motorboaters. The river above Sloan Bridge receives minimal motorboat use.

Although the lower Flathead has some frisky riffles, it's an easy float that beginners can enjoy. It's the kind of river where it's possible to play a guitar or eat a picnic lunch while watching the scenery pass by. But do keep an eye peeled for occasional rocks or obstructions.

Canoes are the craft of choice on a big river like this, as they can be paddled effectively in strong headwinds where rafts can be troublesome. Under normal conditions,

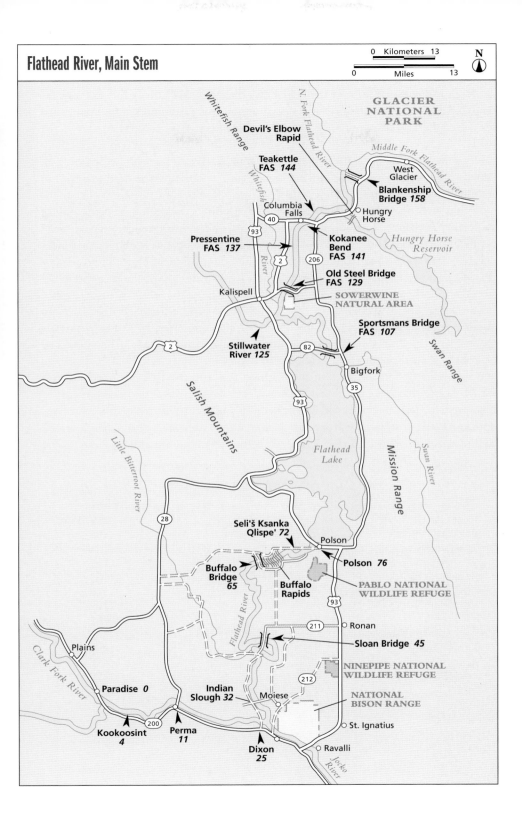

Flathead River, Main Stem

0 Kilometers 13

0 Miles 13

N

GLACIER NATIONAL PARK

Whitefish Range

N. Fork Flathead River

Middle Fork Flathead River

Devil's Elbow Rapid

Teakettle FAS *144*

West Glacier

Blankenship Bridge *158*

Columbia Falls

40

93

Hungry Horse

Pressentine FAS *137*

Kokanee Bend FAS *141*

2

206

Hungry Horse Reservoir

Old Steel Bridge FAS *129*

Kalispell

SOWERWINE NATURAL AREA

Sportsmans Bridge FAS *107*

Stillwater River *125*

82

Bigfork

35

2

93

Salish Mountains

Little Bitterroot River

Flathead Lake

Mission Range

Swan Range

Swan River

28

Seli'š Ksanka Qlispe' *72*

Polson

Polson *76*

Buffalo Bridge *65*

Buffalo Rapids

PABLO NATIONAL WILDLIFE REFUGE

93

Plains

211

Ronan

Flathead River

Sloan Bridge *45*

Clark Fork River

Paradise *0*

Indian Slough *32*

Moiese

212

NINEPIPE NATIONAL WILDLIFE REFUGE

NATIONAL BISON RANGE

200

Kookoosint *4*

Perma *11*

Dixon *25*

Ravalli

St. Ignatius

Jocko River

however, almost any craft will do. Drift boats are also popular as well as small john-boats with trolling motors.

Keep in mind that most of the river flows through the Flathead Indian Reservation, and floaters need a tribal recreational use permit. Camping stamps are needed for overnight trips. Dam proposals have been made for at least six different sites on the lower Flathead. In the late 1970s the US Army Corps of Engineers had several dams under active consideration. They have settled into quiescence in recent years, but dam proposals are like a fungus. You can't always be sure whether they're dead or alive, but it's impossible to kill them. Be vigilant!

Float fishing: The lower Flathead has the dubious distinction of being one of the worst trout-fishing streams in western Montana. Irregular fluctuations from Seli'š Ksanka Qlispe' Dam hurt insect productivity and make some spawning habitat inaccessible. Glacial silts in the river are also thought to contribute to poor fish productivity. On the other hand, the pike and smallmouth bass fishing can be quite good in the summer months and provide good entertainment when other rivers get too warm.

Fisheries biologists report that the average pike caught in the Flathead weighs about 7 pounds, and that pike in the 20-pound class are not at all unusual; however, many "hammerhandles" will be caught before you see one of these behemoths. The northerns were allegedly first introduced in Lone Pine Reservoir about 60 years ago and subsequently introduced into the Flathead River in the 1970s. A fine sport fish for Midwesterners, pike wreak havoc on native trout populations, so do your part to help protect Montana's prized trout populations and enjoy pike tacos after your float. The northerns usually can be found in shallow, weedy backwater areas of the river. Be sure to check the tribal fishing regulations before you head out and have the proper licenses.

Key Access Points along the Flathead River, Main Stem

Access Point	Access Type	(River Mile)
Blankenship Bridge	Ramp	(158)
Teakettle FAS	Ramp	(144)
Kokanee Bend FAS	Ramp	(141)
Pressentine FAS	Ramp	(137)
Old Steel Bridge FAS	Ramp	(129)
Sportsmans Bridge FAS	Ramp	(107)
Polson Park	Ramp	(76)
Seli'š Ksanka Qlispe' Dam	Ramp	(72)
Buffalo Bridge	Ramp	(65)
Sloan Bridge	Ramp	(45)
Indian Slough	Ramp	(32)
Dixon	Ramp	(25)
Perma	Ramp	(11)
Kookoosint	Ramp	(4)
Paradise	Ramp	(0)

14 North Fork Flathead River

The glacial–green waters of the North Fork flow through heavily forested terrain along the western border of Glacier National Park, occasionally providing spectacular glimpses of snowcapped peaks.

Vital statistics: 58 miles from the Canadian border to its juncture with the Middle Fork of the Flathead near West Glacier.

Level of difficulty: Class I with occasional Class II for most of its length. A short section of whitewater between Big Creek and Glacier Rim.

Flow: Annual mean flow: 2,889 cfs near Glacier Rim FAS. Usually good all year, but can get too low above Ford in dry years (below 2,000 cfs). Best conditions are usually from mid-July to mid-August. Don't try floating with flows over 25,500 cfs.

Recommended watercraft: Rafts.

Hazards: Dangerous logjams, narrow channels, and shallow riffles; cold, glacial water.

Where the crowd goes: Big Creek to Glacier Rim.

Avoiding the scene: Polebridge to Big Creek.

Inside tip: Go overnight and howl with the wolves.

Maps: USFS: Flathead; Flathead National Forest and Glacier Natural History Association: Three Forks of the Flathead Wild & Scenic River Float Guide; USGS: Kalispell, MT; Glacier National Park; Montana Afloat: #5 (The Flathead River: North Fork).

Shuttle information: Glacier Raft Company, West Glacier, (406) 888-5454.

River rules: Entire river is closed to bull trout fishing. Catch-and-release for cutthroats. Mouth of Big Creek is closed to fishing June 1 through August 31. Campers beware: The park boundary runs down the middle of the river, and special permits are required to camp within the park (river left).

For more information: Montana Raft Company, West Glacier; Glacier Raft Company, West Glacier; Flathead National Forest, Hungry Horse; FWP, Kalispell.

The Paddling

Born of glacial torrents, the North Fork of the Flathead flows wild and pure out of Canada and then rushes southward 58 miles through Montana, forming the western boundary of Glacier National Park. This beautiful, limpid-green river joins the Middle Fork of the Flathead just below Blankenship Bridge, near West Glacier, to form the main trunk of the Flathead. The entire length of the North Fork is a designated segment of the National Wild and Scenic Rivers System. The entire drainage is an elegant blend of towering mountains, verdant forests, and sparkling waters.

In 1892 a steamboat attempted to ascend the North Fork. An enterprising man by the name of James Talbot conceived this ill-fated venture. Talbot, an early-day boomer, learned of the coal deposits along the North Fork and envisioned that this coal could fuel the construction of a railroad, which would stimulate the growth of his town of Columbia Falls and fatten his wallet at the same time.

The cool, glacial waters of the North Fork are a welcome sight on a hot August afternoon.
RYAN BUSSE

Talbot built a 75-foot steamship, named it The Oakes, and in May 1892 attempted the swollen North Fork. After several days of hard work, the crew was about 10 miles upriver. Somewhere in the vicinity of what we know today as Fool Hen Rapids, the steamer Oakes took on too much water and sank. Though no crew members were lost, they all had to traverse difficult terrain to make their way back to Columbia Falls.

While steamships no longer try the North Fork, an armada of rafters and canoeists challenge it each year. Considering the North Fork's remote setting, access is excellent. Although an unpaved road parallels the river for its entire distance, it rarely can be seen. The North Fork Road, which runs along the west side of the river, has long been a focal point of controversy. Some folks want the road improved to promote tourism and logging. Conservationists and most local residents want it left the way it is—bumpy, narrow, and dusty. In 2011 they got their wish when the government of British Columbia passed legislation to curtail all future permitting for energy development on public land in the North Fork drainage in Canada. South of the border the bipartisan North Fork Protection Bill passed Congress in 2015 and offers similar protections.

A road on the east side of the river in Glacier National Park also parallels the river for much of its length and offers occasional access. Called the "inside" North Fork Road, it leads to Kintla Lake and offers limited river access between Polebridge and the lake.

Most floaters, however, launch from the west side of the river. Developed river access points occur at fairly regular intervals, and there are some undeveloped launch sites off the road.

Floating in Montana begins at the Canadian border river access and continues for the North Fork's entire distance in Montana. From the Canadian border to Polebridge, numerous logjams and fast currents provide serious hazards, particularly when the water is high. While the river is not technically difficult, the high wood content means mistakes can be dangerous. Because the nearby mountains are so high, runoff sometimes extends well into July. Watch for some large standing waves near the mouth of Kintla Creek. Intermediate rafters and canoeists can handle the section from the border to Polebridge.

The easiest section of the river lies between Polebridge and Big Creek. Beginners can handle it when the water is low and weather conditions are favorable, but they should stay clear during higher flows. The North Fork has extremely cold water, and early season spills can be dangerous. Again, watch carefully for logjams and narrow channels. Be wary of shallow riffles where the current is fast. You may tip your canoe if you aren't parallel to the current. Be prepared to jump out and walk your canoe through shallow spots if you get hung up. Floaters often stop at the bridge leading to Polebridge and walk the mile to the famous Polebridge Mercantile for a cold refreshment or their famous baked goods.

The most challenging section of the North Fork lies between Big Creek and the Glacier Rim river access. It's suitable for intermediates in rafts or canoes at moderate flows. Deep runs and pools are interrupted by four significant rapids, the first about 1 mile below Big Creek, the second about 4 miles downstream (a small Class III). About 3 miles before the take-out at Glacier Rim is Fool Hen Rapids, which actually are two Class III rapids less than a mile apart. Big standing waves usually line up below each of the rapids.

Spring runoff on the North Fork typically starts in late May and runs through late June. Best conditions are usually from about mid-July to mid-August. After mid-August, particularly during dry years, the river from the Canadian border to Ford Station can get really scratchy and may be too low to float. From Ford downriver the North Fork is usually floatable unless it's frozen. Fall trips can be outstanding when there's enough water. Get up-to-date information by calling the Forest Service's Hungry Horse Ranger District at the phone number listed in appendix A.

The North Fork's proximity to Glacier National Park makes it an excellent place to spot wild critters of all kinds. Bald eagles and ospreys are common, as are moose, which prefer the willow bottoms. It's a great river to spot river otters, and floaters sometimes even see grizzly bears and wolves.

Float fishing: Fishing on the North Fork is often mediocre, but it's unpredictable. Most of the fish in the river are migratory, so it's a matter of being in the right place at the right time. The North Fork is one of the few remaining rivers in Montana that support a native fishery. The primary species are westslope cutthroat and

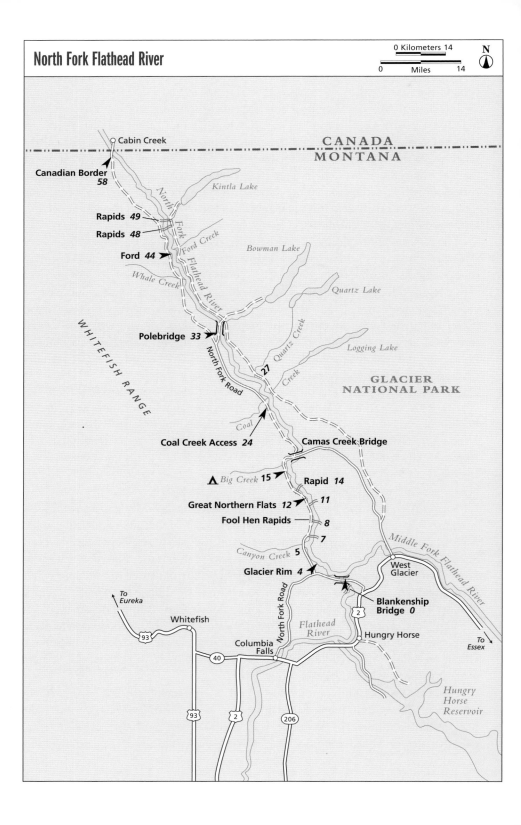

North Fork Flathead River

0 Kilometers 14

0 Miles 14

N

CANADA
MONTANA

Cabin Creek

Canadian Border
58

Kintla Lake

North Fork

Ford Creek

Rapids **49**

Rapids **48**

Bowman Lake

Ford **44**

Flathead River

Whale Creek

Quartz Lake

Polebridge **33**

North Fork Road

Quartz Creek

Logging Lake

27

Creek

GLACIER
NATIONAL PARK

WHITEFISH RANGE

Coal

Coal Creek Access **24**

Camas Creek Bridge

▲ Big Creek **15**

Rapid *14*

Great Northern Flats *12*

11

Fool Hen Rapids

8

7

Canyon Creek **5**

Middle Fork Flathead River

Glacier Rim *4*

West
Glacier

To
Eureka

Blankenship
Bridge *0*

Whitefish

North Fork Road

2

Flathead
River

Hungry Horse

To
Essex

93

Columbia
Falls

40

Hungry
Horse
Reservoir

93

2

206

bull trout (also known as Dolly Varden). Dolly Varden was a character in a Dickens novel distinguished by her gaudy clothes. A member of the char family, this beautifully colored fish lives up to its name. Once native to many Montana rivers, healthy populations remain in only a few of the state's rivers. Westslope cutthroats are listed as a threatened species.

Because the North Fork is a glacial stream, it doesn't have the nutrients that make southwestern Montana trout streams so productive. As a result there are fewer fish, and they grow more slowly. Moreover, some call the cutthroat trout the most gullible fish that swims, making them vulnerable to overfishing. The North Fork is a great place to practice catch-and-release fishing, and when the hatches are on, they are easy to catch, even for novice anglers. Be sure to check the regulations.

Key Access Points along North Fork Flathead River

Access Point	Access Type	(River Mile)
Canadian border	Hand Launch	(58)
Ford	Hand Launch	(44)
Polebridge	Hand Launch	(33)
Coal Creek	Hand Launch	(24)
Big Creek	Hand Launch	(15)
Great Northern Flats	Hand Launch	(12)
Glacier Rim	Hand Launch	(4)
Blankenship Bridge	Ramp	(0)

15 Middle Fork Flathead River

A picturesque wilderness whitewater river, the Middle Fork is both extremely challenging and remote. The Middle Fork roars through the Bob Marshall Wilderness and forms the southern border of Glacier National Park.

Vital statistics: 90 miles from the confluence of Strawberry and Bowl Creeks in the Bob Marshall Wilderness to its juncture with the North Fork of the Flathead near West Glacier.

Level of difficulty: Difficult whitewater in the wilderness section, with Class IV rapids or better at peak flows. Experts only. Class II, III, and IV rapids outside the wilderness.

Flow: Annual mean flow: 2,879 cfs near West Glacier. Wilderness section typically too low by mid-July. The river can be floated all year outside the wilderness. Check the gauge on the West Glacier bridge: Floating is possible when the flows are between 1 and 8 feet.

Recommended watercraft: Rafts.

Hazards: Big rocks, dangerous snags, and deep holes. Cold water and cold air can create hypothermic conditions even in summer.

Where the crowd goes: Moccasin Creek to West Glacier.

Avoiding the scene: The portion within the wilderness.

Inside tip: The Glacier Raft Company provides excellent raft trips at a fair price on the moderate whitewater section near West Glacier. This incredibly scenic float makes a great side trip when visiting Glacier National Park and is sure to please out-of-town visitors.

Maps: USFS: Flathead, Bob Marshall Complex Topographic Map; USGS: Cutbank, MT; Kalispell, MT; Glacier National Park, MT; Flathead National Forest and Glacier Natural History Association: Three Forks of the Flathead Wild & Scenic River Float Guide.

Shuttle information: Glacier Raft Company, West Glacier, (406) 888-5454; Red Eagle Aviation, Kalispell, (406) 755-2376.

River rules: Motors limited to recreation section (downstream from Bear Creek). Maximum size 10 horsepower. Special-use permits for outfitters only. Registration for wilderness floats at Schafer Meadows. Check for special fishing regulations. Park boundary is ordinary high-water mark on park side of river.

For more information: Montana Raft Company, West Glacier; Glacier Raft Company, West Glacier; Great Northern Whitewater, West Glacier; Flathead National Forest, Hungry Horse.

The Paddling

Those who have floated the Middle Fork of the Flathead know why it's called Montana's wildest river. Numerous large boulders have settled in the bottom of this heavily glaciated valley, and the river drops an average 35 feet per mile as it plunges out of one of the largest expanses of wilderness in the Lower 48. Downed trees sometimes block the river, creating serious hazards for floaters but excellent habitat for fish. Throw in the high water volumes during runoff, and the difficulty of getting help if there's trouble, and it's plain why the Middle Fork is not a stream for the fainthearted.

A designated component of the National Wild and Scenic Rivers System for its entire length, the tumultuous Middle Fork gets its start in the untrammeled peaks of

The Middle Fork is renowned for its challenging whitewater. The best floating usually occurs in June before it gets too low.

the Bob Marshall Wilderness. As the late great conservationist Dale Burk explains in his book *Great Bear, Wild River*:

> *The Middle Fork of the Flathead begins hard against the Continental Divide in the steep, highly erosive slopes of mountains where a glacier once rode the earth. . . . It is set amidst startlingly scenic mountains, its channel often literally carved through the sedimentary rock cliffs that sweep straight upward onto slopes so steep they are difficult for a man to hike upon.*

Burk's book chronicles the bitter battle to establish the Great Bear Wilderness. The Great Bear, named for the grizzlies that inhabit the area, became a designated wilderness in 1978. This 285,000-acre area encompasses nearly 50 miles of the Middle Fork.

As might be expected, access to the uppermost sections of the Middle Fork is difficult. The options are to pack in with horses or fly in to the airstrip at Schafer Meadows. A pack trail parallels the river for most of its wilderness flow.

This starting point is located about 27 miles upstream from Bear Creek, where the river first meets civilization. From Bear Creek downstream (about 46 miles), the river parallels US 2.

Most people fly in, which provides an interesting river perspective. From the air the Middle Fork looks like a frothing thread of water, liberally sprinkled with large

While the Middle Fork is famous for its whitewater, during the slow sections fly fishing provides for some much-needed relaxation.

boulders and occasional logjams. Private flights can be chartered out of Kalispell City Airport with Red Eagle Aviation and run about $450 per plane. The weight limit of their Cessnas is 900 pounds of people and cargo, so be prepared and weighed in before you show up for your flight. Booking flights early is also important as the outfitters tend to book the early morning flights. The trail from Schafer Meadows airstrip to the river can be a downright slick, muddy, mosquito-ridden swamp. There is a gurney to help with shuttling your gear to the river, but be prepared for a lot of trips and plenty of time to assemble rafts and get on the water. Luckily camping sites on the upper river are plentiful and it doesn't take long to find your own piece of paradise.

Although outfitted use is popular on the river, to avoid human "logjams," the Forest Service has placed restrictions on the number of commercial outfitters who can operate on the river, but it has not restricted private floaters. The Forest Service limits party size to ten people both for commercial and noncommercial groups.

Although flows average about 1,000 cfs (measured at West Glacier), peak flows can exceed ten times that amount. While the river typically carries about 700 cfs of water in February, flows increase dramatically when the snow melts, sometimes climbing to more than 11,000 cfs at the peak of runoff in early June. The Middle Fork can be unfloatable during these peak discharges and even outfitted trips can get cancelled.

The optimum floating period on the wilderness portion of the Middle Fork is usually from early June through mid-July. Air temperatures dictate the rate of runoff. Keep in mind, however, that even on warm days, water temperatures will be quite low—usually around 40 degrees. Rainstorms, combined with the low water temperatures in the river, make hypothermia a real threat on early season floats.

In a normal year, flows in the upper river drop sharply in mid-July, and floating can become difficult. In low-water conditions, each rapid becomes a maze of exposed rocks that can tear up rafts. Check river conditions with the Forest Service's Hungry Horse Ranger District at Hungry Horse or on the USGS website.

When the river is ripping, it's easy to float from Schafer Meadows to Bear Creek in a day. Most floaters, however, choose to take a couple of days so they can camp and have time to explore the Great Bear Wilderness. While it's possible to get out at Bear Creek, the Essex Bridge is the usual take-out spot as it has more convenient boat access. With these few extra miles, floaters not only catch a couple more good rapids but also get to visit the famous goat lick on the edge of Glacier National Park.

The goat lick is a slumping cliff on the north side of the river where mountain goats come down from the crags to lick exposed mineral salts. It's one of the few places in North America where it's possible to see wild goats next to a wild river. If you've managed to keep your camera dry, it's an excellent place to take pictures. Just don't approach the goats too closely.

The Middle Fork isn't all fun and games. During higher flows in early June, the rapids are challenging and the weather is often very rainy.

RIVER WILD

The wilderness section of the Middle Fork has some challenging rapids, as does the more accessible portion of the river that runs immediately adjacent to Glacier National Park.

Soaking rains may accompany early season Middle Fork trips, and without a wet suit or quality rain gear, hypothermia is possible. This can cause serious errors in judgment, such as not scouting difficult rapids. Be prepared for cold temperatures and adverse weather.

Major rapids on the Middle Fork begin a couple of miles below Schafer Meadows, with a group known as the Three Fork series. The Forest Service rates them Class IV at high flows and Class III at normal flows. These three rapids occur in a 1-mile stretch upstream from Morrison Creek. The largest rapids occur as you enter a tight canyon. Floaters can scout on river left. You can breathe easier for the next 10 miles after Morrison Creek, until you pass Twenty-Five Mile Creek. Below here, for the next 7 miles, is the most difficult water the Middle Fork offers. The toughest rapids are the Spruce Park Rapids, a set of three sharp drops that start just downstream from the Spruce Park guard station. The guard station can be difficult to see on river right, so keep your eyes open. The first rapid can be finicky and our last trip down a lineup of outfitted boats were being lined through the rapid, causing a 2-hour delay for every boat behind them. The rapids have huge waves, big rocks, and turbulence capable of flipping a raft. The Forest Service rates them Class V at peak flows, but under more normal conditions they are Class IV. You'll want to check these out carefully before going through, but the rugged terrain and lack of eddies to pull out make scouting difficult.

The trip through the wilderness section of the Middle Fork can be run by intermediates at lower flows but only by experts when it's high. The rapids change from year to year as boulders tumble into the river and trees lodge in different places. The most difficult rapids lie in a 3-mile canyon below Spruce Park. (For a complete description, see the "River Wild" sidebar.) Refer to your map, but there is an easy hiking trail that serves as an option for floaters who would rather hike their way around Spruce Park Rapids. Just make sure you know exactly where to pick up the hikers once through the canyon!

The remoteness of the upper Middle Fork makes it doubly dangerous. Those who haven't run many rivers as technically difficult as the Middle Fork may want to consider hiring an outfitter. The Hungry Horse Ranger District can provide a list of reputable ones.

Middle Fork float trips require considerable skill and quality equipment. A durable raft (a self-bailer is a must) with a rowing frame is the standard. For safety purposes, it's best to have two or three rafts per party. Be sure to take along extra paddles

After Spruce Park there are no more difficult rapids before the Middle Fork meets US 2 near Bear Creek. Just downstream from Bear Creek, however, are two more Class III rapids known as Staircase and Goat Lick. They are close to the place along the river where exposed natural salts attract mountain goats. The Izaak Walton Inn is nearby also.

Between Essex Bridge and Moccasin Creek, expect mostly Class II water. Watch for a drop called Brown's Hole, about 5 miles below Paola Creek, that's difficult at high water—approach river left. Expert and strong intermediate canoeists can handle this strikingly beautiful section of river except at peak flows. Watch for snags and dangerous logjams.

The Middle Fork's last gasp happens between Moccasin Creek and West Glacier in the 8-mile-long John Stevens Canyon. Cliff walls restrict the river to a narrow channel as it descends over rock ledges. It drops about 35 feet per mile as it dashes through the canyon. Expect to encounter fairly continuous whitewater for 2 to 3 miles through the middle of the canyon, suitable for intermediate and better rafters and kayakers, depending on water levels.

For those who like to know the names, here's a rundown of rapids for John Stevens Canyon: The first two, Tunnel and Bonecrusher, are pretty mild and get you ready for the toughest rapid, known as Jaws. Next comes Narrows, then Repeater, then C.B.T.; shortly before West Glacier is Pumphouse. Most of the rapids are Class II or III, but the Forest Service rates Jaws as Class IV at peak flows.

From West Glacier to the Blankenship Bridge is a good half-day float for beginners in rafts or canoes.

or oars, as they can be snapped off on cliff walls or submerged logs. Wet suits or rain gear is a necessity. This is one river where it's not necessary to remind people to wear life jackets. You may wish you had two. Every boat should have a couple of throw bags for emergency use.

Because the number of good campsites along the river is limited, this river corridor has potential for overuse. Tread lightly, and pack everything out. To avoid problems with grizzly bears, hang food and other bear attractants out of reach and keep a clean campsite. Consult *Bear Aware* by Bill Schneider (FalconGuides, 2004) and *Leave No Trace: Minimum Impact Outdoor Recreation* by Will Harmon (FalconGuides, 1997) for advice on camping safely and responsibly in bear country.

The non–wilderness section of the Middle Fork receives heavy summertime use, much of it from Glacier National Park visitors. The tourists usually get their money's worth. Moose, deer, bears, and a host of smaller mammals and birds often are seen near the river. Cutthroat trout, bull trout, and whitefish—all native fish—swim the waters and occasionally fall prey to artificial flies or wobbling spoons.

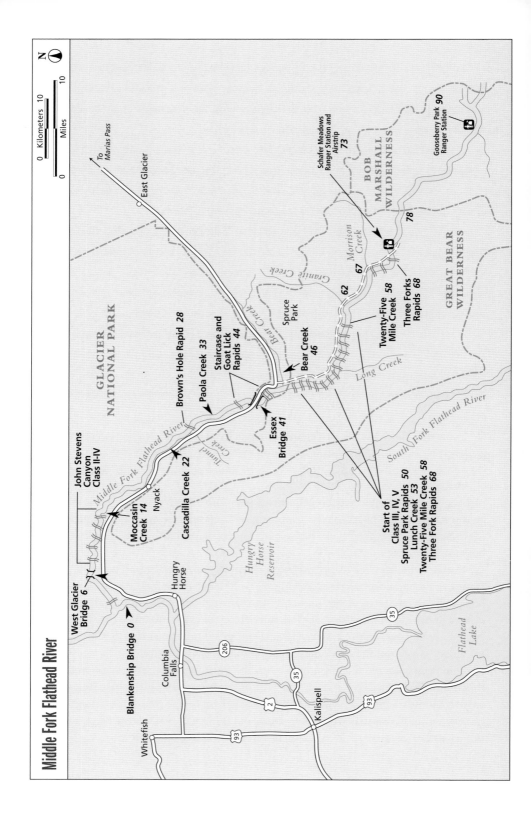

Middle Fork Flathead River

The Middle Fork is one of Montana's best-protected rivers. It flows through the wilderness for half its length, and it forms the southern border of Glacier National Park for the other half. The biggest problem this river faces is potential overuse, but the Forest Service so far has done an excellent job of managing people problems.

Key Access Points along Middle Fork Flathead River

Access Point	Access Type	(River Mile)
Schafer Meadows	Fly-In/Walk-In	(73)
Bear Creek	Hand Launch	(46)
Essex Bridge	Ramp	(41)
Paola Creek	Ramp	(33)
Cascadilla Creek	Ramp	(22)
Moccasin Creek	Ramp	(14)
West Glacier Bridge	Ramp	(6)
Blankenship Bridge	Ramp	(0)

16 South Fork Flathead River

The South Fork is a fairy-tale wilderness river that flows through the heart of the Bob Marshall Wilderness, with crystal-clear waters, native cutthroat trout, and an occasional grizzly bear.

Vital statistics: 100 miles (including 35 reservoir miles) from the confluence of Danaher and Youngs Creeks to the Flathead River at Hungry Horse.

Level of difficulty: Mostly Class I but punctuated by some difficult rapids. The extremely remote Meadow Creek Gorge has Class III and IV rapids (Class V at peak flows) and should only be attempted by experts. Watch for a short set of Class III and IV rapids below Hungry Horse Dam.

Flow: Annual mean flow: 2,310 cfs near Twin Creek. Not recommended at high flows (above 5,500 cfs). Few people risk the South Fork during runoff, which usually peaks in mid-June. July is prime time. In dry years it usually gets too low by early August. For floats starting at Youngs Creek, 2,000 cfs is minimum; 750 cfs is minimum for floats beginning at Big Salmon Creek.

Recommended watercraft: Small rafts, inflatable kayaks, pack rafts.

Hazards: Logjams and shallow riffles in the upper section, major rapids and narrow restrictions in the middle section. Hang your food at campsites, away from bears, porcupines, and squirrels.

Where the crowd goes: Difficult access limits use, but many outfitters take clients from Youngs Creek to the take-out above Meadow Creek Gorge.

Avoiding the scene: Cedar Flats below Meadow Creek down to Hungry Horse Reservoir.

Inside tip: In mid-July the South Fork put-ins can be downright busy. Think about shoulder season opportunities.

Maps: USFS: Flathead, Bob Marshall Complex; USGS: Choteau, MT; Cut Bank, MT; Kalispell, MT; Flathead National Forest and Glacier Natural History Association: Three Forks of the Flathead Wild & Scenic River Float Guide.

Shuttle information: Flathead River Shuttle, (406) 752-5331; Blackfoot Commercial Co., (406) 793-5555.

River rules: No motors, special fishing regulations.

For more information: Flathead National Forest, Hungry Horse; Spotted Bear Ranger Station, on the river.

The Paddling

The famous conservationist Aldo Leopold once wrote, "To those devoid of imagination a blank place on the map is a useless waste; to others, the most valuable part." So it is with the South Fork of the Flathead River, the main travel route through Montana's Bob Marshall Wilderness. The South Fork is Montana's most pristine and inaccessible river, a designated component of the National Wild and Scenic Rivers System for nearly its entire length and arguably one of the most remote rivers in the Lower 48.

Those wishing to float the wilderness portion of the South Fork must either hike or ride horses a considerable distance before they hit the water. Most people approach the river via Holland Lake and Gordon Creek, a distance of about 27 miles. Others pack in over Pyramid Pass and reach the South Fork via Youngs Creek, which is slightly farther. The usual starting point is Big Prairie, as the river is often too low to float after mid-July above this point. Put-ins can sometimes almost feel crowded on the South Fork, despite being so far from civilization. The South Fork has officially made it on the map, so to speak, so don't be disappointed if you have company. Unfortunately, efforts have been recently made to open airstrips on the Bob Marshall Wilderness that would allow easier access for tourists. Some places should just remain difficult to reach.

The trip from Big Prairie to the South Fork access just downstream from Spotted Bear Ranger Station covers about 45 miles and can easily be floated in 4 days. Because equipment must be packed such a long distance, most people make the trip in small rafts, allowing for two people and about 60 pounds of gear per raft. Campsites are easy to find along the river.

Don't forget to pull out before Meadow Creek gorge at the end of your trip. While the gorge can sometimes be runnable in small craft, logjams can pop up overnight and once you're in, you're in. TIM PALMER

From Big Prairie to Salmon Forks, a distance of about 14 miles, you can relax and enjoy the scenery, as there are few or no rapids. This upper section of the river may have logjams that completely block the river, however, so be prepared for portages. The upper section is often too low by mid-August or earlier in dry years, and it may be necessary to drag your raft across some riffles. Salmon Forks can generally be reached the first day.

The next section, between Salmon Forks and Black Bear Creek, is about 12 miles. Here the river increases in depth and begins to form more pools and riffles. The South Fork's water is extraordinarily clear and pure, and the bottom is dotted with brick-red, chalk-white, and aqua-green rocks. The water is so clear that, with polarized sunglasses, it's often possible to see trout coming to your fly well in advance of the strike. While the river speeds up a bit, it's still not very difficult. What's so remarkable about the South Fork isn't that it's so unusually spectacular but that it's so wild and untrammeled. The South Fork looks much like many other broad western Montana valleys, with one exception—it has no roads, no humming of cars, and no houses.

Floaters typically hit the tough part of the South Fork on the third day. While it's only about 9 river miles from Black Bear Creek to Harrison Creek, allow an entire day for this spectacular section. Look for a few rapids right below Black Bear Creek, but the real hazards begin in a narrow canyon just downstream from where Mid Creek pours into the South Fork. A large Forest Service sign just above this point warns boaters that this is the last safe take-out if you intend to portage around the downstream gorge. In the course of the next 2 miles below the sign, the river squeezes into restrictions so narrow in two separate places that a raft cannot pass through. At one of these points, it's possible to stand with one foot on each bank and watch the river flow between your legs.

Less than 1 mile below the second major restriction comes the incredible Meadow Creek Gorge. Be prepared for a spectacular entry. Just above the gorge, there's a tricky little rapid that shoots you around a blind corner, under the Meadow Creek pack bridge, and into the gorge. It's a real thrill—the river is too fast and the cliff walls too steep to permit any scouting of what's coming. Instead you blast into the gorge praying there aren't any serious obstacles or obstructions.

From a sheer geologic perspective, the gorge is the most spectacular part of the trip. Canyon walls rise up nearly 150 feet, as the gorge itself is but a narrow cleft, a ribbon of water in an otherwise solid mass of rock. Often less than 15 feet wide, it's like being in a labyrinth; the canyon twists and turns, and it's impossible to see what lies around the next corner. It's quite dark in the bottom of the canyon and eerily quiet except for one place where a waterfall pounds down from above. While the current in the mile-long gorge is rather swift, it's smooth and there aren't permanent hazards. While winding around the curves, however, one can't help but be apprehensive about the possibility of a logjam in this narrow chasm. It's often possible to look up and see logs that completely bridge the canyon. When in the gorge (and in other narrow spots on the river), you'll want to have a stout stick or a rugged canoe paddle handy

The South Fork of the Flathead is Montana's ultimate wilderness float. Access is difficult, but the rewards are worth the trouble. TIM PALMER

to keep your boat from bouncing off cliff walls. It's such a narrow gorge that standard raft oars on a frame are almost useless.

Immediately past the gorge begins some of the South Fork's most difficult and dangerous whitewater. Large rocks combined with swift current make passage rather technical, and scouting is recommended. The whitewater doesn't last long, however. By the time Harrison Creek enters, the difficult water is behind you.

From Harrison Creek to Spotted Bear, the river is also wild and beautiful and receives only modest use. While the upper section of the river receives heavy outfitter pressure, almost no outfitters take clients through the gorge. Consequently the river below Mid Creek receives much less boat traffic. The road on the east side of Hungry Horse Reservoir is the quickest route to Spotted Bear, although it is dirt for its entirety. It's a 90-minute drive from Hungry Horse to Cedar Flats on the west side of the reservoir. The only access points are the Meadow Creek airstrip or the Cedar Flats river access, off the Meadow Creek Road (FR 2826). The Cedar Flats access involves a steep, 400-yard hike down a narrow trail to the river, but it is possible to wrestle a boat down and the section is runnable for intermediate canoeists midsummer. It's about a 4-hour float from Cedar Flats to the South Fork access—short but spectacular. From Spotted Bear downstream to where Hungry Horse Reservoir impounds the river, there's easy public access on both sides of the road.

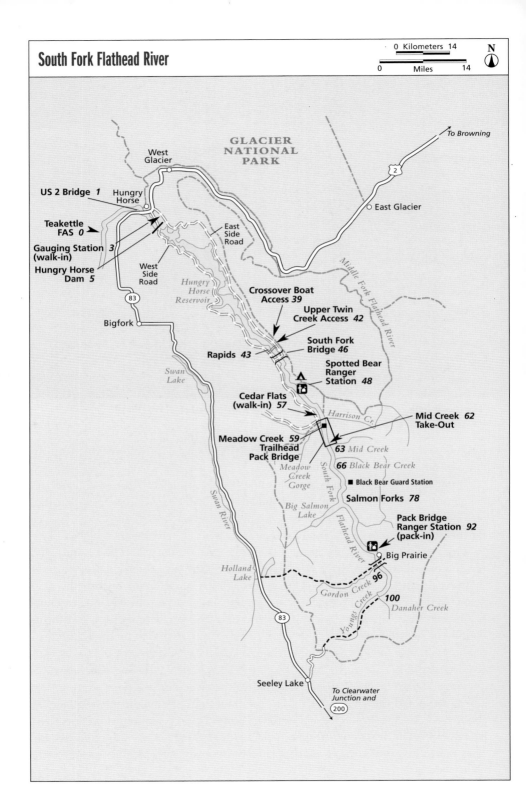

South Fork Flathead River

While floating on the South Fork is only moderately difficult, its extreme isolation makes it far too risky for beginners. Errors here can mean serious discomfort, or even death. Intermediates could make the trip if they go when the water is low and if they portage around Meadow Creek Gorge (about 4 miles by trail—it's best to make arrangements with an outfitter).

Only experts should attempt the hazardous float between Mid and Harrison Creeks. While the gorge itself is not that dangerous if you portage the narrow restrictions, the hazard level is high, and there's little margin for error if you make a mistake. Anyone floating below the warning sign should get out and scout each dangerous point. Except at the highest flows, it's possible to get out and scout except where the river rushes under the Meadow Creek pack bridge. It's easy to hear the roar of the obstructions well in advance. At the two restrictions where portages are mandatory, the routes are obvious along the canyon walls. The first one is short, and the second one is a few hundred yards long.

No official access exists on the 5 miles of the South Fork that flows below Hungry Horse Reservoir. An unofficial access point is about 3 miles north of US 2. This section of river has Class III whitewater and fluctuates significantly based on dam releases. Use caution; several people have drowned in this section after floating mishaps.

Float fishing: Don't leave your fishing rod at home. The South Fork is arguably one of the most robust native cutthroat and bull trout fisheries in the state. Although its popularity as a fishing river has surged in recent years due to an increase in outfitted floats and numerous magazine features, the South Fork will not disappoint. Although the floating window is somewhat short, cutthroats and bulls are eager to put on weight while bug life is plentiful. Special regulations designed to protect large fish have resulted in sizable numbers in the 12- to 18-inch range. Moreover, cutthroats are notoriously easy to catch. This is the only river in Montana where it is legal to target and fish for threatened bull trout. As this large, migratory fish makes its way upriver to spawn in the fall, they aggressively chase and feed on smaller cutthroats. It is not uncommon to catch bull trout over 10 pounds. Check with FWP for licensing requirements.

Key Access Points along South Fork Flathead River

Access Point	Access Type	(River Mile)
Big Prairie	Pack-In	(96)
Mid Creek take-out	Pack-In	(62)
Cedar Flats	Walk-In	(57)
South Fork Access	Hand Launch	(47)
Upper Twin Creek Access	Hand Launch	(42)
Crossover Boat Access on Hungry Horse Reservoir	Ramp	(39)
Gauging Station	Walk-In	(3) (walk-in)
Teakettle FAS	Ramp	(2 miles on the main stem Flathead)

17 Gallatin River

Originating in Yellowstone National Park, the alpine-surrounded Gallatin River provides great whitewater and good fishing as it courses through one of the most scenic valleys in Montana. The Gallatin River actually consists of two forks, the East Gallatin and the West Gallatin Rivers. Because the West Gallatin is substantially larger, it's generally recognized as the main stem river. While both branches are floatable, they differ sharply in character.

Vital statistics: 100 miles from the Wyoming border to the Missouri River near Three Forks. The East Gallatin River, a major tributary of the Gallatin, is also floatable for about 20 miles from Bozeman to its confluence with the main stem near Manhattan.

Level of difficulty: A difficult whitewater stream with Class II, III, and IV rapids in the upper 40 miles. Very technical; experts only at high flows.

Flow: Annual mean flow: 810 cfs near Gallatin Gateway. Often too low by late July. On the lower river (measured at Gallatin Gateway), 500 cfs is a minimum flow and 2,500 cfs is a maximum flow. For the Mad Mile, 8,000 cfs should be maximum for whitewater enthusiasts.

Recommended watercraft: Rafts or kayaks on the upper whitewater section; all crafts are suitable below the confluence with the East Gallatin.

Hazards: Large rocks, tricky currents, large waves, diversion dams, and logjams on the Gallatin. Barbed-wire fences, sharp bends, low water, and narrow brushy channels on the East Gallatin.

Where the crowd goes: Big Sky to Squaw Creek.

Avoiding the scene: Shed's Bridge FAS to Missouri Headwaters State Park.

Inside tip: Great fall duck hunting from Logan to Trident. A birder's paradise.

Maps: USFS: Gallatin; USGS: Bozeman, MT; River Rat Maps: Gallatin; Montana Afloat: #11 (The Gallatin River).

Shuttle information: Bob's Shuttle Service, (406) 595-0587.

River rules: No fishing from boats from Yellowstone National Park to the confluence with the East Gallatin.

For more information: Yellowstone Raft Company, Big Sky; FWP, Bozeman.

The Paddling

The Gallatin River springs from the snow-clad peaks of the Madison and Gallatin Mountain ranges and courses 100 miles before joining the Madison and Jefferson Rivers at Three Forks. The Gallatin comes close to being an alpine stream as it spills through the scenic Gallatin Canyon, where frequent rapids alternate with deep, green pools alive with trout.

After its start in Yellowstone National Park, the Gallatin dashes its way through beautiful forested country, providing good fishing and excellent whitewater boating along the way. The upper 40 miles of the Gallatin River contain some of Montana's finest whitewater with an abundance of technical rapids, tight turns, big rocks, and

House Rock in the Gallatin canyon is a formidable rapid for whitewater paddlers. JOHN TODD

large waves. While much of Montana's whitewater consists of large drops separated by long stretches of flatwater, the Gallatin distinguishes itself with its quantity of white-water as well as its quality. Some stretches have nearly continuous action. Almost all the Gallatin's whitewater is easily accessible, as the river flows mostly through public land and generally runs close to US 191. Even though the Gallatin is a small river, it can sustain good boating well into summer.

The Indians knew this area as "the valley of the flowers." Despite ever-increasing development, it remains one of Montana's loveliest valleys.

Lewis and Clark named the river for President Thomas Jefferson's secretary of the treasury, Albert Gallatin. Captain William Clark explored the Gallatin Valley in July 1806 on his return trip from the Pacific. He wrote in his journal: "I saw Elk, Deer and Antelope, and great deal of old signs of buffalo. Their roads is in every direction . . . emence quantities of beaver on this Fork . . . and their dams very much impede the navigation of it."

Had Captain Clark proceeded farther upstream, he would have discovered some challenging rapids that would have tested the Corps of Discovery's buffalo-skin boats. Modern-day explorers, however, find the whitewater much to their liking.

The sinuous East Gallatin winds through open meadows and agricultural country. With its brushy banks, deep holes, and sometimes silty bottom, it resembles the Beaverhead, only smaller. Its high nutrients make for a good fishery, but access is difficult and fences are common.

Floating on the East Gallatin is usually possible except in dry years. With normal flows, floating is possible as high as the Cherry River FAS in Bozeman. This winding upper section can be handled by intermediate canoeists and rafters. Practiced beginners can give it a try below Dry Creek, although the sharp bends and occasional brush piles necessitate constant maneuvering. Because the river is flanked by private lands, it is occasionally blocked by barbed-wire fences and is so narrow and winding, it's rather difficult to float, but this doesn't stop some adventurous floaters.

County road bridges provide the primary access for East Gallatin float trips, and they occur at fairly regular intervals. Most of the river receives only moderate floating pressure.

The main stem Gallatin is a river for experienced floaters. From Taylor Creek to the West Fork, intermediate canoeists and rafters can test their skills. During peak flows, however, canoeists will have problems with high waves. Below the West Fork the Gallatin is extremely challenging all the way to Squaw Creek, and only experts or solid intermediates should try it. The most difficult section runs for 2 miles directly below the highway bridge at Cascade Creek. Large rocks in the river spawn tricky currents and frothing water.

The often-photographed House Rock Rapid, the most formidable of all, is visible from the highway, and crowds often gather to watch intrepid boaters. At peak flows only experienced floaters with high-flotation life jackets, helmets, and wet suits should try this stretch.

Although the Gallatin loses its whitewater below the mouth of the Gallatin Canyon, it remains difficult until it reaches the East Gallatin near Manhattan. The river frequently channels and has numerous logjams that sometimes completely block the

BIG FUN ON THE GALLATIN

The upper 40 miles of the Gallatin River contain some of Montana's finest whitewater. Most of the whitewater fun takes place in May and June; the water generally gets low by mid-July. The action starts right where the Gallatin leaves Yellowstone National Park near Taylor Creek (boating is not permitted inside the park boundary). From the park boundary to Big Sky (where the West Fork enters), intermediate rafters and strong intermediate canoeists will have fun. The river is broad and shallow with tight turns. It's a Class II run with some big waves. A favorite run is from Red Cliff to Big Sky, a distance of about 8 miles. The river above Red Cliff doesn't get much floating use. It's typically too low for boats by mid-July. Watch for downed trees.

As the Gallatin churns downstream, it grows increasingly difficult. Big Sky to Greek Creek features tight turns and challenging rapids as the river picks up volume. There's a particularly challenging spot near where Portal Creek spills in. Intermediate rafters can handle it, but it's on the margin for canoeists. It's mostly Class II, but Portal Creek is a difficult Class III.

The real heavy-duty Gallatin whitewater lies between Greek Creek and the Squaw Creek Bridge. Not long after Greek Creek, the canyon narrows and the river changes. The turns get tighter, the river grows rockier, and the whitewater becomes more continuous. It gets hard to find eddies where it's easy to pull out and bail or take a break. Between Greek Creek and the Cascade Creek Bridge (also known as the "35-mile-per-hour bridge") lie several tricky rapids, including a treacherous bend known as Screaming Left Turn and a boat-eating keeper called Hilarity Hole. While the rapids can be intense (this section rates a solid Class III), the most difficult whitewater comes between Cascade Creek and the Squaw Creek Bridge. At high flows this final 3 miles is for experts only, so don't miss the take-out at Cascade Creek (on the left side of the river, opposite the highway) if you're not up to the run.

Below the Cascade Creek Bridge the whitewater is nearly continuous, with big rocks and big water in the narrowly constricted river. This section contains the Gallatin's most famous and most photographed whitewater, House Rock Rapid. Immediately downstream lie a boulder field and a swift section known as the Mad Mile. Again, this section is for properly equipped experts, running in groups. Super-expert canoeists have run this section in recent years, but it requires a great deal of flotation and really exceptional skills. This section contains many Class III rapids and a couple of Class IVs.

The last section of good whitewater lies between Squaw Creek and the bridge at the mouth of the Gallatin Canyon. This popular section has some Class III water. Watch for a dangerous diversion dam about 1 mile before the take-out.

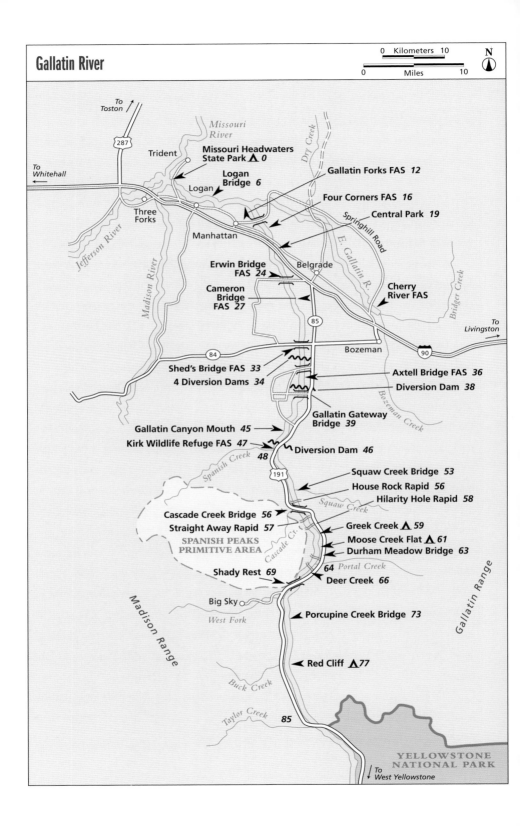

Gallatin River

0 Kilometers 10

0 Miles 10

N

To Toston

Missouri River

Dry Creek

Trident

Missouri Headwaters State Park ⛰ 0

Gallatin Forks FAS 12

To Whitehall

287

Logan Bridge 6

Logan

Four Corners FAS 16

Central Park 19

Three Forks

Manhattan

Springhill Road

Jefferson River

Madison River

E. Gallatin R.

Erwin Bridge FAS 24

Belgrade

Cherry River FAS

Cameron Bridge FAS 27

Bridger Creek

To Livingston

85

Bozeman

90

84

Shed's Bridge FAS 33

4 Diversion Dams 34

Axtell Bridge FAS 36

Diversion Dam 38

Bozeman Creek

Gallatin Gateway Bridge 39

Gallatin Canyon Mouth 45

Kirk Wildlife Refuge FAS 47

Diversion Dam 46

Spanish Creek 48

191

Squaw Creek Bridge 53

House Rock Rapid 56

Hilarity Hole Rapid 58

Squaw Creek

Cascade Creek Bridge 56

Straight Away Rapid 57

SPANISH PEAKS PRIMITIVE AREA

Greek Creek ⛰ 59

Moose Creek Flat ⛰ 61

Durham Meadow Bridge 63

Cascade Cr.

Shady Rest 69

64 Portal Creek

Deer Creek 66

Big Sky

West Fork

Porcupine Creek Bridge 73

Madison Range

Gallatin Range

Red Cliff ⛰ 77

Buck Creek

Taylor Creek 85

YELLOWSTONE NATIONAL PARK

To West Yellowstone

river. Combine that with occasional diversion dams (especially in the area immediately below Axtell Bridge), and it all adds up to frustrating floating. Rafters are smart to pass up this section. Only expert canoeists or kayakers should try it during runoff. Afterward, intermediates can handle it if there's enough water. Irrigation dewatering may deter summer floating in some sections.

The two forks of the Gallatin join about 2 miles north of Manhattan (at Gallatin Forks FAS) and provide easy floating, suitable for beginners, for about the next 6 miles downstream to Logan Bridge. Between Logan and Trident (another 6 miles downstream) occasional logjams and sharp bends increase the hazard level. Like the last few miles of the Jefferson and Madison Rivers, the last segment of the Gallatin is alive with wildlife, including waterfowl, deer, and an occasional moose.

Float fishing: Biologists report trout numbers as high as 3,000 fish per mile on the upper Gallatin. While the river isn't renowned for huge trout, there are some nice browns below Erwin Bridge. Anglers should be aware that the entire West Gallatin—from Yellowstone National Park to its confluence with the East Gallatin—is closed to fishing from boats. The Montana Fish and Game Commission established this closure to alleviate conflict between floaters and bank anglers. Because the Gallatin is classified as a navigable river, it remains open to floaters who are not fishing.

Key Access Points along the Gallatin River

Access Point	Access Type	(River Mile)
Red Cliff	Hand Launch	(77)
Porcupine Creek Bridge	Hand Launch	(73)
Shady Rest (Big Sky)	Hand Launch	(69)
Deer Creek	Ramp	(66)
Durham Meadow Bridge	Hand Launch	(63)
Moose Creek Flat	Ramp	(61)
Greek Creek	Hand Launch	(59)
Cascade Creek Bridge	Hand Launch	(56)
Squaw Creek Bridge	Hand Launch	(53)
Kirk Wildlife Refuge FAS	Hand Launch	(47)
Gallatin Canyon Mouth Harringer Bridge	Hand Launch	(45)
Axtell Bridge FAS	Hand Launch	(36)
Shed's Bridge FAS	Hand Launch	(33)
Cameron Bridge FAS	Hand Launch	(27)
Erwin Bridge FAS	Hand Launch	(24)
Central Park	Hand Launch	(19)
Four Corners FAS	Hand Launch	(16)
Gallatin Forks FAS	Hand Launch	(12)
Logan Bridge	Hand Launch	(6)
Missouri River Headwaters State Park	Ramp	(0)

18 Jefferson River

Once traversed for its entire distance by the Lewis and Clark Expedition, the Jefferson meanders peaceably through thick cottonwood bottoms while providing good fishing and excellent wildlife viewing.

Vital statistics: 83 miles from the confluence of the Big Hole and Beaverhead Rivers to its juncture with the Madison and Gallatin Rivers to form the Missouri River near Three Forks.
Level of difficulty: Class I, suitable for practiced beginners its entire length.
Flow: Annual mean flow: 1,979 cfs near Three Forks. Usually floatable all year but sometimes suffers summertime dewatering below Silver Star. Don't float the Jefferson with flows over 12,000 cfs (Twin Bridges gauge).
Recommended watercraft: Suitable for all crafts.
Hazards: Logjams, protruding trees, and narrow channels. Dangerous diversion dams.
Where the crowd goes: Twin Bridges on the Beaverhead River to Kountz Bridge.

Avoiding the scene: Downstream from Cardwell Bridge.
Inside tip: Several undeveloped hot springs occur along the river.
Maps: USFS: Beaverhead, Deerlodge; USGS: Dillon, MT; Bozeman, MT; River Rat Maps: Jefferson; Montana Afloat: #10 (The Jefferson River).
Shuttle information: Canoeing House, Three Forks, (406) 285-3488; Bob's Shuttle, (406) 555-1234.
River rules: No boats over 10 horsepower.
For more information: Four Rivers Fishing Company, Twin Bridges; Frontier Anglers, Dillon; FWP, Bozeman.

The Paddling

The Beaverhead and Big Hole Rivers merge near Twin Bridges to form the Jefferson, which then flows generally northeast for more than 80 miles. The river winds and braids repeatedly through mostly arid benchland and irrigated farmland, encompassing a wide band of thick, brushy river bottom.

For those who like to drift back in history as they float down rivers, the Jefferson offers a gold mine of river lore. Not only did Lewis and Clark travel its entire length, but famous mountain man John Colter also made his legendary run along the Jefferson's brushy banks.

In the spring of 1808, Colter and a companion were each paddling a canoe down the Jefferson when they were accosted by Blackfeet Indians, a tribe vigorously resisting the invasion of the white man. The Blackfeet motioned for them to come to shore. Colter's companion balked, which was a fatal mistake. He was killed on the spot, and Colter was captured.

Since Colter's scalp would be a substantial prize, the Indians decided it should go to the fleetest brave. Colter was stripped of his clothes and shoes and given a chance to run for his life. When the chief inquired about the white man's speed, the clever Colter responded that he was a poor runner. The Blackfeet gave Colter a head start—all the speedy fur trapper needed. He ran about 5 miles before diving into the Jefferson and finding a hiding spot under a logjam. Although the Indians searched the river extensively, they failed to find the well-hidden mountain man.

Colter's ordeal, however, had only begun. When night fell, he began the long trek to the nearest civilization—a fort at the mouth of the Bighorn River, 250 miles distant. Even though he had neither food nor clothing, Colter reportedly covered the distance in 11 days, losing so much weight that his friends didn't recognize him when he appeared at the fort.

Captain Lewis's August 2, 1805, description of the Jefferson River and its valley remains quite accurate today. His journal reads:

> . . . we found the current very rapid waist deep and about 90 yds. wide. bottom smooth pebble with a small mixture of coarse gravel . . . The valley along which we passed today, and through which the river winds it's meandering course is from 6 to 8 miles wide and consists of a beautiful level plain with but little timber, and that confined to the verge of the river; the land is tolerably fertile, and is either black or dark yellow loam, covered with grass from 9 inches to 2 feet high. the plain ascends gradually on either side of the river to the bases of two ranges of high mountains. the tops of these mountains are yet covered partially with snow, while we in the valley are nearly suffocated with the intense heat of the midday sun; the nights are so cold that two blankets are not more than sufficient covering.

The Corps of Discovery had an arduous journey as they lined their boats up the brushy Jefferson. Hot weather, mosquitoes, and slippery rocks plagued the crew. Today modern explorers encounter some of the same problems. Captain Lewis even got lost on the Jefferson and was forced to spend the evening on an island. During his restless night he heard a large splash, which he feared was the dreaded "white" bear, the grizzly. River rats no longer have to deal with Old Griz on the Jefferson, but present-day explorers will be pleased to find parts of the Jefferson much as Lewis and Clark saw it. The picturesque Tobacco Root Mountains (still largely roadless) rise to the east, while the more rounded Highland Mountains enliven the view on the west side. Most of the river bottom remains undeveloped, although cattle have replaced the elk Lewis and Clark saw.

Water quality is the biggest change since frontier days, and it's the biggest drawback to a Jefferson float. Irrigation runoff and grazing practices create turbidity that often clouds the river. Although the Jefferson is usually clear in late summer and fall, rainstorms can muddy the river in short order. In addition, excessive nutrients in the water often foster rapid growth of algae in summer, creating a nuisance for anglers and swimmers. In late summer the river can be too low to float due to heavy agricultural irrigation in the valley.

Near Cardwell, the Jefferson is wide and slow, perfect for lazy day floats where crowds are few.

With proper caution the entire Jefferson can be floated by beginners. Much of the river is broad and slow moving, although the river sometimes channels and picks up speed. Logjams, protruding trees, and narrow channels are the major hazards.

In the upper sections the river is quite removed from civilization. Occasional diversions and riprap, however, will remind you that man isn't far away. The diversions below Parson's Bridge and at the Parrot Castle FAS are hazardous. Adequate in-stream flows to protect fish and wildlife are sorely needed.

Below the Parrot Castle access and the Renova Bridge, the river divides into two channels of nearly equal size for about 8 miles, forming a large island. This section of the river is particularly scenic as it sweeps by the Tobacco Roots. About 3 miles below Cardwell Bridge FAS, the river enters a narrow canyon, as does the old highway, which parallels the river for the next several miles. As the river cuts through the canyon, it forms many deep pools as well as a few fast runs. Steep limestone walls and colorful rock formations make it an interesting section. The popular Lewis and Clark Caverns, which were never actually visited by Lewis and Clark, can be viewed from the river just a few miles below Cardwell.

As the river approaches Three Forks, it again becomes isolated. It braids into several channels as it winds through brushy, lowland habitat for its last few miles before helping to form the Missouri. The numerous channel changes and occasional downed trees make this the trickiest section. Still, beginners can handle it if the water isn't high.

Jefferson River

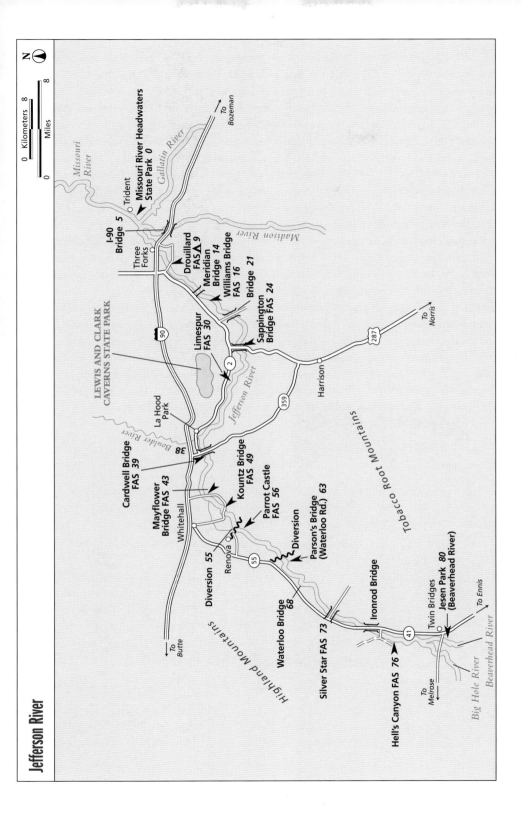

The last few miles of the Jefferson are a great place for wildlife viewing. Ducks and geese nest in this area, and the brush is alive with whitetails. The area also has a few moose, so keep your eyes peeled for the king of the deer family.

The floating pressure the Jefferson receives is light and well distributed. Most floaters are anglers from Butte and surrounding communities. This river offers excellent potential for multiday float trips, and you could start on the Big Hole or Beaverhead and take an extended trip right through the heart of Lewis and Clark country. The Jefferson River Chapter of the Lewis and Clark Trail Heritage Foundation has done an excellent job preserving land and designating camping areas along the river. Consider supporting their efforts to preserve the rich history of the Jefferson; contact information is in appendix B.

Float fishing: While fishing sometimes is excellent on the Jefferson, water clarity and water temperature are crucial components of a good fishery. Most anglers float the upper stretches and favor big wet flies or streamers. Browns inhabit the river (fewer than 800 per mile below Ironrod Bridge) along with a few rainbows (catch-and-release only) and whitefish. In recent years the "Jeff" has been plagued with high temperatures, often reaching upward of 75 degrees Fahrenheit. As a result fish kills are somewhat common, and FWP often closes the river to fishing when temperatures soar in late summer (initiated when water temps reach 73 degrees or more for 3 consecutive days). Many groups and agencies are stepping up to address the low, warm flows in the Jefferson. If you are interested in helping keep the Jeff running cold and clear, contact the Jefferson River Watershed Council (see appendix B).

Key Access Points along the Jefferson River

Access Point	Access Type	(River Mile)
Jesen Park, Twin Bridges	Ramp	(80)
Hell's Canyon FAS	Ramp	(76)
Silver Star FAS	Ramp	(73)
Waterloo Rd. Parson Bridge	Hand Launch	(63)
Parrot Castle FAS	Walk-In	(56)
Kountz Bridge FAS	Ramp	(49)
Mayflower Bridge FAS	Ramp	(43)
Cardwell Bridge FAS	Ramp	(39)
Limespur FAS	Walk-In	(30)
Sappington Bridge FAS	Ramp	(24)
Williams Bridge FAS	Ramp	(16)
Meridian Bridge	Ramp	(14)
Drouillard FAS	Ramp	(9)
Missouri River Headwaters State Park	Ramp	(0)

19 Judith River

This excellent canoeing stream flows through isolated breaks country that features white cliffs, deep coulees, and hoodoo rock formations.

Vital statistics: 130 miles from the confluence of the Middle and South Forks to the Missouri River.

Level of difficulty: Mostly Class I except for a 1-mile Class II rapid beginning 1 mile upstream from the Highway 81 bridge. Suitable for intermediates in canoes or practiced beginners in rafts.

Flow: Annual mean flow: 60 cfs near Utica. Too low to float by mid-July except in wet years.

Recommended watercraft: Canoes.

Hazards: Barbed wire (even some electric fences!), many rocks, ledges across the river, downed trees in lower river, and rattlesnakes.

Where the crowd goes: Nowhere. Most floating occurs between the Highway 81 bridge (east of Denton) and Anderson Bridge.

Avoiding the scene: Just show up.

Inside tip: In wet years a fall trip may be possible.

Maps: USFS: Lewis & Clark (Jefferson Division); USGS: White Sulphur, MT; Roundup, MT; Lewistown, MT.

Shuttle information: Hole in the Wall Adventures, Lewistown, (406) 538-2418; Missouri River Canoe Company, Virgelle, (406) 378-3110.

River rules: Be respectful of private property as very little public land adjoins this remote prairie stream.

For more information: BLM, Lewistown.

The Paddling

The fast-flowing Judith River gets its start in the Little Belt Mountains and then courses through forests, badlands, and arid prairies for 130 miles before meeting the Missouri River not far from Judith Landing. This must have been the point in Lewis and Clark's journey where they got lonely for female companionship—Captain Clark named the Judith for Julia "Judy" Hancock (whom he later married), and not far upstream Captain Lewis named the Marias (Maria's River) after Maria Wood, a favorite cousin.

The Judith is a small stream floatable only early in the season or in wet years. It's largely unfloatable above Hobson, as beaver dams and fences create frequent barriers. Between Hobson and the Highway 81 bridge, occasional county bridges provide access. A 1-mile rock garden beginning 1 mile upstream from the Highway 81 bridge has some moderate rapids (Class II). Otherwise the river is mostly flat but swift-flowing water with rocks, ledges, and wood in the river.

The small amount of floating that does occur on the Judith takes place mainly between the Highway 81 bridge and the Missouri River, where the river flows through a secluded canyon. This river has a surprisingly lively flow for a prairie stream, rushing down a rocky streambed with occasional ledges. Rugged terrain surrounds

Near the junction with the Missouri, the Judith River winds its way through dramatic breaks and cottonwood bottoms.

the river, including sandstone cliffs, clay banks, and slightly timbered hillsides. There aren't many trees, just occasional groves of cottonwoods and intermittent buffalo berry bushes, Russian olives, and willows. The river is extremely isolated, with only a handful of ranch houses near the river. We floated the Judith one October, and a rancher told us we were the first floaters she had seen in 30 years. While this river sees a few floaters every year, it's very remote, and you'll feel like an explorer. It's an outstanding river for canoeing, as it requires constant maneuvering. Wildlife viewing is great; expect to see deer, coyotes, eagles, and pheasants. The Judith has places with more wild asparagus than we've seen on any other Montana river.

The biggest problem with Judith River floats is the barbed-wire fences. They're very floater-unfriendly—some are even electrified! They are difficult to portage around; lifting them is the best bet, but at higher flows keep your eyes peeled downriver so you aren't surprised. Lots of barbed wire translates into lots of cows, and the Judith has its share. Heavy cow use has rendered many potential campsites undesirable. Public land along the Judith is limited, however, so you may have to take what you can get. Your best bet to stay on public land and avoid conflict is by using onXmaps or a similar GPS app.

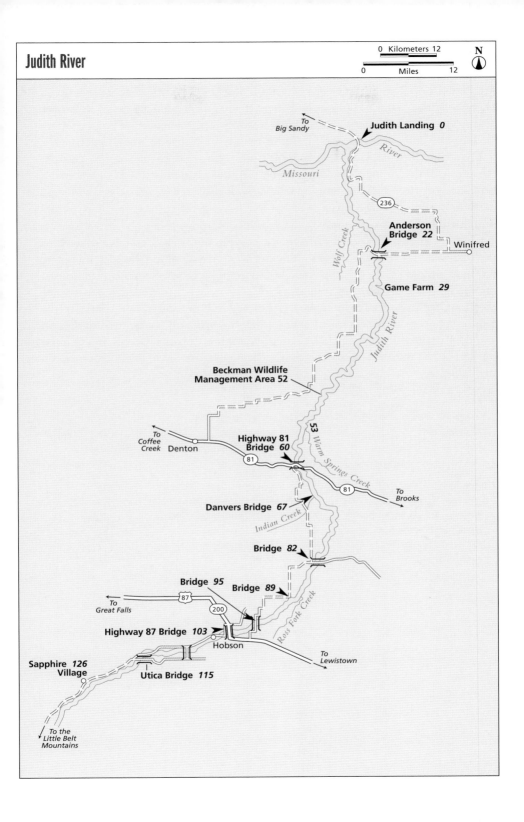

Judith River

0 Kilometers 12
0 Miles 12
N

To Big Sandy
Judith Landing *0*

River

Missouri

236

Wolf Creek

Anderson Bridge *22*
Winifred

Game Farm *29*

Judith River

Beckman Wildlife Management Area *52*

53

Warm Springs Creek

To Coffee Creek
Denton
Highway 81 Bridge *60*

81

81
To Brooks

Danvers Bridge *67*

Indian Creek

Bridge *82*

Bridge *95*   Bridge *89*

87
To Great Falls

200

Highway 87 Bridge *103*

Ross Fork Creek

Hobson
To Lewistown

Sapphire *126* Village

Utica Bridge *115*

To the Little Belt Mountains

In a normal year, floating on the Judith is possible until mid-July (it can pick up with fall rains). If you see lots of rocks above the surface and the water looks low just above the Highway 81 bridge, you should definitely not try the float between Danvers Bridge and the Highway 81 bridge. If you put in at the Highway 81 bridge, Warm Springs Creek, about 7 miles downstream, provides a significant boost of water (at least 100 cubic feet per second). The Highway 81 bridge to Anderson Bridge is a 2-day trip when days are long and the water is up. Add another day to go from Anderson Bridge to Judith Landing. While the Judith is almost all Class I water, this brisk-flowing river with its profusion of rocks will challenge inexperienced canoeists.

With a few less barbed-wire fences, a few less cows right next to the river, and some better public-land campsites, the Judith could provide a truly first-class river experience. The BLM studied the river for possible Wild and Scenic River status in the mid-1980s. If you take a trip on this river, you may wish to follow up by calling the BLM in Lewistown (see appendix A) and urging it to get involved with protecting the Judith's considerable natural attributes.

Float fishing: While the upper reaches of the North and South Forks of the Judith support trout populations, the lower Judith is primarily a warmwater fishery. If you do plan on bringing your rod, be prepared to throw plastics, worms, and spinners for burbot and catfish. Both species are excellent table fare for an exploratory trip on the Judith.

Key Access Points along the Judith River

Access Point	Access Type	(River Mile)
Highway 87 bridge	Hand Launch	(103)
Bridge	Hand Launch	(95)
Bridge	Hand Launch	(89)
Bridge	Hand Launch	(82)
Danvers Bridge	Hand Launch	(67)
Highway 81 (Denton) bridge	Hand Launch	(60)
Beckman Wildlife Management Area	Hand Launch	(52)
Anderson Bridge	Hand Launch	(22)
Judith Landing	Ramp	(0)

20 Kootenai River

This big, clear river courses through heavily forested mountains, providing good fishing and excellent scenery along the way. Home to the impressive Kootenai Falls downstream from Libby.

Vital statistics: 100 miles in Montana (50 reservoir miles) from the Canadian border north of Eureka to the Idaho border. Second-largest river in Montana in water volume.

Level of difficulty: Mostly Class I with a couple of difficult sections that are Class II and III. China Rapids and Kootenai Falls Gorge are Class IV and V, respectively.

Flow: Annual mean flow: 13,340 cfs at Leonia, Idaho. The river is dam controlled, and large fluctuations in volume are not uncommon. Floatable all year. Optimum floating between 7,000 and 11,000 cfs.

Recommended watercraft: Drift boats and rafts, canoes for intermediate paddlers.

Hazards: Large waves and choppy water. Avoid Kootenai Falls. Experts only for Kootenai Falls Gorge, immediately below the falls for about 2 miles.

Where the crowd goes: Libby Dam to Libby.

Avoiding the scene: Troy to Leonia.

Inside tip: Float immediately below Libby Dam in the fall to watch eagles, as many as 160 in a single day.

Maps: USFS: Kootenai-Kaniksu East; USGS: Kalispell, MT.

Shuttle information: Kootenai River Outfitters, Troy, (406) 295-9444; Dave Blackburn's Kootenai Angler, Libby, (406) 293-7578.

River rules: Check for special fishing regulations.

For more information: FWP, Kalispell; Kootenai National Forest, Libby; US Army Corp of Engineers, Libby Dam; Kootenai Angler, Libby.

The Paddling

The Kootenai rises in British Columbia and flows southwest in a great loop through northwestern Montana. Its total length exceeds 480 miles, and it is the second-largest river in Montana in water volume. *Kootenai* (or *kutenai*) is an Indian word meaning "deer robes." The first white man to navigate the Kootenai was David Thompson, who paddled a birch-bark canoe down the river in 1808 and later founded a settlement near Libby. The river has an interesting history. Steamboats traveled on it for a short time while the mining industry was booming.

Once known as Montana's "dream stream," the US Army Corps of Engineers turned much of the Kootenai River into a nightmare. Prior to 1972 floaters could cruise for nearly 150 miles through rugged mountains and undisturbed river bottoms on a stream that may have had the best native cutthroat fishery in the country. Then came Libby Dam, which reduced floating on the Kootenai to less than 50 miles and turned the river into fluctuating, mud-lined Koocanusa Reservoir. Koocanusa is not a Tribal name; rather it was the product of a naming contest. The name borrows its first three letters from Kootenai, its next three from Canada, and its last three from USA.

Below Troy, the Kootenai appears placid, but beware as powerful currents and hydraulics can upset novice boaters.

Floating on the Kootenai starts below Libby Dam and continues to the Idaho border and beyond. Drift boats, canoes, and rafts all work well. While most of the river is broad and swift flowing, occasional rapids and big standing waves require some caution. Jennings Rapid, just below the Fisher River, requires care. Because of the fluctuations in the amount of water discharged from Koocanusa Reservoir, river levels can rise sharply, by as much as 2 to 4 feet. Because of these fluctuations and occasional rapids, beginners should steer clear of the Kootenai above the falls.

About 10 miles below the Libby Bridge, as the river approaches Kootenai Falls, lies a long, difficult section of river known as China Rapids. As the story goes, the rapids got their name in the 1860s when a party of Chinese miners from British Columbia tried to raft down the river with a load of gold dust. They took the river rather than an overland route because they feared their fortune would be stolen by other miners. As the raft hit the rapids, however, the heavy gold shifted and the raft upended. Only one miner made it to shore to tell the story, and the river kept the gold.

All but expert kayakers (with or without gold) should portage around China Rapids (Class IV). Expert rafters and kayakers can try it, but be sure to scout it first. Don't forget to check the flows before any Kootenai River trip.

The power line above Kootenai Falls marks a good take-out point for floaters. Don't worry about missing the power line; you'll see and hear the falls in plenty of time. Obviously floaters should be careful not to venture too close. Early settlers called it "Disaster Falls" for good reason. Kootenai Falls is the largest undammed falls in the state.

Immediately below the falls the river remains fast and turbulent for about 2 miles. Only experts in kayaks and large rafts should try it. Don't forget that the extreme water fluctuations caused by the dam make this section different each time. Each of the five major rapids (Class IV) in this 2-mile gorge should be inspected on foot before going through. Once you commit to floating this gorge, the steep walls will prevent you from turning back.

Below Troy, as the river leaves the highway, lies the last Montana vestige of the Kootenai as it once was. Although railroad tracks parallel the river, you still get a feeling of isolation on this big river, particularly below where the Yaak River enters.

While the transparent Kootenai remains large and fast flowing, practiced beginners can handle this section. High waves create the biggest hazard, and they can swamp open canoes. Most of the choppy water can be skirted if paddlers are alert. The most serious high waves are in the section below Troy at the Yaak River confluence. If you're in a raft, they provide a real roller-coaster ride.

Access points are limited below Troy. Floaters can get out easily at Leonia, Idaho, just across the border, or continue to float all the way to Bonner's Ferry, 20 miles into Idaho.

Although the Kootenai is flanked by a highway and train tracks for nearly its entirety, the river offers plenty of solitude in this forgotten corner of Montana.

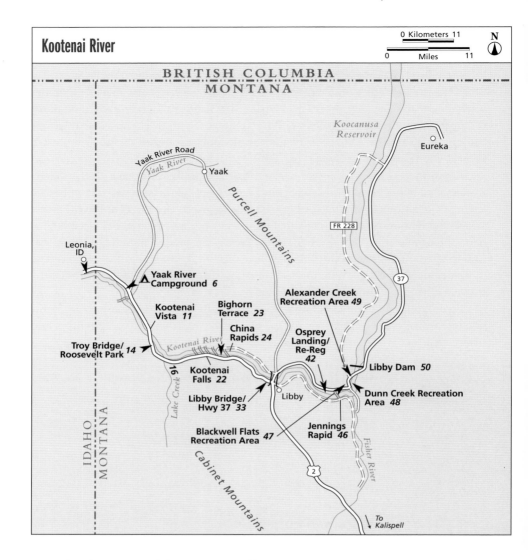

0 Kilometers 11

0 Miles 11

N

BRITISH COLUMBIA
MONTANA

Koocanusa Reservoir

Eureka

Yaak River Road

Yaak River

Yaak

Purcell Mountains

FR 228

Leonia, ID

Yaak River Campground *6*

Kootenai Vista *11*

Bighorn Terrace *23*

Alexander Creek Recreation Area *49*

China Rapids *24*

Osprey Landing/ Re-Reg *42*

37

Troy Bridge/ Roosevelt Park *14*

Kootenai River

Libby Dam *50*

Kootenai Falls *22*

Lake Creek

16

Libby

Dunn Creek Recreation Area *48*

Libby Bridge/ Hwy 37 *33*

Blackwell Flats Recreation Area *47*

Jennings Rapid *46*

IDAHO

MONTANA

Fisher River

2

Cabinet Mountains

To Kalispell

Isolated portions of the Kootenai still contain abundant wildlife. The king of all anglers, the osprey, can often be seen diving for fish. Bighorn sheep live on the cliffs near the falls, and whitetails walk most of the thickets. The Kootenai is one of the few rivers in Montana where black bears are commonly sighted prowling in late spring. Bald eagles concentrate along the river in winter, as do waterfowl.

Floating pressure on the Kootenai has increased with tales of great fishing. In comparison to southwestern Montana rivers, however, pressure is light and comes mostly from local people, as this neglected corner of the state is far from everywhere. Some people use motorboats on the river.

Trivia buffs will be interested to learn that the lowest point in Montana is where the Kootenai leaves the state near Leonia, Idaho. The elevation is 1,820 feet, substantially lower than most places in Montana.

Float fishing: The Kootenai has a substantial fishery, which produces large numbers of rainbow trout and whitefish. Both species of fish grow quickly; 3-pound trout are quite common. The Kootenai has earned the reputation of being the best "big fish" fishery in northwestern Montana, and the state record rainbow trout—33 pounds, 1 ounce—was caught in the Kootenai in the section immediately below the dam. Many believe the fish directly below the dam grow to such an enormous size by feeding on small kokanee salmon that are chopped up in the dam's turbines. Although a good deal of fish habitat has been destroyed to accommodate the railroad, the Kootenai is still a productive river, with great insect hatches throughout the summer and fall. Catch-and-release fishing from Libby Dam to Kootenai Falls for trout 13 to 18 inches has increased this size class remarkably.

In addition to trout, the unusual and rare white sturgeon resides in the Kootenai below the falls. These large fish, which can weigh more than 100 pounds, are an endangered species. At the turn of the 20th century, old-timers used to think it was great sport to dynamite these big fish at the large pool at the base of the falls. They floated out to the pool on rafts and dropped the charges into the water. During one such foray a misplaced charge blew up the raft and all the anglers. Fishing with hook and line—as well as dynamite—is now prohibited for these disappearing behemoths.

Key Access Points along the Kootenai River

Access Point	Access Type	(River Mile)
Libby Dam	Hand Launch	(50)
Alexander Creek Recreation Area	Ramp	(49)
Dunn Creek Recreation Area	Ramp	(48)
Blackwell Flats Recreation Area	Ramp	(47)
Canoe Gulch	Ramp	(45)
Osprey Landing/Re-Reg	Ramp	(42)
Libby Bridge/Highway 37	Ramp	(33)
Bighorn Terrace	Ramp	(23)
Troy Bridge/Roosevelt Park	Ramp	(14)
Kootenai Vista	Ramp	(11)
Yaak River Campground (North)	Gravel	(6)
Leonia, Idaho	Ramp	(0)

21 Madison River

Montana's most famous fishing river, the rapid-flowing Madison cuts a beautiful swath through a broad valley, passing by lush meadows and broken timber.

Vital statistics: 133 miles (23 reservoir miles) from the Wyoming border to its juncture with the Jefferson and Gallatin Rivers to form the Missouri River near Three Forks.

Level of difficulty: All Class I except for two sections—below Quake Lake and Bear Trap Canyon—that have difficult rapids.

Flow: Annual mean flow: 1,753 cfs downstream from Ennis Lake. Usually floatable all year. In dry years, Varney to Ennis Lake can be marginal because the river braids extensively. Bear Trap Canyon may be unfloatable at peak flows (over 3,000 cfs). Minimum Bear Trap flows are 1,000 to 1,200 cfs. Below Ennis Lake, floating is best below 4,500 cfs.

Recommended watercraft: Raft.

Hazards: Fast water with frequent rocks in the upper river. Low bridges with debris around the pilings, logjams, snags, and a diversion dam just below Varney. Bear Trap Canyon and the difficult water below Quake Lake.

Where the crowd goes: For anglers, Lyons Bridge to Ennis. For whitewater enthusiasts, the Bear Trap Canyon. For inner-tubers, Warm Springs to Greycliff.

Avoiding the scene: Ennis to Ennis Lake on the upper Madison (though it's all crowded in the summer). Greycliff to Missouri Headwaters State Park on the lower river.

Inside tip: Fish the often-neglected lower river in spring and fall when water temperatures are cool. The entire river has seemingly recovered from whirling disease that especially crippled the fishing on the upper river, which is predominantly a rainbow fishery. But don't pass up the lower river either, where large brown trout are more common. Be sure to fish the side channels.

Maps: BLM: Bear Trap Canyon Wilderness Visitor's Guide; USFS: Gallatin (West), Beaverhead Interagency Travel Plan (East); USGS: Ashton, ID; Bozeman, MT; River Rat Maps: Madison.

Shuttle information: Above Ennis: Driftaway Shuttles, (406) 682-3088; below Ennis: River Gal Shuttles, (406) 685-3500.

River rules: No motors over 10 horsepower anywhere. No motors in Bear Trap Canyon. No floating in Yellowstone National Park. Quake Lake to Lyons Bridge and Ennis Bridge to Ennis Lake are closed to fishing from boats. Check ever-changing fishing regulations. No float camping, except at designated areas. Fire pans and self-registration required in Bear Trap Canyon. New outfitting regulations and nonresident floating restrictions are being considered by FWP. Check regulations before heading out.

For more information: Madison River Fishing Company, Ennis; The Tackle Shop, Ennis; FWP, Bozeman; BLM, Dillon.

The Paddling

The Madison River is to fisherman as the Grand Canyon is to whitewater enthusiasts. It's the angler's equivalent of a trip to Mecca. This is a place where fly fishing existed long before it became a hobby for the rich and famous, although the Madison sure has plenty of that as well these days. As its reputation evolves, the beautiful Madison probably remains Montana's most famous river.

The Madison River's popularity is well founded. Originating from pristine sources high in Yellowstone National Park, the Madison flows gin-clear and undisturbed through lush meadows and broken timber. Within the park, elk and bison graze along the shores, and trumpeter swans dip their graceful necks underwater to reach vegetation. It's a "Peaceable Kingdom" setting. The only downside is that the park gets extremely crowded in summer. As mentioned, floating the Madison within the boundaries of Yellowstone is prohibited.

Two dams and a natural lake check the flow of the river outside the park. First comes Hebgen Dam, built in 1915, which backs up the Madison to within 2 miles of the park boundary. A few miles below Hebgen Dam is Quake Lake, a small lake formed by a major earthquake and subsequent landslide in 1959. Then, some 60 miles downstream, lies the Madison Dam, a small hydropower project built around the turn of the 20th century. The Madison Dam forms Ennis Reservoir and marks the artificial distinction between the upper and lower river.

Floating on the upper Madison usually begins about 4 miles downstream from Quake Lake at Raynolds Pass FAS. The 4-mile section immediately below Quake Lake is extremely dangerous because of fast water, big drops, and sharp, jagged rocks. The sharp rocks are remnants of the 1959 earthquake, and even thrill-seekers tend to avoid this whitewater (or at least wear the proper padding!). It should be good floating in a few hundred years—once the fast-flowing waters round off the sharp edges.

Most of the 40-mile stretch between Quake Lake and Varney Bridge flows swiftly but at a uniform depth. The river gushes in a wide, shallow channel averaging about 3 or 4 feet deep and resembles a long, continuous riffle. Occasional large boulders present the only hazard for floaters. The cannonball-size rocks that blanket the bottom

Although known for its spectacular fishing, the Madison also boasts impressive whitewater in Beartrap Canyon. JOHN TODD

of the river have a slick coating of algae that results in treacherous footing. Practiced beginners in rafts or canoes can handle this section, but watch out for those rocks!

The river winds through highly scenic country, with the lofty Madison Range to the east and the sage-covered foothills of the Gravelly Mountains to the west. Access is excellent, and much of the land bordering the river is publicly owned. There are numerous picnic areas, campgrounds, and fishing access sites.

The section of river from Varney Bridge to Ennis Lake braids into several channels where logjams and downed trees are common. Beginners should stay clear. Low summer flows may require floaters to drag their crafts over sandbars. The section of river from Ennis Bridge to the lake is an excellent area to view wildlife. Look for deer, moose, mink, and beaver, as well as raptors and shorebirds. Several great blue heron rookeries can be found as well. Keep in mind that fishing from a boat in this section is prohibited, although floating is fine.

Floating pressure on the upper river is quite high. Recreational studies reveal a 500 percent increase in angler pressure over the past three decades. The upper river now supports over 60,000 anglers annually. Dozens of professional outfitters offer guide services on this upper section, and it's very popular with tourists and out-of-state anglers. The large number of floaters has created a conflict between float anglers and bank anglers, and that's why some sections have been closed to fishing from boats. FWP is currently negotiating additional rules to curtail conflict between outfitted use, personal use, and wade anglers. Check the current regulations before heading onto the river.

The upper Madison has received a great deal of national attention in recent years because of whirling disease, an infectious fish microbe that in the early to mid-1990s reduced rainbow trout populations by as much as 90 percent. Luckily, the fishery has rebounded dramatically and is all but recovered. Be sure to check current fishing regulations.

The lower Madison (below Ennis Lake) isn't nearly as popular as the upper section. While this part of the river was once one of the most productive trout streams in Montana, thermal problems and dewatering have affected the fishery.

Fisheries biologists have learned that during the hot summer months, Ennis Lake acts as a giant solar collector, and its water temperature sometimes gets as high as 85 degrees Fahrenheit. Since the lake has filled in with silt and become very shallow, it has no thermocline (a natural dividing point between warm and cold water). All the lake water gets warm, then flows over the dam and heats up the river downstream. Since trout do best with cold water temperatures, their growth rates have been dramatically affected below Ennis Dam. Fish numbers remain fairly good (more than 3,000 fish per mile) until the Greycliff FAS. In addition, plant and insect life has changed.

While all this is of grave concern to trout anglers, swimmers and inner-tubers certainly don't mind the warm water temperatures. Consequently the lower river near MT 84 has become a popular recreation site during the heat of summer.

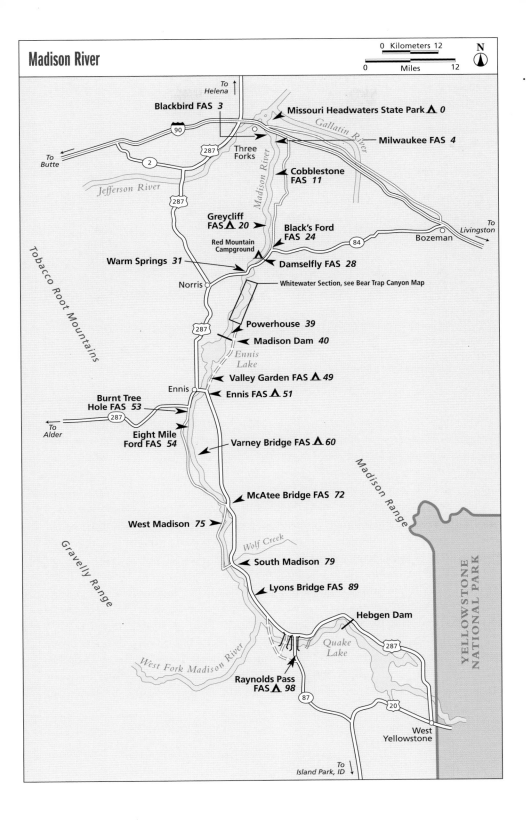

Madison River

0 Kilometers 12
0 Miles 12

N

To Helena

Blackbird FAS *3*

Missouri Headwaters State Park ▲ *0*

Gallatin River

Milwaukee FAS *4*

90

287

Three Forks

Madison River

To Butte

2

Cobblestone FAS *11*

Jefferson River

287

Greycliff FAS ▲ *20*

Black's Ford FAS *24*

To Livingston

Bozeman

84

Red Mountain Campground

Warm Springs *31*

Damselfly FAS *28*

Norris

Whitewater Section, see Bear Trap Canyon Map

287

Powerhouse *39*

Madison Dam *40*

Ennis Lake

Valley Garden FAS ▲ *49*

Ennis

Ennis FAS ▲ *51*

Tobacco Root Mountains

Burnt Tree Hole FAS *53*

287

To Alder

Eight Mile Ford FAS *54*

Varney Bridge FAS ▲ *60*

Madison Range

McAtee Bridge FAS *72*

West Madison *75*

Gravelly Range

Wolf Creek

South Madison *79*

Lyons Bridge FAS *89*

Hebgen Dam

Quake Lake

287

West Fork Madison River

Raynolds Pass FAS ▲ *98*

87

20

YELLOWSTONE NATIONAL PARK

West Yellowstone

To Island Park, ID

Key Access Points along the Madison River

Access Point	Access Type	(River Mile)
Raynolds Pass FAS	Ramp	(98)
Lyons Bridge FAS	Ramp	(89)
South Madison	Walk-In	(79)
West Madison	Walk-In	(75)
McAtee Bridge FAS	Ramp	(72)
Varney Bridge FAS	Ramp	(60)
Eight Mile Ford FAS	Ramp	(54)
Burnt Tree Hole FAS	Ramp	(53)
Ennis FAS	Ramp	(51)
Valley Garden FAS	Ramp	(49)
Madison Dam	Hand Launch	(40)
Powerhouse	Hand Launch	(39)
Warm Springs	Ramp	(31)
Damselfly FAS	Ramp	(28)
Black's Ford FAS	Ramp	(24)
Greycliff FAS	Ramp	(20)
Cobblestone FAS	Walk-In	(11)
Milwaukee FAS	Ramp	(4)
Blackbird FAS	Ramp	(3)
Missouri Headwaters State Park	Ramp	(0)

Floating on the lower river can begin right below the dam—although not for everyone. Below the dam lies the rugged, inaccessible Bear Trap Canyon, which has some outstanding rapids. The BLM currently manages this 9-mile section of the river, known as the Bear Trap Canyon Recreation Area. It encompasses 36,700 acres and is a designated wilderness.

The Bear Trap has a few hazards other than tough whitewater. Rattlesnakes inhabit the canyon, and if you believe all the stories, they're more common here than earthworms. Ticks are numerous in spring. Poison ivy awaits you. Still want to go? Grizzly bears occupy the area as well.

The BLM has published an excellent map of the river and the Bear Trap Canyon. The Bear Trap Canyon Wilderness Visitor's Guide has an excellent topographic map as well as photos of the approaches to the four major rapids. It's available free of charge by contacting the BLM (see appendix A).

After the Madison exits Bear Trap Canyon, it's pretty tame. Once the river leaves MT 84, access is limited and the river is more remote. Access points at Greycliff, Cobblestone (no boat ramp, walk-in access only), and Three Forks occur in about equal intervals in the 24-mile section from the MT 84 bridge to the headwaters of the Missouri.

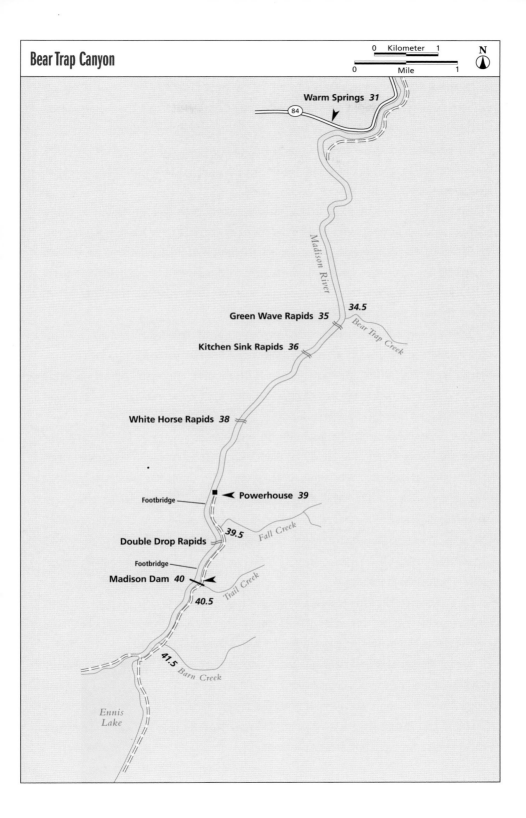

Bear Trap Canyon

0   Kilometer   1
0   Mile   1

N

Warm Springs *31*

84

Madison River

34.5

Green Wave Rapids *35*

Bear Trap Creek

Kitchen Sink Rapids *36*

White Horse Rapids *38*

Footbridge — ◄ **Powerhouse** *39*

39.5   *Fall Creek*

Double Drop Rapids

Footbridge —

Madison Dam *40* ◄

Trail Creek

40.5

41.5 *Barn Creek*

Ennis Lake

THE BEAR TRAP

The 1,500-foot-high cliffs above the Madison River serve as a backdrop for one of Montana's most scenic whitewater trips—the run through Bear Trap Canyon Wilderness. The Bear Trap offers excitement for experts in large rafts or kayaks. Small rafts or open canoes should stay away.

The canyon starts at the outlet to Ennis Lake and continues until MT 84 meets the river, slightly less than 10 miles downstream. A narrow dirt road, a hazard in itself, leads to the put-in. The take-out point is the BLM's Warm Springs access.

Although dams regulate flows on the Madison, neither Ennis Lake nor Hebgen Lake is a storage reservoir. So when there's a high influx of water, it gets passed downriver. Flows vary from 900 to 10,000 cfs, based on the season. Optimal flow for floating activities is about 1,500 to 2,200 cfs. The Bear Trap Canyon gets exceedingly dangerous when flows hit 4,000 to 5,000 cfs. Look for a river flow sign about 200 yards upstream from the powerhouse. It displays current water levels and is updated daily.

Intense rapids with considerable stretches of easy water in between characterize the Bear Trap Canyon. There are four primary rapids, and all have unmarked portage routes for those not along for the thrills. The first whitewater is Double Drop Rapids, which you'll miss if you put in too close to the powerhouse. The next major whitewater, White Horse Rapids, lies about 2 miles downstream. It's a long set of big waves.

After White Horse comes the most difficult and dangerous rapids in the Bear Trap, the Kitchen Sink—Class IV even at low flows and Class V when the water is up. It's a tricky, dangerous piece of whitewater that people without the proper skills should not attempt. It has large waves, big drops, lots of rocks, and two turns. A wave that lurches back over a large rock—which some people think looks like a drain at the bottom of a sink—gives this rapid its name. According to the BLM, at least eight people have lost their lives here in the last 20 years. At peak flows it's a life-threatening Class V. The remoteness of this rapid accentuates the danger. It's almost exactly in the middle of the canyon.

The last major whitewater is known either as Green Wave Rapids or The Dumplings. Some creative mind decided that this series of huge rocks in the river looks like dumplings floating in a bowl of chicken broth. These rapids are about 4 miles before the take-out.

Quality equipment is important on a tough run like the Bear Trap Canyon, but experience and judgment are just as critical. Only strong intermediates or better should try the Bear Trap at normal flows, and only experts should attempt it at high water. This isn't the place for flimsy rafts and horse-collar life jackets. Several outfitters run trips in the Bear Trap Canyon if you want to check out the river with experienced people first.

The lower sections of the Madison are quite isolated and can have excellent fishing in spring and fall. Hundred-foot gray cliffs tower over the river, and many vantage points offer spectacular views of the Spanish Peaks. Because of high winds that stir up mud in Ennis Lake, the lower Madison sometimes gets dirty even at non-runoff times.

Float fishing: Since fishing is the main attraction on the Madison, it's only fair to tell you why. Between the 1920s and 1970s, over 3 million fish were stocked in the Madison, bolstering the population and introducing several nonnatives (brown trout and rainbows). Since the 1970s Montana FWP has phased out many of their stocking programs and wisely focused on habitat protection and enhancement. Fisheries biologists, who survey the river regularly, report that sections of the river contain as many as 2,000 brown trout per mile. These fish are wild—they're not raised in a hatchery, anymore at least—and average about a pound each. For those who think big, biologists occasionally capture fish in the 5- to 7-pound range when doing fish surveys.

The Madison salmon fly hatch usually occurs on the upper river in late June. During this time incredible numbers of large stoneflies buzz through the air like miniature helicopters, and the fish go wild. So do the anglers, and the river gets so thoroughly flailed that there's foam all the way to Three Forks.

22 Marias River

The isolated Marias River originates east of Glacier National Park and features spectacular badlands and sandstone cliffs reminiscent of the Missouri River.

Vital statistics: 171 miles (26 reservoir miles) from the confluence of the Two Medicine River and Cut Bank Creek to its juncture with the Missouri River near Loma.

Level of difficulty: Class I, suitable for beginners its entire length.

Flow: Annual mean flow: 915 cfs near Chester. The BOR tries to maintain a minimum flow of 500 cfs from Tiber Dam; it's too low to float below 350 cfs. Optimum flows are 700 to 1,500 cfs below Tiber Dam. Typically gets too low for floating in summer above Tiber Reservoir in dry years.

Recommended watercraft: Canoes and rafts; drift boats between Tiber and Highway 223.

Hazards: Extreme temperatures, relentless wind, mosquitoes, rattlesnakes, and unpaved roads that become impassable after rainstorms.

Where the crowd goes: No crowd on this river.

Avoiding the scene: Above Tiber Reservoir.

Inside tip: Apparently a great river for conceiving children. My brother's middle name is Marias. Upland bird-hunting opportunities abound.

Maps: USGS: Cut Bank, MT; Shelby, MT; Great Falls, MT.

Shuttle information: John's Shuttle Service, Fort Benton, (406) 622-3652.

River rules: No hunting on the Brinkman Game Preserve (special permit only for whitetail), a state wildlife refuge that borders the river for 10 miles immediately below the Highway 223 bridge.

For more information: BLM, Havre; FWP, Great Falls; Coyotes Den Sports, Chester; BOR, Tiber Dam.

The Paddling

Known to the Indians as "the river that scolds at all others," the slow-moving but scenic Marias River is one of Montana's finest canoeing streams. While its headwaters actually originate near Glacier National Park, the river begins about 12 miles south of the town of Cut Bank, where Cut Bank Creek and the Two Medicine River join. While floating is possible from this point down to Tiber Reservoir, access is somewhat challenging, and this section receives little pressure. Most floaters go below the reservoir, where fishing is better and the scenery more appealing.

The Marias has a rich historical background. Lewis and Clark camped at the river's mouth, near the present-day site of Loma, on June 3, 1805. Captain Lewis named the river Maria's River in honor of his cousin, Miss Maria Wood. Obviously not much of a ladies' man, Lewis later apologized in his journal for naming such a silt-laden, unromantic river in honor of his beloved cousin. Historians later dropped the apostrophe.

Lewis and Clark had to make a critical decision when they reached the mouth of the Marias. The explorers were unsure which branch was the main fork of the Missouri. The Marias most resembles the part of the Missouri the crew had already traversed, as it is slow and turbid. The other fork—which we now recognize as the main stem Missouri—flowed clear and seemed to lead to the mountains. Almost all the crew thought the Marias was the main fork of the Missouri. Lewis and Clark, however, thought differently. After several days of careful deliberation, they made the correct decision.˙

What if Lewis and Clark had proceeded up the Marias instead of the Missouri? They might have been forced to retrace their path, losing valuable time that could have meant a late, dangerous trip across the mountains in November. On the other hand, they might have found Marias Pass near Glacier National Park, the lowest and least formidable path across the Continental Divide.

The beauty of the rolling prairies that surround the Marias captivated both Lewis and Clark. Lewis wrote in his journal:

> [The river] passes through a rich fertile and one of the most beautifully picturesque countries that I ever beheld, through the wide expanse of which innumerable herds of living anamals are seen, it's borders garnished with one continued garden of roses, while it's lofty and open forrests are the habitation of miriads of the feathered tribes who salute the ear of the passing traveler with their wild and simple, yet sweet and cheerfull melody.

No less ecstatic, Captain Clark reported:

> [T]he country in every derection around us was one vast plain in which innumerable herds of Buffalow were seen attended by their shepperds, the wolves; the solatary antelope which now had their young were distributed over it's face; some herds of Elk were also seen; the verdue perfectly cloathed the ground, the weather was pleasant and fair.

Above Tiber Reservoir the Marias flows some 50 miles from the confluence of the Two Medicine River and Cut Bank Creek. Although this section sees little use, this piece of river is extremely beautiful and abounds with wildlife. With the creation of the Marias River Wildlife Management Area in 2008, additional access and public lands have added to the allure of this stretch of water. South of Shelby, along the banks of the Marias, is the location of the greatest slaughter of Native Americans by US troops in American history—known today as the Baker Massacre of 1870. This horrific incident left over 200 Blackfeet Indians dead, mostly women and children. Between Tiber Reservoir and the Missouri River, the Marias flows past towering sandstone cliffs and fascinating badlands formations. Thick cottonwood groves often line the river. It's like a mini Missouri River, but the scenery is up-close and personal.

Like the nearby Missouri, the Marias is slow moving and muddy, except for the approximately 15-mile section immediately below the dam, where the water is clearer and colder. There's remarkable trout fishing in this section, especially for large fish, including the newly minted state record brown trout, weighing in at 32 pounds. The fishery is now improving because the BOR has changed the flow regime from Tiber Reservoir to more closely mimic natural runoff.

There's good access to the river right below the dam, and two county roads and a state highway cross the river in the next 20 miles. After the Highway 223 bridge, the river remains quite isolated for the rest of its course. Beginners can handle the Marias. Although the dam can cause water fluctuations, they usually aren't major. In extremely dry years the Marias can get too low to float.

Although you won't experience all the wildlife Lewis and Clark did (they saw wolves, grizzlies, buffalo, and elk), many species still roam the hills and bottoms of the Marias. Both mule and white-tailed deer are fairly common. Large numbers of waterfowl typically congregate on the river in spring and fall. Eagles often winter along the Marias, and coyotes can be seen almost any time. One friend reported he saw over fifty of the much-maligned song-dogs on one trip.

Hunters should be aware of the Brinkman Game Preserve, a state wildlife refuge that extends from the Highway 223 bridge east for about 10 river miles. It ends at the Liberty-Hill county line. This little-known refuge, which encompasses nearly 13,000 acres of public and private land, was created by the Fish and Game Commission in 1926. Its boundaries are poorly marked. Hunting is not permitted along this section of river except for deer hunting (by permit only).

Beaver occasionally can be spotted along the Marias, but they aren't as numerous as they once were. In 1831 James Kipp thought it was such good beaver country

The Marias River winds a green ribbon of life through otherwise arid river breaks and cliffs.
BEN LAMB

Marias River

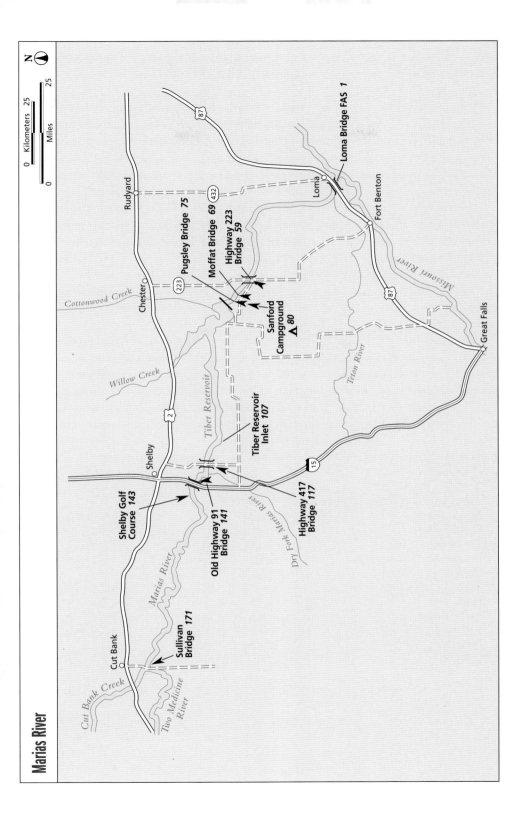

that he built Fort Piegan at the mouth of the Marias. He reportedly acquired over 2,400 "plews" in his first 10 days of business, but the trade didn't last and the fort was abandoned.

Summers along the Marias are generally short, but they can be devilishly hot. This area experiences extreme temperature fluctuations, and water temperatures in the river can get very warm in summer. Natural siltation, along with irrigation returns, accounts for the poor water quality found in most of the river. The soil in this area is the famed Missouri River gumbo—rock-hard when dry and stickier than tarpaper when wet.

Because of the impermeability of this soil, small pools of water form when it rains. These provide excellent breeding grounds for a particularly voracious race of mosquitoes. Numerous and quite large, they're sometimes mistaken for small ducks. Take plenty of repellent, and wear long pants and long sleeves.

In addition to the swarms of mosquitoes, this region of the state is notably one of the windiest. If you are paddling a fully loaded canoe, stay close to the shore to avoid being swamped. In some areas the wind is fully capable of blowing you right back to your put-in.

Float fishing: If it's trout you're after, head below Tiber Reservoir and throw something big to the large browns that stack up below the dam. The next 20 miles below the dam are also quite productive and have a diverse mix of coldwater and warmwater species, making for an interesting catch. The topwater action can be quite good in the summer months with prolific mayfly hatches and hoppers that keep the fish looking up. Warmwater fish such as walleye, sauger, carp, northern pike, catfish, and goldeye inhabit the lower sections of the river, and the experienced worm dunker can do quite well. Goldeye usually bite on artificial lures as well as bait.

Key Access Points along the Marias River

Access Point	Access Type	(River Mile)
Sullivan Bridge	Hand Launch	(171)
Shelby Golf Course	Hand Launch	(143)
Old Highway 91 bridge	Hand Launch	(141)
Highway 417 bridge	Hand Launch	(117)
Sanford Campground/Tiber Dam	Ramp	(80)
Pugsley Bridge	Ramp	(75)
Moffat Bridge	Ramp	(69)
Highway 223 bridge	Ramp	(59)
Loma Bridge FAS	Ramp	(1)

23 Milk River

Named for its whitish color, the lengthy Milk River winds through remote prairies and seldom-visited cottonwood bottoms alive with wildlife.

Vital statistics: 437 miles from the outlet of Fresno Reservoir west of Chinook.

Level of difficulty: Class I its entire length, suitable for beginners except at high flows.

Flow: Annual mean flow: 656 cfs near Nashua. Floatable all year, except in its uppermost reaches. A 200 cfs minimum is needed below Dodson.

Recommended watercraft: Canoes.

Hazards: Diversion dams, barbed-wire fences, and mosquitoes.

Where the crowd goes: Nowhere. Dodson to Vandalia is popular with walleye anglers.

Avoiding the scene: The Milk's origin to the Highway 213 bridge (just before it enters Canada) is quite remote, with clearer water.

Inside tip: An excellent choice for a long-distance float trip. For better public land access, float through the Milk River and Lost River Wildlife Management Areas.

Maps: USGS: Cut Bank, MT; Shelby, MT; Havre, MT; Glasgow, MT.

Shuttle information: Good luck. Bring an extra vehicle or a bike.

River rules: Tribal fishing licenses required for Blackfeet, Fort Belknap, and Fort Peck Indian Reservations.

For more information: BLM, Havre; FWP, Glasgow; BOR, Billings.

The Paddling

While not a classic beauty, the Milk River contains some of the least-explored water in Montana. At first glance the sluggish and turbid Milk might not seem as appealing as famous rivers like the Blackfoot or Madison. But those who seek solitude, wide-open spaces, and excellent wildlife viewing opportunities won't be disappointed.

The Milk River country is a land of varied landscapes, ranging from rolling hills and badlands to low buttes and shallow valleys. It has a rough, primitive beauty composed of windswept plains once covered by glaciers.

Captain Meriwether Lewis noted the most salient characteristic of this major river while traveling up the Missouri in 1805. He wrote, "The water of this river possesses a peculiar whiteness, being about the colour of a cup of tea with the admixture of a tablespoonfull of milk." Always the astute observer, Lewis named it the Milk River.

While most people think of the Milk as a cloudy river, it flows out of the undisturbed slopes of Glacier National Park as a clear mountain stream. It then enters Canada north of Cut Bank. After a 100-mile loop, the Milk returns to Montana a changed stream. The Canadians aren't to blame, however, as most of the siltation is natural. While it was once thought the Milk's bluish-white color resulted from glacial till, it's now thought the color originates from fine sand picked up in a deep gorge near Writing-on-Stone Provincial Park in Alberta.

The Milk does carry a heavy sediment load in spring. Some say it's so muddy you can see the deer and raccoon tracks float by. Others claim you can walk across it during runoff. Despite all the jokes about the Milk, it winds through beautiful prairie country that's teeming with wildlife. The river occupies a broad floodplain, which geologists speculate was created by the Missouri River in preglacial times. The Milk doesn't have the rugged breaks of nearby rivers such as the Missouri and Marias. Tall cottonwoods and thick brush envelop the river, creating excellent habitat for deer, beaver, mink, and great blue herons. Sandhill cranes stalk the shallows, and white pelicans reside nearby. Heron and cormorant rookeries can be found along the more isolated sections. The Milk often hosts large concentrations of waterfowl during migration. It also replenishes the wetlands and prairies of Bowdoin National Wildlife Refuge, which boasts over 250 bird species.

Other once abundant species are now represented only by their ghosts. Lewis and Clark reported seeing buffalo, wolves, and grizzlies, but they all flickered out of existence around the turn of the 20th century, as did the plains elk. The Milk River country was renowned for its thundering buffalo herds and the Blackfeet Indians who hunted them. Today the river provides essential spawning for migratory birds and native fish.

The Milk River sees little floating traffic; however, it is frequented by many species of wildlife.

Milk River

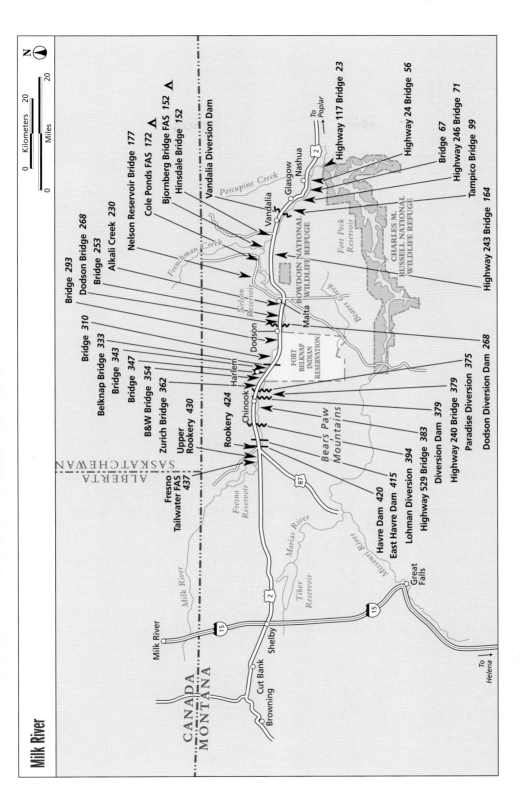

CANADA
MONTANA

ALBERTA
SASKATCHEWAN

Milk River

Shelby

Cut Bank

Browning

To
Helena

Great
Falls

Tiber Reservoir

Marias River

Missouri River

Fresno Reservoir

Bears Paw Mountains

Milk River

Chinook

Harlem

Dodson

Malta

Nelson Reservoir

Frenchman Creek

Vandalia

Nashua

Glasgow

Porcupine Creek

To
Poplar

FORT BELKNAP INDIAN RESERVATION

Beaver Creek

BOWDOIN NATIONAL WILDLIFE REFUGE

Fort Peck Reservoir

CHARLES M. RUSSELL NATIONAL WILDLIFE REFUGE

Fresno Tailwater FAS 437

Upper Rookery 430

Rookery 424

Zurich Bridge 362

B&W Bridge 354

Bridge 347

Bridge 343

Belknap Bridge 333

Bridge 310

Bridge 293

Dodson Bridge 268

Bridge 253

Alkali Creek 230

Nelson Reservoir Bridge 177

Cole Ponds FAS 172

Bjornberg Bridge FAS 152

Hinsdale Bridge 152

Vandalia Diversion Dam

Highway 117 Bridge 23

Highway 24 Bridge 56

Bridge 67

Highway 246 Bridge 71

Tampico Bridge 99

Highway 243 Bridge 164

Dodson Diversion Dam 268

Paradise Diversion 375

Highway 240 Bridge 379

Diversion Dam 379

Highway 529 Bridge 383

Lohman Diversion 394

East Havre Dam 415

Havre Dam 420

N

0   Kilometers   20

0   Miles   20

Key Access Points along the Milk River

Access Point	Access Type	(River Mile)
Fresno Tailwater FAS	Ramp	(437)
Upper Rookery	Hand Launch	(430)
Rookery	Hand Launch	(424)
Highway 529 bridge	Hand Launch	(383)
Highway 240 bridge	Hand Launch	(379)
Zurich Bridge	Hand Launch	(362)
B&W Bridge	Hand Launch	(354)
Bridge	Hand Launch	(347)
Bridge	Hand Launch	(343)
Bridge	Hand Launch	(310)
Bridge	Hand Launch	(293)
Dodson Bridge	Hand Launch	(268)
Bridge	Hand Launch	(253)
Alkali Creek FAS	Hand Launch	(230)
Nelson Reservoir Bridge	Hand Launch	(177)
Cole Ponds FAS	Ramp	(172)
Highway 243 bridge	Hand Launch	(164)
Bjornberg Bridge FAS	Hand Launch	(152)
Hinsdale Bridge	Hand Launch	(152)
Tampico Bridge	Hand Launch	(99)
Highway 246 bridge	Hand Launch	(71)
Bridge	Hand Launch	(67)
Highway 24 bridge	Hand Launch	(56)
Highway 117 bridge	Hand Launch	(23)

The Milk is Montana's longest tributary to the Missouri, coursing eastward before meeting "Old Misery" near Fort Peck. For almost 200 miles the river parallels both the tracks of the old Great Northern Railway (Montana's "High Line" railroad, often spelled "Hi-Line") and US 2.

Because the river meanders so repeatedly, the actual river distance is over 500 miles. While the Milk never strays far from US 2, it's usually distant enough that the highway can't be seen or the motors heard. It's an ideal river for floaters seeking an extended trip away from people.

Floating on the Milk in Montana begins below Fresno Dam and continues to where the Milk meets the Missouri. It's all suitable for beginners. The only hazards on this meandering stream are occasional diversion dams and barbed wire across the stream. Watch for major diversions at Vandalia and Dodson. The Milk can get very high during runoff and is known to flood significant portions of north central Montana. Flooding typically peaks on the Milk in early May. Mosquitoes can be fierce along the Milk in June and July.

In 2013 Montana FWP purchased and developed the Lost River Wildlife Management Area (WMA) north of Havre near the Canadian border (named the Lost River because the Milk already has a WMA named after it downstream near Hinsdale). This 13-square-mile public land purchase allows floaters exceptional hunting and camping opportunities on a remote section of this stream. Pheasants and white-tailed deer abound along the lush river bottom.

Designated access to the Milk is almost nonexistent. FWP has one site west of Havre (Fresno Tailwater FAS) and two west of Hinsdale (Bjornberg Bridge FAS and Alkali Creek), and there are public parks at Hinsdale and Malta.

Float fishing: Most people who float the Milk are anglers. The Milk sustains at least forty-two species of fish, including walleye, sauger, catfish, and northern pike. Limited trout fishing is available a few miles below Fresno Dam. Anglers often have good luck where tributaries such as Whitewater, Frenchman, and Beaver Creeks enter. Probably the most popular section lies between Dodson and Vandalia, which FWP biologists rate as among the best walleye fishing stream in the state, frequently producing walleyes over 10 pounds.

24 Missouri River

The river that carried Lewis and Clark across much of Montana is a trout-filled mountainous stream in its upper reaches and a broad, scenic prairie river in its lower two-thirds. This is a trip through history.

Vital statistics: 734 miles (223 reservoir miles) from Three Forks to the Montana-North Dakota border. America's longest river, nearly 2,500 miles.

Level of difficulty: Class I, suitable for beginners its entire length, except below Morony Dam in Great Falls (4 miles of Class III rapids).

Flow: Annual mean flow: 7,696 cfs at Fort Benton. Plenty of water all year in this big river.

Recommended watercraft: Drift boats, rafts, canoes.

Hazards: Strong winds, sudden storms, mosquitoes, and plenty of rattlesnakes.

Where the crowd goes: The 149-mile Wild and Scenic section, especially between Coal Banks and Judith Landings. Holter Dam to Pelican Point receives heavy fishing pressure.

Avoiding the scene: Fred Robinson Bridge to Turkey Joe. For a long trip, Fort Peck Dam to the North Dakota border.

Inside tip: Float from Fred Robinson to Fort Peck Reservoir in September to see and hear one of the last remaining prairie elk herds in the nation on the Charles M. Russell National Wildlife Refuge.

Maps: BLM: Upper Missouri National Wild & Scenic River (maps 1 and 2, 3 and 4); USFS: Helena; USGS: Bozeman, MT; White Sulphur, MT; Great Falls, MT; Shelby, MT; Lewistown, MT; Jordan, MT; Wolf Point, MT; River Rat Maps: Upper Missouri River & Chain of Lakes Complex—Three Forks to Wolf Creek; Upper Missouri #2—Holter Dam to Fort Benton; Montana Afloat: #16 (The Missouri River).

Shuttle information: CrossCurrents, Craig, (406) 235-3433; The Trout Shop, Craig, (800) 337-8528; Upper Missouri River Guides, Fort Benton, (406) 622-3652; Hole in the Wall Adventures, Lewistown, (406) 538-2418.

River rules: Check with FWP regarding ever-changing trout-fishing and warmwater-fishing regulations. Registration required for floating Wild and Scenic section of the Missouri (at Fort Benton, Coal Banks Landing, and Judith Landing). Seasonal motor restrictions (June 15 to September 15) on the Wild and Scenic section to alleviate conflict with floaters.

For more information: BLM, Lewistown or Fort Benton; Montana River Outfitters, Great Falls; Missouri River Outfitters, Fort Benton; Lewis and Clark Trail Adventures, Missoula.

The Paddling

Known as "Old Misery" to early explorers and fur trappers who fought its tricky currents and fickle moods, the Missouri River has carried boatloads of Montana history-makers on its waters. Pathway for the expansion of the West, the Missouri provided the major water route to the Rocky Mountains from the time of Lewis and Clark until the coming of the railroads in the late 1800s.

Although the river once bustled with activity, it now offers solitude and a deep sense of the past. Nearly every bend has a story to tell, and despite all the mishaps that have occurred on this historic river, even beginning floaters can handle the Missouri for its entire length in Montana.

The Blackfeet, Assiniboine, Gros Ventre, and Cree Indians ruled the lands along the Missouri before settlers arrived. In 1805 and 1806 Lewis and Clark traversed the entire length of the Missouri River and its tributaries in Montana. Fur trappers invaded soon after. Steamboats came next, proceeding as far up the Missouri as Fort Benton. The ships brought gold-seekers, sodbusters, homesteaders, shopkeepers, and other opportunists. Livestock came to Montana in the 1880s, and cattle operations still dominate the Missouri River area today.

Colorfully named landmarks reflect the Missouri's rich and romantic past. Places like Gates of the Mountains, Citadel Rock, Hole-in-the-Wall, Slaughter River, Bull-whacker Creek, Drowned Man's Rapids, Steamboat Rock, and Woodhawk Creek all played a role in Montana history. Floaters looking for Lewis and Clark information will find a treasure trove, but two books stand out. First is Bernard DeVoto's classic book, *The Journals of Lewis and Clark*. It's an excellent distillation of the journals, with explanatory footnotes. The other is Stephen Ambrose's *Undaunted Courage*.

Pioneers weren't able to deal with the river's wandering ways and set out to harness it. Dams now check the Missouri for most of its 2,500-mile flow. In Montana nearly a third of the Missouri lies stilled behind concrete and earth. First come Canyon Ferry, Hauser, and Holter Dams, three dams in succession that lie east and northeast of Helena and impound the river for nearly 70 miles. Then near downtown

The Wild and Scenic section of the Missouri River is one of the most famous stretches of stream in the state. JOHN TODD

Great Falls lie five run-of-the-river dams that check the famous falls where Lewis and Clark made an arduous 17-mile portage. Finally—and most significantly—the huge Fort Peck Dam in eastern Montana drowns nearly 100 miles of river and creates the fourth-largest reservoir in the world.

The 149-mile segment of the Missouri between Fort Benton and the Fred Robinson Bridge endures as the only major portion of the 2,500-mile-long Mighty Mo that has been protected and preserved in a free-flowing and natural state. After a hard-fought battle, it became a part of the National Wild and Scenic Rivers System in 1976. In 2001 President Clinton used his executive powers to designate nearly half a million acres adjacent to the Wild and Scenic section as the Upper Missouri River Breaks National Monument. It's very popular, attracting river rats and history buffs from all over the country.

Like a great fallen tree with its branches ensnarled in the mountains, the Missouri starts near Three Forks at the confluence of the Jefferson, Madison, and Gallatin Rivers. The river flows freely for about 35 miles before being trapped by the Canyon Ferry-Hauser-Holter complex of impounded lakes.

Float fishing (upper): The river between Townsend and Three Forks has experienced a burst of popularity as anglers have discovered the exceptionally large trout that reside here. Fairly isolated, the area has beautiful rolling hills and wooded islands. Water quality isn't always the best here, and hot summer days can raise water temperatures. Toston Dam, which lies about halfway between Three Forks and Canyon Ferry and creates a few miles of slack water, blocks upstream movement of trout. The Toston-to-Townsend float is popular in fall, when the brown trout are spawning and the fish are concentrated below the dam. Carp have slowly invaded this section of the river and provide sport opportunities for those willing to target the "golden bones" of the Missouri.

Except for a short float from Hauser Dam to Holter Reservoir that is popular with motorboats, the next floating opportunity starts below Holter Dam near Wolf Creek, where the river flows through a narrow canyon. Lewis and Clark watched mountain goats and bighorn sheep prance along the cliffs here. Although I-15 is close to the river and subdivisions sometimes mar the scenery, the Missouri between Helena and Great Falls remains magical. The water flows clear, and the fishing is excellent. Access is easy with the Missouri River Recreation Road paralleling the river for 35 miles.

Float fishing (mid-river): According to state fisheries studies, the Missouri between Wolf Creek and Craig ranks with the Beaverhead and Big Hole Rivers for trophy trout production. In recent years the rainbow and brown trout populations have surged. As of 2019 this section has dipped slightly but contains a healthy 3,200 fish per mile; of those, in the Craig section, there are 390 brown trout over 10 inches per mile. It's easy floating all the way to Great Falls except for some difficult water about 1.5 miles below Hardy Bridge.

The well-known falls of the Missouri preclude floating through Great Falls, but expert kayakers can try surfing the waves just downstream from Black Eagle Dam that on rare occurrences come into form—most notably a frothing monster known as "the serpent's tongue" at 25,000 cfs. Other floaters may want to put in right below Morony Dam and try the short section of whitewater (about 2.5 miles) that lasts until about 1 mile beyond Belt Creek. Less-skilled paddlers can launch at Carter Ferry to avoid the whitewater. After Carter Ferry the river is easy for the rest of its way across Montana. The biggest danger is the wind that can create waves and make maneuvering a boat nearly impossible. Although old maps may show rapids, they're only dangerous if you're piloting a steamboat.

The Missouri begins to change character once it cuts into the plains near Great Falls, picking up sediment and getting more turbid. The Sun River pushes the first mud into the Missouri, and the Marias River completes the job. At runoff times it justly earns its nickname, "Big Muddy." Some farmers claim to fill pipes with Missouri River water and then saw them into disks to use as grindstones.

The "wild" Missouri starts at Fort Benton, a historic Montana town with a great museum. For the first 40 miles below Fort Benton, canyon walls slope obliquely toward the river as the Missouri slowly sheds itself of civilization. Most of the land along this section is privately owned. After passing Virgelle and Coal Banks Landing, the river becomes completely isolated as the sloping canyons turn into sheer white cliffs that rise directly from the river's edge. Wind and rain have shaped the soft rock into peculiar formations, guaranteed to mesmerize river explorers.

This bizarre but attractive country enchanted Captain Lewis. Always the person for detail, his 1805 description of the river and its scenery is hard to top:

> The hills and river Clifts which we passed today exhibit a most romantic appearance. . . . The water in the course of time in decending from those hills and plains on either side of the river has trickled down the soft sand clifts and woarn it into a thousand grotesque figures. . . . As we passed on it seemed as if those seens of visionary inchantment would never have an end. . . .

After nearly 35 miles of white cliffs, the scenery changes to rugged badlands. A maze of coulees and ravines, this legendary Missouri River Breaks country invites exploration. Below Cow Island Landing the valley broadens and the bluffs are lower and more distant. Dense cottonwood stands dominate the river bottom for most of the remaining distance to the Fred Robinson Bridge.

The BLM has developed an excellent map of the Wild and Scenic portion of the river. These water-resistant maps provide a mile-by-mile guide to the river as well as other important logistical considerations. They may be purchased at most BLM offices in Montana.

Those looking for a 1-day trip on the "wild" Missouri usually float between Fort Benton and Loma. Depending on how fast you paddle (and whether there's wind), Coal Banks Landing to Judith Landing takes 2 or 3 days, as does the section from Judith Landing to the Fred Robinson Bridge. Most people allow 5 to 7 days to float the entire 149 miles. While the widely spaced access points preserve the primitive nature of the river, they make shuttling vehicles difficult and somewhat expensive.

The Wild and Scenic portion of the Missouri grows more popular every year, and high national interest in the Lewis and Clark Expedition could lead to levels of use that compromise solitude. Floaters traveling between Fort Benton and the Fred Robinson Bridge between Memorial Day and the weekend after Labor Day must register with the BLM (it's free). Self-registration is available at Fort Benton, Coal Banks Landing, and Judith Landing.

While you may encounter large numbers of people at major put-in points, this is a big river, and people seem to spread out during the day. Unfortunately, campsites on public land are limited, as is shade. Mature cottonwoods are dying, and there is little new growth, mainly due to cattle grazing along the banks and controlled flows that hinder growth. Cow pie campsites are unfortunately somewhat common. Measures need to be taken by the BLM to protect existing trees and provide for regeneration of new trees.

The BLM estimates that at least 8,000 people float the "wild" Missouri each year. Floaters should be prepared for an irritant you wouldn't expect on a Wild and Scenic River: motorboats. The droning of motors off the canyon walls diminishes the primitive experience that is a key part of this trip. Motorboats also make the river seem smaller and more crowded. BLM says the river has a tradition of motorboat use and contends the decision to allow motors was made after extensive public participation. There is a no-wake restriction (about 5 miles per hour), and only downstream travel is allowed for motorboats on the Wild and Scenic sections from the weekend before Memorial Day to the weekend after Labor Day.

Although beginners can handle the Missouri, hazards exist. Thunderstorms can be severe and can occur suddenly. The Missouri's strong winds are legendary. Stay close to shore if the winds get brisk, and stop if they worsen. But if the wind is steady and in your favor, take advantage of it. Rig a poncho or ground cloth (be creative!) between your canoe paddles for a sail. The person in the bow holds the sail between his legs (to drop or adjust depending on the wind), while the person in the stern uses another paddle as a rudder. You will fly!

Be sure to take along drinking water. The river water is unsafe to drink unless boiled or filtered and even then it will be an inconvenience. There is potable water at Coal Banks Landing, Hole-in-the-Wall, and Judith Landing. When camping overnight, take along gas stoves for cooking; firewood is scarce. Beware of camping in cottonwood groves when winds are strong, as the trees snap easily. Be sure to camp and hike only on public land unless you have permission to access private land. Vault toilets have been installed at most campsites. Downstream from Virgelle, few official campsites exist and there are no official toilets. Be prepared to pack out your waste! Rattlesnakes are common along the river and have been encountered at every campsite. Don't forget to bring a first-aid kit, and consider packing along a satellite phone for the more remote sections as you won't find any cellphone reception.

Multiday trips on the Missouri's white cliffs section are renowned for their beauty and history.
JOHN TODD

If you're looking for wildlife, head for the prairie dog towns—they're usually a center of activity. More than thirty different species of Great Plains wildlife use the dog towns, especially burrowing owls. Floaters also have an excellent opportunity to see Rocky Mountain bighorn sheep. These animals were reintroduced into the Missouri Breaks country in the 1960s to replace the Audubon sheep that had been wiped out after the settlement of the white man. Today there are large populations on both sides of the river below Judith Landing.

Bird-watchers will enjoy the river. Kingbirds perch along the river and grab insects, while many warblers sing from the brush. Pheasants use the thick vegetation often found on islands, and great blue herons and Canada geese appear along the shores. Look for white pelicans either floating on the river or circling overhead.

The spiny softshell turtle, uncommon in Montana, can sometimes be spotted sunning on a beach. Don't pick them up—they may bite. The Missouri has excellent populations of warmwater fish species, including catfish, sauger, paddlefish, sturgeon, and northern pike. Night fishing for catfish is a pleasant way to spend a warm summer evening. Or leave a baited hook out overnight and have fish for breakfast.

While most people head for the "wild" Missouri, the 25 miles of river below Fred Robinson Bridge (James Kipp Recreation Area) is equally primitive and spectacular. Bounded on each side by the Charles M. Russell National Wildlife Refuge (CMR), an incredibly productive prairie elk herd roams the bottoms and sometimes can be

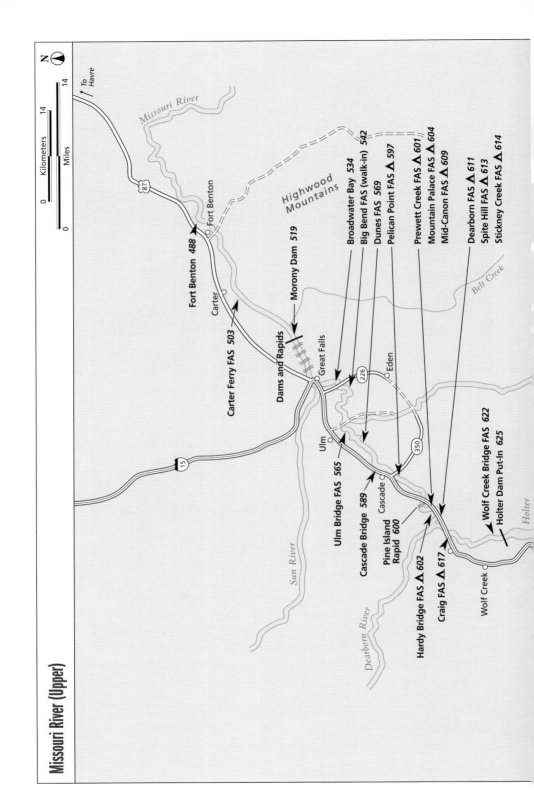

Missouri River (Upper)

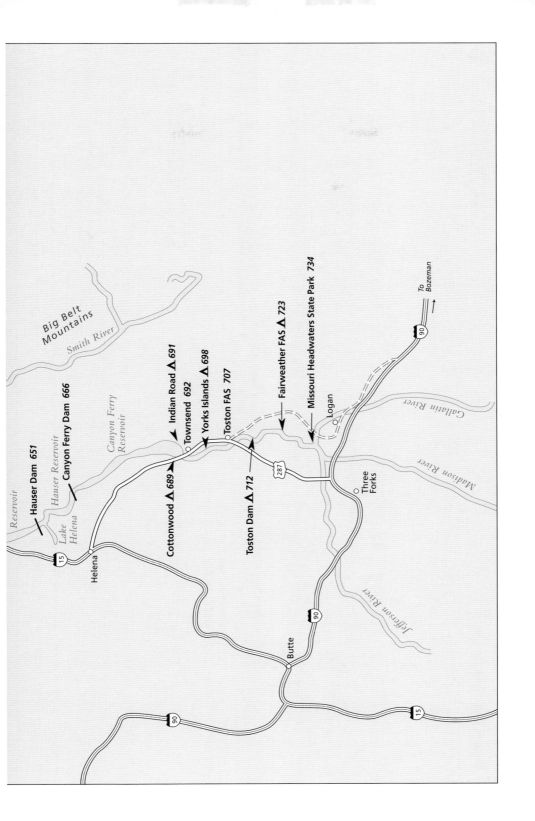

Missouri River (Wild and Scenic)

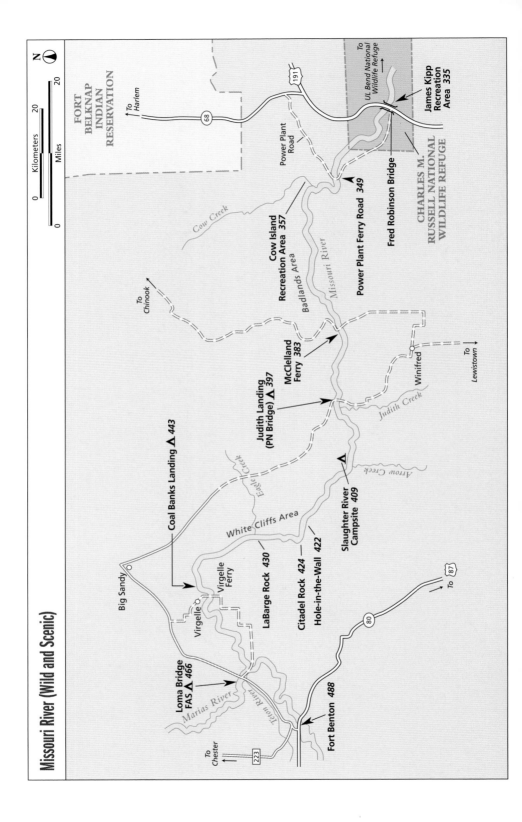

Missouri River (Lower)

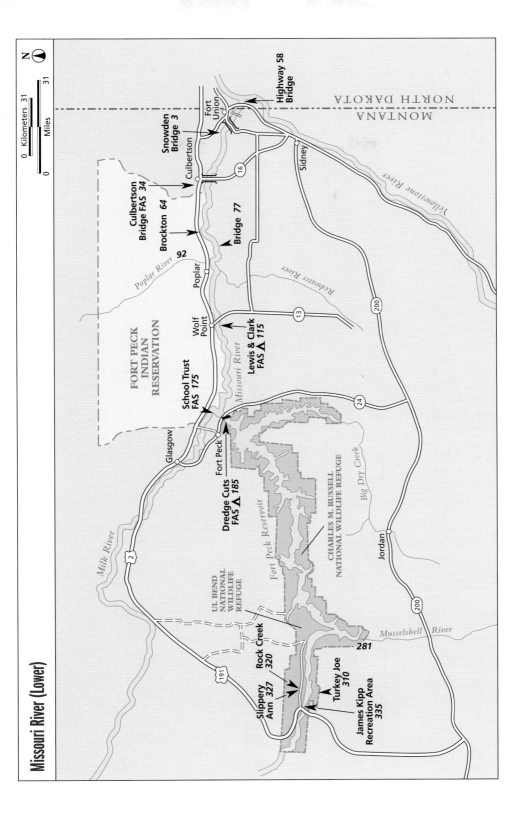

Highway 58 Bridge

Snowden Bridge 3

Fort Union

Culbertson

Culbertson Bridge FAS 34

Brockton 64

Bridge 77

Sidney

16

Poplar River 92

Poplar

FORT PECK INDIAN RESERVATION

Redwater River

13

200

School Trust FAS 175

Wolf Point

Lewis & Clark FAS △ 115

Missouri River

Glasgow

Fort Peck

Dredge Cuts FAS △ 185

24

2

Milk River

Fort Peck Reservoir

CHARLES M. RUSSELL NATIONAL WILDLIFE REFUGE

Big Dry Creek

Jordan

200

191

UL BEND NATIONAL WILDLIFE REFUGE

Rock Creek 320

Slippery Ann 327

281

Turkey Joe 310

James Kipp Recreation Area 335

Musselshell River

MONTANA
NORTH DAKOTA

N

0 Kilometers 31
0 Miles 31

Key Access Points along the Missouri River

Access Point	Access Type	(River Mile)
Missouri Headwaters State Park	Ramp	(734)
Fairweather FAS	Ramp	(723)
Toston Dam	Walk-In	(712)
Toston FAS	Ramp	(707)
Yorks Islands FAS	Ramp	(698)
Indian Road (Townsend)	Ramp	(691)
Cottonwood	Ramp	(689) (reservoir)
Holter Dam	Walk-In	(625)
Wolf Creek Bridge FAS	Ramp	(622)
Craig FAS	Ramp	(617)
Stickney Creek FAS	Ramp	(614)
Spite Hill FAS	Ramp	(613)
Dearborn FAS	Ramp	(611)
Mid-Canon FAS	Ramp	(609)
Mountain Palace FAS	Ramp	(604)
Hardy Bridge FAS	Hand Launch	(602)
Prewett Creek FAS	Ramp	(601)
Pelican Point FAS	Ramp	(597)
Cascade Bridge	Hand Launch	(589)
Dunes FAS	Hand Launch	(569)
Ulm Bridge FAS	Ramp	(565)
Big Bend FAS	Hand Launch	(542)
Broadwater Bay	Ramp	(534)
Morony Dam	Hand Launch	(519)
Carter Ferry FAS	Ramp	(503)
Fort Benton	Ramp	(488)
Loma Bridge FAS	Ramp	(466)
Coal Banks Landing	Ramp	(443)
Judith Landing	Ramp	(397)
McClelland Ferry	Ramp	(383)
Power Plant Ferry Road	Ramp	(349) (south side)
James Kipp Recreation Area	Ramp	(335)
Slippery Ann	Hand Launch	(327)
Rock Creek	Ramp	(320)
Turkey Joe	Ramp	(310) (reservoir)
Fort Peck Dredge Cuts FAS	Ramp	(185)
School Trust FAS	Ramp	(175)
Lewis and Clark FAS	Ramp	(115)
Bridge	Hand Launch	(77)
Brockton	Hand Launch	(64)
Culbertson Bridge FAS	Ramp	(34)
Snowden Bridge FAS	Ramp	(3)
Highway 58 bridge (North Dakota)	Ramp	(0)

seen swimming the river or grazing on the islands. Deer, sage grouse, and coyotes are also common. Floating ends where the river backs up to form Fort Peck Reservoir at Turkey Joe.

The prehistoric paddlefish is also a denizen of this section of the Missouri. Spring triggers a spawning run of these strange fish up the Missouri from Fort Peck Reservoir. Fish as heavy as 141 pounds have been caught near the Fred Robinson Bridge. Paddlefish, however, aren't taken by conventional fishing methods. Heavily weighted treble hooks are used to snag these fish, which may live 30 years or more. These fish require a specific tag to harvest. They feed on plankton, which are rarely larger than the period at the end of this sentence. Similarly, prehistoric pallid sturgeon occupy the Missouri, although their populations are at risk because of limited spawning habitat. They must be released immediately.

Below Fort Peck Reservoir the Missouri remains primitive, and the rough breaks country gently merges with woodlands as the river approaches North Dakota. Although US 2 is never far away, this section of the river is quite isolated for its entire 185-mile course. If you don't like the crowds on the "wild" Missouri, this section will please the crustiest of river hermits. Count on seeing plenty of wildlife, and for those seeking the unusual, this is probably the best spot in Montana to see a whooping crane. They migrate through this part of Montana in spring and fall along with tens of thousands of ducks and geese.

25 Powder River

A remote eastern Montana river, described by pioneers as "a mile wide and an inch deep," which flows through some of Montana's most uninhabited, desolate badlands and prairies.

Vital statistics: 218 miles from the Wyoming border to its juncture with the Yellowstone River near Terry.

Level of difficulty: All Class I, suitable for beginners, except for 200 yards of Class II+ rapids beginning at Mile 8.

Flow: Annual mean flow: 584 cfs near the Highway 12 bridge. Can get too low by late summer. At least 750 cfs is needed for floating.

Recommended watercraft: Canoes.

Hazards: Fences, mud and quicksand, rattlesnakes, and hard-to-see sandbars.

Where the crowd goes: It just isn't done. Most accessible is the 30-mile stretch from the Highway 12 bridge at Locate to the Yellowstone.

Avoiding the scene: The higher in the drainage you go, the more remote it gets. Some motorboat traffic near the mouth of the Yellowstone. It's downright lonely at the top.

Inside tip: Take a spring float to look for turkeys. Beware of high water in May.

Maps: USFS: Custer (Ashland Division); USGS: Ekalaka, MT; Miles City, MT.

Shuttle information: Inquire at Red Rock Sporting Goods, Miles City, (406) 232-2716.

River rules: Mostly private land; camp within the high-water mark.

For more information: BLM, Miles City; FWP, Miles City.

The Paddling

The Powder River may well be Montana's most remote non–wilderness river. Although there are a few isolated ranches or abandoned homesteads nearby, you'll rarely see a light at night or hear a motor. The river enters Montana not far from Kaycee, Wyoming, and flows north for 218 miles before meeting the Yellowstone River not far from Terry. The Powder channels and braids through cottonwood bottoms for most of its course. Noted for its shifting channels and hidden sandbars, the Powder carries more sediment than probably any other Montana river. "Too thin to plow and too thick to drink" is a favorite local description.

But the Powder is quite scenic and extremely isolated. The uppermost parts in Montana flow through rugged badlands, which then give way to cottonwood bottoms. In the last 14 miles, downstream from the Coal Creek Bridge, the river stops braiding, the cottonwoods disappear, and the Powder turns into an arid, wide-open river that's quite unique. At one place, about 8 miles above where the Powder hits the Yellowstone, exposed bedrock juts up in the river and creates rapids that last for about 200 yards. Intermediate rafters or canoeists can handle this hazard (known locally as Ed's Rapids) or walk around it.

The Powder River earns its name from the fine sand along a portion of its banks. Tim Palmer

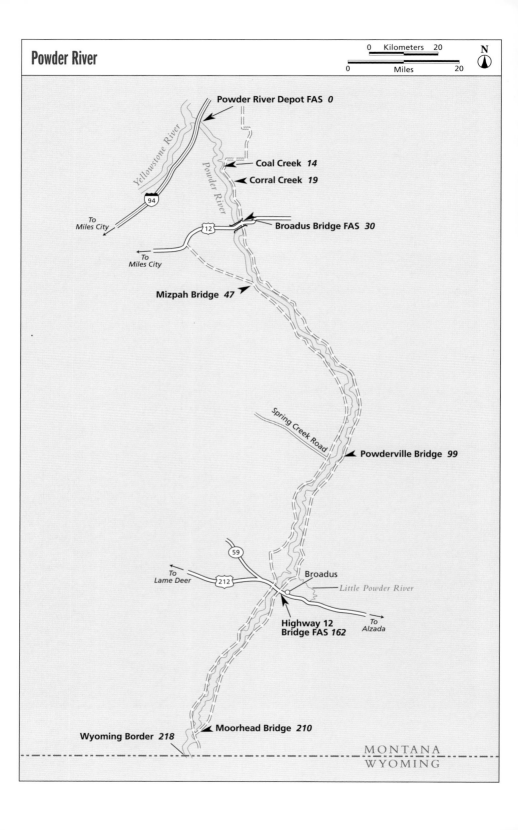

Powder River

Powder River Depot FAS *0*

Yellowstone River

Powder River

94

Coal Creek *14*

Corral Creek *19*

To Miles City

12 **Broadus Bridge FAS** *30*

To Miles City

Mizpah Bridge *47*

Spring Creek Road

Powderville Bridge *99*

59

To Lame Deer

212 **Broadus**

Little Powder River

Highway 12 Bridge FAS *162*

To Alzada

Moorhead Bridge *210*

Wyoming Border *218*

MONTANA

WYOMING

Since the Powder is quite shallow, the floating season is short. In a typical year, flows will be too low by late July. River trips in the fall are rarely possible, which is really too bad given the hunting opportunities that abound. Turkeys and mule deer are plentiful, as are sharp-tailed grouse, sage grouse, and antelope. The Powder River basin was one of the last areas in the nation that had free-roaming bison herds, and it's still possible to find bones and teeth in the riverbank. This is also a great area for fossils; several dinosaur finds have been made nearby.

The floating is easy on the Powder, suitable for practiced beginners in rafts or canoes. There really aren't many hazards except for an occasional downed tree and barbed-wire fence. But the fences aren't even much of a problem—they get washed out during the season when you'd want to be floating.

The Powder has great appeal for those who like long, isolated trips. We heard of one canoeist who floated the entire river by himself (218 miles in Montana and 185 miles in Wyoming) in 32 days. Public land along the river is quite limited; access points are far apart and consist mainly of county road bridges. You'll be treated like an explorer if anyone encounters you on this river.

Float fishing: The best floating and fishing is below where the Little Powder River enters near Broadus. A local biologist who has done fish surveys on the Powder tells us his favorite stretch is from Mizpah to Locate (the Highway 12 bridge). At high flows it took him less than 8 hours to cover this 17-mile section. This same biologist reports that the Powder is one of Montana's best spawning streams for shovelnose sturgeon and catfish. Their spawning runs coincide with spring runoff and the floating season.

Key Access Points along the Powder River

Access Point	Access Type	(River Mile)
Moorhead Bridge	Hand Launch	(210)
Broadus Bridge FAS	Hand Launch	(162)
Powderville Bridge	Hand Launch	(99)
Mizpah Bridge	Hand Launch	(47)
Highway 12 bridge	Hand Launch	(30)
Corral Creek	Hand Launch	(19)
Coal Creek	Hand Launch	(14)
Powder River Depot FAS	Hand Launch	(0)

26 Red Rock River

Small, windy, and remote, the Red Rock River originates in one of Montana's most scenic high-altitude valleys.

Vital statistics: 113 miles (27 miles of lakes and reservoir) from Lillian Lake to where it enters Clark Canyon Reservoir.

Level of difficulty: Class I its entire length. Sharp turns, fast currents, and logjams below Lima Reservoir require at least intermediate skill.

Flow: Annual mean flow: 143 cfs near Monida. Usually too low by midsummer.

Recommended watercraft: Canoes.

Hazards: Logjams, swift currents, sharp bends, barbed wire, and diversion dams below Lima Reservoir. Above the reservoir, beware of remoteness and bad weather.

Where the crowd goes: Nowhere. The "wilderness" section between Upper and Lower Red Rock Lakes is the most popular.

Avoiding the scene: Not an issue.

Inside tip: Good wildlife viewing for trumpeter swans, which regularly use the river between Lower Red Rock Lake and Brundage Bridge.

Maps: USFS: Beaverhead Interagency Travel Plan (East and West); USGS: Ashton, ID; Dubois, WY; USFWS: Red Rock Lakes Recreation Guide.

Shuttle information: Check with the Dell Mercantile, Lima, (406) 276-3231; alternatively pack a bike, as the distances are not extremely far.

River rules: The river between Upper and Lower Red Rock Lakes is open to floating between September 1 and freeze-up (typically late October) but closed to fishing. No motors in Red Rock Lakes National Wildlife Refuge. Check with refuge for updated regulations.

For more information: Red Rock Lakes National Wildlife Refuge, Lima; FWP, Bozeman; BOR, Billings.

The Paddling

If you're bothered by the heavy traffic on the upper Beaverhead, try driving a little farther south to the Red Rock River. This little-known stream, which empties into Clark Canyon Reservoir, receives only modest floating pressure.

Between Lima and Clark Canyon, the Red Rock closely resembles the Beaverhead, both in scenery and fishing. It's a little smaller, but it turns and twists in the same distinctive fashion and has similar outstanding trout habitat. In its upper reaches in the isolated Centennial Valley, the river flows through Red Rock Lakes National Wildlife Refuge, a unique high-altitude marsh that teems with birdlife. Much of the 32,000-acre refuge is designated wilderness, one of the largest roadless wetlands in the United States.

The Red Rock River gets its start amid the towering peaks of the Centennial Mountains, just west of Yellowstone National Park. Herds of cattle were driven into the valley in 1876, a hundred years after the Revolutionary War, giving the area its name. Cattle remain the predominant sign of man's presence.

The upper sections of the Red Rock River are flanked to the south by the towering Centennial Range.

Most people know the Red Rock Lakes National Wildlife Refuge as the place where trumpeter swans were rescued from extinction. In the 1930s these majestic white birds numbered less than seventy, and many ornithologists predicted their demise. Stringent protection brought them back to where they now number close to 2,500 and are expanding their range. These large birds, which may weigh as much as 35 pounds and have a wingspan of 8 feet, have a distinct, low-pitched bugling call that seems to resound across the entire valley.

Floating on the Red Rock begins within the refuge after a short paddle across Upper Red Rock Lake. A canoe is the craft of choice. The river snakes its way through a maze of marshy islands before emptying into Lower Red Rock Lake. Since there is little current, it's possible to lose your way while picking a path through the marsh. A detailed map of the refuge and the 7-mile trip between the lakes is available at the refuge headquarters. Beware, however: During the summer and fall the lake levels can be frustratingly low, leaving paddlers scooping more mud than water.

Wildlife viewers have spotted over 200 species of birds on the refuge, and at least 18 species of waterfowl nest there. Shorebirds including long-billed curlews, avocets, and willets frequent the mudflats bordering the marshes, while gulls, terns, and pelicans wheel overhead. Sandhill cranes are common, particularly in the meadows bordering the upper lake.

Allow a full day for the trip between the lakes, as the slack water requires more paddling than on a normal river. To protect nesting waterfowl, no boats are allowed

The Red Rock has become increasingly popular with wade anglers; however, because of challenging access, floating remains the best option.

on this section before September 1. Check at the refuge headquarters for information on boating regulations.

Between the refuge boundary and Lima Reservoir, the thick marsh gradually gives way to open range. The river is quite isolated and can only be reached by a few county roads. The only time of year this section sees any traffic is during waterfowl season. It's an excellent float to see waterfowl almost any time, and trumpeter swans use the river extensively.

Floating the Red Rock from Lima Dam to Kidd is possible, but it's strictly for the adventuresome. Be on the lookout for blind corners with barbed-wire fences, downed trees, and low bridges. It's only recommended for experienced boaters who don't mind occasional portages. The sharp turns, fast currents, and occasional logjams found below Lima Dam require intermediate skill. It's best floated in a canoe, as the river is rather small and winding for rafts. Moreover, hitting barbed wire can be a deflating experience. Low flows in dry years may preclude floating by midsummer.

The river grows increasingly larger as it approaches Clark Canyon Reservoir. Below Kidd the river is much less hazardous. This section has great fishing, but the only access other than floating is by making friends with Ted Turner, as he owns a large ranch along the river. If you float this section, be sure to stay within the high-water mark.

Red Rock River

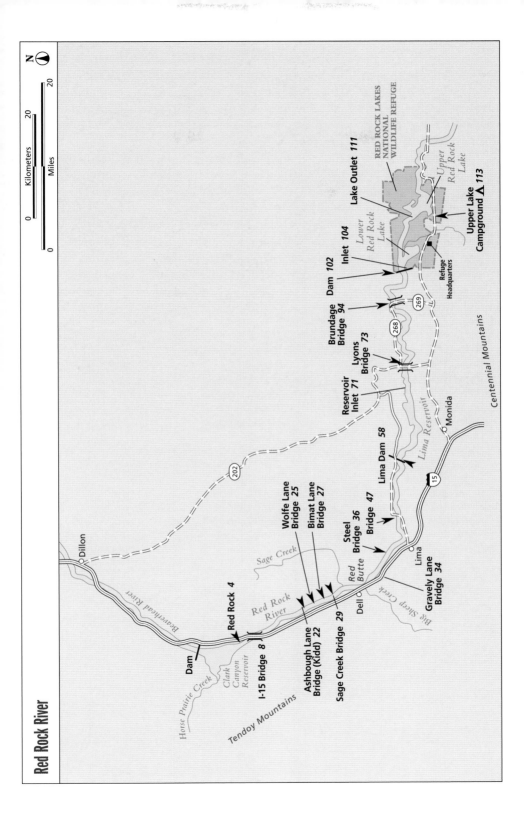

RED ROCK LAKES NATIONAL WILDLIFE REFUGE

Lake Outlet 111

Upper Red Rock Lake

Upper Lake Campground △ 113

Inlet 104

Dam 102

Lower Red Rock Lake

Brundage Bridge 94

Refuge Headquarters

Lyons Bridge 73

Reservoir Inlet 71

Lima Dam 58

Lima Reservoir

Monida

Steel Bridge 36

Bridge 47

Centennial Mountains

Wolfe Lane Bridge 25

Bimat Lane Bridge 27

Red Butte

Lima

Ashbough Lane Bridge (Kidd) 22

Sage Creek Bridge 29

Gravely Lane Bridge 34

Dell

Big Sheep Creek

Dam

Red Rock 4

I-15 Bridge 8

Clark Canyon Reservoir

Horse Prairie Creek

Red Rock River

Sage Creek

Beaverhead River

Dillon

Tendoy Mountains

N

Kilometers
0   20

Miles
0   20

Access to the Red Rock downstream from Lima is exclusively by county bridges, and most are overgrown with brush or blocked by barbed wire. Although the State of Montana has affirmed that county bridges provide legal access for floaters and anglers, some landowners disagree and have filed lawsuits. Be aware that the size of the county right-of-way can vary significantly. Be sure you know the law (see appendix D) when floating sections with difficult or controversial access.

Float fishing: Between the reservoir and the refuge, the water is slightly turbid and fishing is erratic at best. Reports indicate some trout present (cutthroats and grayling), as well as ling. The water is slow and flat and easy for beginners. The best fishing opportunity is undoubtedly between Kidd and Clark Canyon Reservoir. This section has minimal wade-fishing access, but has plenty of good fishing for browns and rainbows if you're willing to work for them. Below the Lima Reservoir the fishery tends to resemble more of a tailwater, and large fish often sit in skinny water. Don't forget that the section between Upper and Lower Red Rock Lakes is closed to fishing. Fishing above Upper Red Rock Lake can be very productive in the spring, but is better suited for wade fishing.

Key Access Points along the Red Rock River

Access Point	Access Type	(River Mile)
Upper Lake Campground	Walk-In	(113)
Dam	Hand Launch	(102)
Brundage Bridge	Hand Launch	(94)
Lyons Bridge	Hand Launch	(73)
Lima Dam	Walk-In	(58)
Bridge	Hand Launch	(47)
Steel Bridge	Hand Launch	(36)
Sage Creek Bridge	Hand Launch	(29)
Bimat Lane Bridge	Hand Launch	(27)
Wolfe Lane Bridge	Hand Launch	(25)
Kidd Bridge	Hand Launch	(22)
Red Rock	Hand Launch	(4) (Clark Canyon Reservoir)

27 Rock Creek

This well-graveled, clean–flowing mountain stream gushes past spectacular palisades and through thick pine forests, providing some of the best fishing in western Montana.

Vital statistics: 51 miles from the confluence of its two forks above Gilles Bridge to its juncture with the Clark Fork River.

Level of difficulty: All Class I except for a short Class II whitewater section through the Dalles. All suitable for intermediates in rafts.

Flow: Annual mean flow: 513 cfs near the mouth. Usually too low for floating by mid-July. Minimum flow is 650 cfs; 2,800 cfs is maximum. Flows between 1,000 and 1,500 cfs are optimum.

Recommended watercraft: Small rafts.

Hazards: Dangerous logjams, swift currents, narrow channels, and standing waves.

Where the crowd goes: Windlass to the White Bridge (and just about everywhere else) during the salmon fly hatch.

Avoiding the scene: Get up early or float late.

Inside tip: During a high-moisture year, try a fall overnight trip on the upper river.

Maps: BLM: #21 (Missoula East), #22 (Philipsburg), #23 (Wisdom); USFS: Lolo, Deerlodge; USGS: Butte, MT; Montana Afloat: #3 (Rock Creek).

Shuttle information: Right Turn Clyde Shuttles, (406) 240-5455 or call the Rock Creek Mercantile at (406) 825-6440.

River rules: No float fishing from July 1 to November 30. Outfitters not allowed from Elkhorn Landing to Valley of the Moon and through the Dalles section. Outfitters cannot float on weekends or on Memorial Day from Welcome Creek to Elkhorn. Check fishing regulations with FWP.

For more information: FWP, Missoula; Grizzly Hackle, Missoula; Missoulian Angler, Missoula; Rock Creek Mercantile, Rock Creek.

The Paddling

What is the difference between a creek and a river? Only the name. Rock Creek, which starts west of Philipsburg and flows for more than 51 miles before hitting the Clark Fork about 20 miles east of Missoula, has the attributes and flow of many small Montana rivers. This world-class trout stream courses through a largely undeveloped valley, flowing past thick forests and stunning rock formations. Many of the heavily timbered hillsides give way to grassy meadows near their crests. The fishery is extremely prolific and, as a result, Rock Creek continues to be one of the most famous trout streams in the state.

The creek gets its name from the rockslides that stretch down the mountainsides and occasionally into the stream. It's one of the best rivers in the state for seeing bighorn sheep, especially on the hills near Solomon Creek at the lower end of the river and near Windlass Bridge on the upper river. Moose and black bears are common along the river, as are western tanagers and ruffed grouse.

Rock Creek is one of only a few Montana streams where agencies have restricted fishing from boats. Because it's a small stream that receives heavy use from anglers on foot, conflict between floaters and waders increases as water levels decrease. All fishing from boats is prohibited between July 1 and November 30. While state law guarantees the right to float navigable rivers like Rock Creek at any time, agencies can restrict the ability to float and fish. People who float Rock Creek in summer should expect to encounter a steady stream of anglers who may have to move out of the stream channel to avoid you. They won't be happy. Since the creek is usually too low for floating anyway, we suggest you avoid it during the summer fishing season.

Almost all Rock Creek floating takes place from May 15 to July 1, coincidental with the salmon fly hatch. For nonfishing people, this is the hatch of giant stoneflies that brings large trout to the surface. Rock Creek can become extremely crowded during this time, especially on the upper river.

Floating can begin where the West and Middle Forks come together. The river is always swift and flows over a cobbled bottom. Logjams and snags pose the biggest hazards, and there are occasional big waves. Although Rock Creek contains only Class I water except for a short section through the Dalles, it's too difficult for beginners in canoes or rafts at the higher flows typically encountered in May and June. The Dalles is mostly Class II and III water that intermediate rafters can handle. A road parallels the river for its entire length, but it's usually unnoticeable.

The upper river has some exceptional scenery as it winds past brightly colored rock outcroppings. Sunsets are spectacular. Public land adjoins much of the river. A popular float at high flows is the 22-mile section between Gilles Bridge and White Bridge. At high flows it takes about 6 hours.

The Dalles is a 4-mile section of whitewater that lies between Harry's Flat and Welcome Creek. The stream constricts into a narrow channel that contains many large boulders. The rapids are not particularly difficult, mostly Class II or easier. The Welcome Creek Wilderness lies immediately adjacent to the river and has excellent hiking. A swinging bridge provides access for hikers and is the unofficial end of the Dalles whitewater section.

Logjam problems can be acute on the lower river, particularly in the vicinity of the Valley of the Moon. Most years, large jams completely block the river downstream from Elkhorn. Check with local sources, including the Rock Creek Mercantile and the Missoula fly shops listed in appendix A, for current information. For an easily accessible half-day float, put in at Lower Fire Ring and float to Elkhorn. Check out the Elkhorn take-out before floating, however, as the entrance to the side channel can become choked with wood.

Float fishing: Rock Creek comes into shape usually when other rivers in the area are high and brown, meaning this stream gets a lot of action in the months of May and June. It's a tough river to fish from a boat as there are few eddies or slow sections. This is combat fishing at its finest—throwing huge salmon flies and golden stones under overhanging willows while flying down the river at close to 10 miles per hour! Make sure all your gear is properly secured in your boat before shoving off, because it may be the last stop you'll make. Be aware of logjams, especially in the area

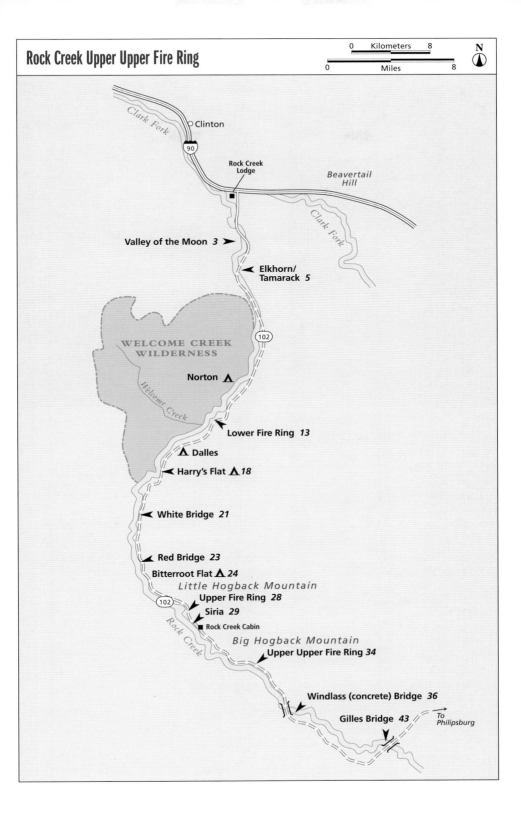

Rock Creek Upper Upper Fire Ring

0   Kilometers   8

0   Miles   8

N

Clark Fork ○ Clinton

90

Rock Creek
Lodge

*Beavertail
Hill*

Clark Fork

Valley of the Moon *3* ➤

◄ Elkhorn/
Tamarack *5*

102

WELCOME CREEK
WILDERNESS

Welcome Creek

Norton ⋀

◄ Lower Fire Ring *13*

⋀ Dalles

◄ Harry's Flat ⋀ *18*

◄ White Bridge *21*

◄ Red Bridge *23*

Bitterroot Flat ⋀ *24*

Little Hogback Mountain

Upper Fire Ring *28*

Siria *29*

■ Rock Creek Cabin

102

Rock Creek

Big Hogback Mountain

Upper Upper Fire Ring *34*

Windlass (concrete) Bridge *36*

Gilles Bridge *43*

*To
Philipsburg*

If you're floating Rock Creek, fishing is likely on your mind. Don't forget to stop and wade fish as the current is swift, with few eddies.

near the microburst where there are usually plenty of downed trees and obstructions. This section is aptly named "the warzone." Usually portages are flagged early season to alert floaters of upcoming danger.

Key Access Points along Rock Creek

Access Point	Access Type	(River Mile)
Gilles Bridge	Hand Launch	(43)
Windlass (concrete) Bridge	Hand Launch	(36)
Upper Upper Fire Ring	Dirt Ramp	(34)
Siria	Hand Launch	(29)
Upper Fire Ring	Dirt Ramp	(28)
Red Bridge	Dirt Ramp	(23)
White Bridge	Dirt Ramp	(21)
Harry's Flat	Walk-In	(18)
Lower Fire Ring	Hand Launch	(13)
Elkhorn/Tamarack	Dirt Ramp	(5)
Valley of the Moon	Walk-In	(3)

28 Ruby River

This small, sinuous stream snakes its way through the historic Ruby Valley, providing excellent fishing along its way.

Vital statistics: 103 miles (3 reservoir miles) from its headwaters south of Alder to its confluence with the Beaverhead River.

Level of difficulty: Class I all the way. Practiced beginners can handle this river at low flows.

Flow: Annual mean flow: 210 cfs below Ruby Reservoir. Frequently too low for floating by late July, especially above the reservoir.

Recommended watercraft: Canoes, small pontoons.

Hazards: Extremely sharp bends, brushy banks, narrow channels, protruding trees, barbed-wire fences, diversion dams, and cranky landowners; contentious access.

Where the crowd goes: Nowhere in particular. Silver Springs to Twin Bridges is most popular.

Avoiding the scene: Upstream from Ruby Reservoir is isolated and difficult to reach—perfect for explorers.

Inside tip: Floating can get you to some great, otherwise inaccessible fishing.

Maps: BLM: #33 (Butte South), #34 (Dillon); USFS: Beaverhead Interagency Travel Plan (East); USGS: Dillon, MT; Bozeman, MT; Ashton, ID; Dubois, ID.

Shuttle information: Check at Harman's Fly Shop, Sheridan, (406) 842-5868; or Four Rivers Fishing Company, Twin Bridges, (406) 684-5651.

River rules: Check with FWP concerning floater access. Spillway area below dam is closed to fishing.

For more information: FWP, Bozeman; Four Rivers Fishing Company, Twin Bridges; Harman's Fly Shop, Sheridan.

The Paddling

With its well-developed curves and bends, the Ruby River makes an excellent little sister to the Beaverhead, the river it flows into near Twin Bridges. The river slinks and turns through the picturesque Ruby Valley, former home of outlaws and gold miners. Piles of gravel that line the banks of many of the Ruby's tributaries are remnants of the area's gold rush legacy. Robber's Roost, a famous roadhouse located between Sheridan and Laurin, was once a favorite hangout for outlaws and bandits who preyed upon gold miners.

The Shoshone Indians called this river Passamari, meaning "water of the cottonwood groves." When Lewis and Clark passed through, Captain Lewis named it "Philanthropy," for what he considered one of Thomas Jefferson's three cardinal virtues (he named the Big Hole River "Wisdom" and the Jefferson River "Philosophy").

Pioneers later downgraded the name to Stinkingwater River after a large number of buffalo carcasses befouled the water one spring. Now it's called the Ruby for the garnets that sharp-eyed people still pick out of the stream's gravel.

The float season for the Ruby River is brief, and by July the river can often be too low for floating. BEN LAMB

This small river originates in the Snowcrest Mountains and flows north for about 40 miles before reaching Ruby Reservoir. Below the reservoir it flows nearly 50 miles before meeting the Beaverhead. The river above the reservoir is small with sharp bends, barbed wire, and occasional obstructions. It requires small crafts and large patience; it's often too low to float by August. Almost all floating on the Ruby takes place below the reservoir.

Then there's the access problem. Most land along the Ruby is private, and landowners are quite sensitive about trespassers. The Ruby has excellent fishing, and some landowners charge hefty fees to access the river. The problem? People floating the river can fish for free, and landowners resent it (as do their paying clients). Fortunately, Montana law says that all navigable rivers are property of the state. Landowners may charge fees for crossing their private property, but they cannot interfere with recreation within the high-water mark. Recent court cases have upheld stream access of prescriptive easements along the Ruby, and contentious bridges, such as Seyler Lane, still allow excellent access to the lower river.

While the Ruby is smaller than the Beaverhead, it has the same brushy banks and excellent trout habitat. It's predominantly a brown trout fishery below the dam and mostly cutthroats and rainbows above. While it's difficult to fish from a boat on the Ruby, a canoe can be useful for reaching inaccessible portions of the river. The Ruby's brushy habitat and frequent backwater sloughs also generate outstanding birdlife. It's a great area for sandhill cranes.

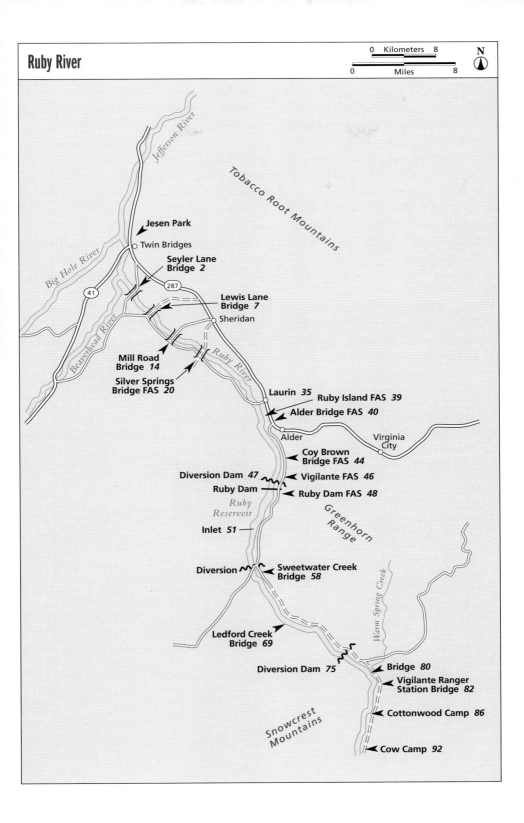

Because of limited access, the small size of the river, and long float distances between access points, the Ruby gets very little floating pressure. This river has so many bends that you should plan on traveling about 3 river miles for every air mile. Access is strictly by fishing access sites and county bridges. Most floating occurs between the Silver Springs access and Twin Bridges. A small canoe is the best craft; it can handle sharp turns and narrow channels and can be portaged easily. Moreover, barbed wire and sharp willows will puncture all but the sturdiest rafts.

While the Ruby isn't difficult, it takes considerable skill to negotiate the repeated sharp bends, narrow channels, diversion dams, and protruding trees. Beginners should stay away when the river is high. But beware of flows getting too low, which often happens because of heavy irrigation demands.

While Lewis and Clark called the Ruby "mild and placid," they didn't encounter present-day hazards such as barbed wire around blind corners, water diverted from the river, and landowners who feel they own the river. It makes one pine for the old days.

Float fishing: Much of your time floating the Ruby will likely be spent navigating its many bends and braids. Fishing from a boat is quite challenging. Plan on getting out and wade fishing if you float this stream. Few people float the Ruby, and as a result fishing from a boat (or boat access) is one surefire way to beat the crowd and find less-pressured fish.

Key Access Points along the Ruby River

Access Point	Access Type	(River Mile)
Cow Camp	Hand Launch	(92)
Cottonwood Camp	Hand Launch	(86)
Vigilante Ranger Station Bridge	Hand Launch	(82)
Bridge	Hand Launch	(80)
Ledford Creek Bridge	Hand Launch	(69)
Sweetwater Creek Bridge	Hand Launch	(58)
Ruby Dam FAS	Walk-In	(48)
Vigilante FAS	Walk-In	(46)
Coy Brown Bridge FAS	Walk-In	(44)
Alder Bridge FAS	Hand Launch	(40)
Ruby Island FAS	Hand Launch	(39)
Silver Springs Bridge FAS	Hand Launch	(20)
Mill Road Bridge	Hand Launch	(14)
Lewis Lane Bridge	Hand Launch	(7)
Seyler Lane Bridge	Hand Launch	(2)
Jesen Park, Twin Bridges (Beaverhead River)	Ramp	(0)

29 Smith River

One of Montana's premier floating streams, the Smith River cuts a narrow swath through a spectacular canyon. Its colorful cliffs, abundant wildflowers, outstanding wildlife, and excellent fishing bring people back year after year.

Vital statistics: 125 miles from the confluence of its two forks to its juncture with the Missouri River near Ulm.

Level of difficulty: At normal flows Class I, except for 2 Class II rapids. Suitable for practiced beginners in rafts and intermediates in canoes. Requires continuous maneuvering.

Flow: Annual mean flow: 148 cfs near Fort Logan. Usually floatable until early July. In a drift boat don't try it below 400 cfs. In a raft you need at least 200 cfs. If you read water well, you can get by with as little as 150 cfs in a non-aluminum canoe.

Recommended watercraft: Rafts.

Hazards: Sharp bends with currents flowing into cliff walls, snags, narrow channels, and float-through fences; sudden, intense lightning or windstorms. Rattlesnakes, bears, and raccoons may cause problems if you fail to keep a clean camp.

Where the crowd goes: Camp Baker to Eden Bridge.

Avoiding the scene: Go in early spring or during the fall in the non-permit season.

Inside tip: After the river drops below floatable levels, summer rainstorms sometimes raise flows enough for spur-of-the-moment canoeists.

Maps: USFS: Lewis and Clark (Jefferson Division), Helena; USGS: White Sulphur, MT; Great Falls, MT; River Rat Maps: Smith; Montana Afloat: #9 (The Smith River).

Shuttle information: Charlie's Think Wild Shuttle Service, White Sulphur Springs, (406) 547-6338; Smith River Shuttle, Eden Bridge, (406) 866-3522.

River rules: Float fee and permit required. No motors. Camping in designated sites only. Campers must declare their campsites prior to departure at Camp Baker. Maximum group size 15. No more than 4 nights camping from June 10 to July 10. No dogs. Floaters must have certified bearproof coolers/dry boxes or an electric bear fence. Check on special fishing regulations.

For more information: FWP, Great Falls or Camp Baker; Charlie's Think Wild Shuttle Service, White Sulphur Springs; Montana River Outfitters, Great Falls; US Weather Service, Great Falls.

The Paddling

Henry David Thoreau once wrote, "He who hears the rippling of rivers will never despair of anything." The bubbling waters of the Smith River have that magical ability to soothe one's soul. Squadrons of floaters seek a special kind of spiritual salvation along the Smith's shores each year.

Located south of Great Falls, the Smith rises out of the Castle Mountains, crooks by White Sulphur Springs, and then courses between the Big Belt and Little Belt Mountains before meeting the Missouri River. Lewis and Clark named the river in

The Smith River is Montana's only river requiring a permit to float. And for good reason—the Smith flows through an impressive canyon with an abundance of camping options.
ALEC UNDERWOOD

1805 in honor of Robert Smith, President Thomas Jefferson's secretary of the navy. The river winds by Fort Logan (first known as Camp Baker), a military outpost established in 1869 to protect ranchers and miners from Indians.

Although the Smith is small in comparison to many other Montana rivers—and frequently is too low for floating in late July and August—it's a high-quality stream cast in a primitive setting. The heart of the river, and the highlight of all float trips, is a deep limestone canyon that envelops the river. Long riffles alternate with deep pools on this emerald-colored stream, creating excellent trout habitat. Towering rock formations and thick forests alive with wildlife complete the scene.

Given these alluring qualities, it's only natural that many people want to float the Smith. To protect and maintain this river's natural qualities, FWP manages the river under a permit system. Competition for permits is stiff during the prime floating months of May, June, and July. Applications are taken beginning January 1, and permits are issued after February 15. Permit fees vary depending on whether you're a Montana resident or nonresident. In addition to the permit fee, floater fees are also required at Camp Baker, and vary by age and residency status. If you don't get a permit, call FWP in Great Falls to check for cancellations. Maximum group size per permit is fifteen.

Most Smith River floats start at Camp Baker and end at Eden Bridge, 60 miles downstream. Although it's possible to start as high in the drainage as where the two major forks of the river join, not many do. For those who try, it's an early season proposition; heavy irrigation usually precludes floating by mid-July. Only intermediates or better should try the Smith above the Fort Logan Bridge. Beware of a short, rocky canyon with some difficult rapids not far below the Buckingham Bridge.

The Smith also receives modest pressure near its mouth, below Eden Bridge. It's a flat, lazy river that flows mostly through open farmland before meeting the Missouri about 20 miles downstream at Ulm. Although the scenery isn't spectacular, it can have good brown trout fishing in the fall as far downstream as the Truly Bridge.

The popular float from Camp Baker to Eden Bridge takes a minimum of 2 nights and 3 full days at normal water levels. The average trip lasts 4 days, but many people take 5 days. While most think a slow trip is best, two canoeists hold the speed record: Camp Baker to Eden Bridge twice in one day! The trips took place at peak flows and maximum daylight.

The shuttle between Camp Baker and Eden Bridge is roundabout, so allow yourself several hours each way if you do it yourself. There are two options: The shorter route is a dirt road that's dusty when dry and nearly impassable when wet. The longer but more comfortable route is via US 89. The other possibility is to use one of the commercial shuttle services listed above. Smith River Shuttle does a fantastic job and once went so far as to re-weld my trailer so it would be roadworthy for my drive home. For a complete list of shuttle services, contact FWP's Great Falls office.

About 60 percent of floaters use rafts, and about 30 percent use canoes; the rest use inflatable kayaks, rowboats, and drift boats. Drift boats are a poor choice during low-water conditions—even at high water a hard boat is tough to keep clear of rocks. Canoes, however, shine when the river gets scratchy, particularly ones made of synthetic materials that slide over rocks without damage. Canoes have good maneuverability and better speed, and they handle headwinds more effectively.

After leaving Camp Baker, grassy hillsides eventually give way to rock outcroppings and sheer walls as the river approaches the canyon. By the time floaters reach Tenderfoot Creek, cliffs rise sharply on both sides of the river. Colorful lichens adorn stone walls, as do swallow's nests and occasional Indian pictographs.

Wildlife viewing can be outstanding, especially in the early morning or late evening. Mule deer can be seen bouncing up hillsides, and beaver, mink, and muskrat are common streamside denizens. Birds to look for include kingfishers, spotted sandpipers, golden eagles, dippers, great horned owls, and an assortment of warblers. On a recent trip we counted eighty-two bird species.

Floaters today may even see an animal Lewis and Clark never saw in Montana—the raccoon. This masked mammal has extended its range west during the last century. One may invade your campsite looking for unsecured food. More troublesome are the black bears that frequent river camps along the Smith. While there haven't been any bear attacks along the river, several problem bears have been killed by wildlife officials in recent years, as they have become habituated to campers that don't keep a clean camp. Remember to be "bear aware" and bring the required bearproof coolers/dry boxes and/or electric fence to secure your food items. FWP requires floaters to declare their boat campsites before they leave Camp Baker. There's competition for the best campsites, and they are issued on a first-come, first-served basis. FWP has restricted dogs on the Smith because of waste in campsites and the nuisance to other floaters and wildlife, so leave the pooch at home unless you are floating during bird-hunting season when they are allowed.

May 15 to July 1 is the prime Smith River floating period, so those seeking solitude go in April and September. Peak flows usually occur in late May and early June, and the floating season typically is over by mid-July. When irrigation ceases in September, flows may pick up enough for a fall float. The minimum flow for a raft is about 200 cfs; for a canoe, about 150 cfs. Check flow conditions on the internet by searching "Montana current streamflow" and selecting the USGS website (it's updated every 4 hours). Or you can do it the old way by calling FWP in Great Falls.

The Smith is a fairly easy river to float. Practiced beginners in rafts will do fine except at high flows. Canoeists require more experience to negotiate the repeated sharp turns and the occasional small rapids. The most significant rapids occur near mile 35, just before and after the Rattlesnake Bend campsite. Other hazards include frequent rocks (many just under the surface and difficult for the uninitiated to detect), sharp bends into cliff walls, rocky shallows, and occasional snags. While fences may cross the river in low periods, they almost always have float gates that permit easy passage.

The most popular (and permitted) section of the Smith River starts at Camp Baker, near White Sulphur Springs, and ends 60 miles downstream at Eden Bridge. ALEC UNDERWOOD

Smith River

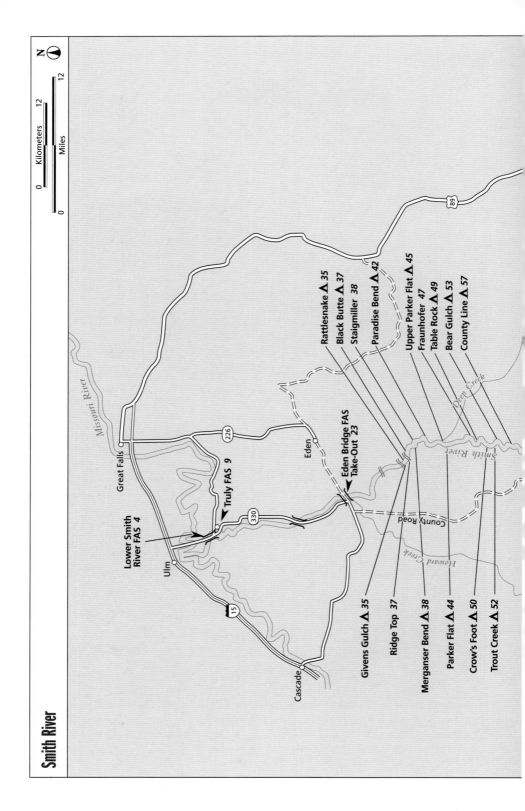

Givens Gulch ▲ 35
Ridge Top 37
Merganser Bend ▲ 38
Parker Flat ▲ 44
Crow's Foot ▲ 50
Trout Creek ▲ 52

Rattlesnake ▲ 35
Black Butte ▲ 37
Staigmiller 38
Paradise Bend ▲ 42
Upper Parker Flat ▲ 45
Fraunhofer 47
Table Rock ▲ 49
Bear Gulch ▲ 53
County Line ▲ 57

Lower Smith
River FAS 4

Truly FAS 9

Eden Bridge FAS
Take-Out 23

Great Falls

Missouri River

Ulm

Eden

Cascade

Deep Creek

Howard Creek

County Road

Smith River

226

330

15

89

N

0   Kilometers   12
0   Miles   12

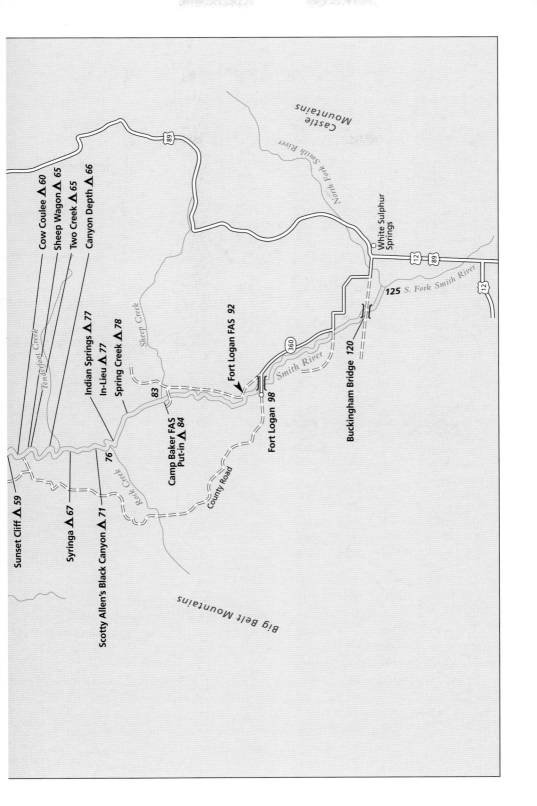

Castle Mountains

North Fork Smith River

White Sulphur Springs

89

12 89

12

125 S. Fork Smith River

Sunset Cliff △ 59

Cow Coulee △ 60
Sheep Wagon △ 65
Two Creek △ 65
Canyon Depth △ 66

89

Syringa △ 67

Scotty Allen's Black Canyon △ 71

76

Indian Springs △ 77
In-Lieu △ 77
Spring Creek △ 78

83

Camp Baker FAS
Put-in △ 84

Rock Creek

Sheep Creek

Fort Logan FAS 92

Fort Logan 98

360

Smith River

Buckingham Bridge 120

County Road

Big Belt Mountains

Key Access Points/Designated Campsites along the Smith River

Access Point	Access Type	Campsite	(River Mile)
Fort Logan FAS	Ramp		(92)
Camp Baker FAS	Ramp		(84)
Spring Creek			(78)
In-Lieu			(77)
Indian Springs			(77)
Rock Garden			(77)
Rock Creek			(76)
Scotty Allen's Black Canyon			(71)
Syringa Camp			(67)
Canyon Depth			(66)
Two Creek			(65)
Sheep Wagon			(65)
Cow Coulee			(60)
Sunset Cliff			(59)
County Line			(57)
Bear Gulch			(53)
Trout Creek			(52)
Crow's Foot			(50)
Table Rock			(49)
Fraunhofer			(47)
Upper Parker Flat			(45)
Parker Flat			(44)
Paradise Bend			(42)
Staigmiller			(38)
Merganser Bend			(38)
Black Butte			(37)
Ridge Top			(37)
Givens Gulch			(35)
Rattlesnake			(35)
Eden Bridge FAS	Ramp		(23)
Truly FAS	Ramp		(9)
Lower Smith River FAS	Hand Launch		(4)

The biggest hazard with the Smith is its remoteness. If you hit a spell of bad weather, there's no choice but to stick it out. Be prepared for rain or cold weather. All floaters—especially canoeists—should avoid overloading their craft with equipment or people. An overladen boat does not handle properly. Don't carry three people in a canoe unless the boat is designed for it.

Despite the Smith's outstanding attributes, every silver lining has a cloud. Those who have floated the Smith for a long time have noted the ever-growing number of cabins and houses along the river. These subdivisions threaten the Smith's natural qualities. Another serious Smith River problem is the proliferation of leafy spurge—a noxious weed that chokes out native plants and reduces forage for wildlife. This plant, which has a bright yellow flower that blooms in July, has taken over much of the river bottom and most large meadows. FWP, the USDA Forest Service, and Meagher and Cascade Counties are working cooperatively to battle this invader with biological and chemical control, as well as landowner and floater education.

Unfortunately, the largest threat to the Smith River is a proposed copper mine near Tenderfoot Creek. While thus far river conservationists have successfully delayed the mine from starting, it's likely only a matter of time before the character of the river is changed forever. While the Smith is an obvious candidate for the National Wild and Scenic Rivers System, most local landowners oppose the concept of federal management. Nevertheless, many landowners want to preserve the river corridor and might support a locally developed cooperative management plan similar to the one that now protects a sizable part of the Blackfoot River. Such an effort could be the best prescription for protecting the Smith from irresponsible development.

Float fishing: Fishing can be excellent on the Smith, although it ebbs and flows based on water levels and wintertime ice-scouring episodes. Above the canyon the river supports mainly rainbow trout with occasional browns. In the canyon expect a mixture of browns and rainbows. Browns predominate below the canyon. There is a prolific golden stonefly hatch in late June, and if there is enough water, spruce moths can appear in high numbers by mid-July. Native cutthroats can be caught throughout. Check regulations for special restrictions.

30 Stillwater River

The Stillwater is a fast, rocky mountain river that flows through timbered bottomlands and past large ranches with the spectacular Beartooth Mountains as a backdrop.

Vital statistics: 68 miles from its headwaters in the Beartooth Mountains southwest of Absarokee to its confluence with the Yellowstone River near Columbus.

Level of difficulty: A challenging whitewater river. Class IV and V rapids in its upper reaches; Class II and III from Cliff Swallow downstream.

Flow: Annual mean flow: 947 cfs near Absarokee. Often too low by August above Absarokee, but usually has adequate flows all year below Absaroka FAS. Float the river with at least 300 cfs (about 1.5 feet), and don't go when it is over 2,000 cfs (about 3 feet).

Recommended watercraft: Rafts, kayaks.

Hazards: Logjams, snags, boulders, and diversion dams. Extremely dangerous low bridges at high flows.

Where the crowd goes: Absaroka to Fireman's Point.

Avoiding the scene: Cliff Swallow to Absaroka.

Inside tip: Great milkshakes and burgers at the Dew Drop Inn in Absarokee.

Maps: USFS: Custer (Beartooth), Gallatin-East; USGS: Billings, MT.

Shuttle information: Stillwater Anglers, Columbus, (406) 322-4977.

River rules: None.

For more information: Absaroka River Adventures, Absarokee; Adventure Whitewater, Red Lodge; Beartooth Whitewater, Red Lodge; FWP, Billings; Custer National Forest (Beartooth Division), Red Lodge.

The Paddling

Mention the Stillwater River and somewhere a kayaker's heart pounds a little faster, for the Stillwater is anything but still. Named by Captain Clark, who must have stumbled onto one of this river's few quiet spots, this picturesque stream dashes madly from the Beartooth Mountains, cascades through sizable boulder fields, and only slows down in its lower reaches before meeting the Yellowstone River near Columbus. It's one of the top whitewater streams in the state.

While the Corps of Discovery never tested the Stillwater's rapids, Captain Clark camped at the mouth of the river for a week and built two canoes for the trip down the Yellowstone. The dugouts were 28 feet long, 16 or 18 inches deep, about 16 to 24 inches wide, ax-hewn, and hollowed by fire. They proved excellent boats to carry the intrepid explorers down the Yellowstone—Clark's group averaged more than 30 miles per day.

Thanks to Congress's 1978 designation of the Absaroka–Beartooth Wilderness, the headwaters of the Stillwater are protected. It's possible for kayakers to float about 5 miles of the river within the wilderness, but the only access is via foot or horse. The upper river has a distinct alpine flavor, with heavy timber running to the edge of the river. Downed trees—a result of forest fires—have made floating the upper stream extremely difficult.

Just downstream from Woodbine Rapids is Chrome Mine Rapids. Located adjacent to the Mouat Mine, it is also extremely challenging. Both rapids require careful scouting and top-quality equipment, including wet suits, helmets, and high-flotation life jackets. From Mouat Mine to Cliff Swallow, the river remains tumultuous but not quite as dangerous.

In an average year the Stillwater above Absarokee usually gets too low for floating by mid-July. Below Absarokee the river typically holds up throughout the summer.

While the Stillwater sees plenty of kayakers, more rafters and canoeists have discovered it in recent years. For those interested in boating the Stillwater, the Beartooth Paddlers Society extends an open invitation for people to show up at the Moraine or Cliff Swallow access points on nearly any Saturday or Sunday during the peak floating season (usually about mid-May to mid-July). It's a good opportunity to go down the river with experienced people.

Contrary to its name, the upper Stillwater contains challenging whitewater. Downstream, the gradient decreases as it joins the Yellowstone. TIM PALMER

STILL WATERS RUN STEEP

Whitewater action on the Stillwater starts at the end of the road near the Woodbine Campground, where the rapids are extremely formidable. Woodbine Rapids lasts for about a mile and at high flows contains some Class IV water as well as one Class V drop. At peak flows, even experts consider these rapids unrunnable. Below Woodbine there's near-continuous whitewater for the next 1.5 miles before hitting Chrome Mine Rapids, opposite the old Mouat Mine. This extremely difficult spot lasts about 300 yards and is a bona fide Class V. Few people run this rapid. Those who do should scout it carefully and wear top-quality equipment, including wet suits, helmets, and high-flotation life jackets. At peak flows it's Class VI—unrunnable.

Chrome Mine Rapids starts out with an 8-foot waterfall and then dashes through a plethora of rocks. An upset spells extreme punishment and possible death. This entire 3-mile section is only for the best of the kayak experts. It is probably the toughest 3 miles of whitewater in Montana.

After the Chrome Mine Rapids, the river calms down for the next 10 miles before reaching the Moraine access. This stretch is almost all Class I and II water. The next 9-mile stretch between Moraine and Cliff Swallow is a popular whitewater run that's mostly Class III, with some Class IV at higher flows. Sharp turns and abrupt drops characterize this section. The biggest rapids are named for nearby access points: First comes Moraine Rapids, then Castle Rock, then finally Roscoe Rapids about 2 miles upstream from Cliff Swallow. You'll want to stop and scout all these spots. This section of river is suited for advanced intermediate and expert kayakers and rafters.

Inexperienced people who want to try out the Stillwater can also contact the guiding services listed in appendix A. Call these experts if you have any questions about flows or where to float. They're happy to help out.

With its broad, gravel bottom and large cottonwood groves, some people compare the Stillwater to western Montana's Bitterroot. The Stillwater has extraordinary water quality for a river so far east. Like the Bitterroot, the Stillwater has many new houses popping up along its shores, and floating pressure on the river has escalated markedly in the last decade.

Although the Stillwater now flows clean and pure, its future is cloudy. Directly adjacent to the main river and the West Fork of the Stillwater lies a mineralized zone known as the Stillwater Complex. This area, which is about 15 miles long and 2 or 3 miles wide, contains one of the country's richest supplies of minerals, including copper, chrome, nickel, and platinum.

Boaters should be aware of a number of low bridges that span the river between Woodbine and Cliff Swallow; there's a particularly bad one at mile 39. At high flows these bridges can be too low for rafts to pass under. They are very dangerous, so be sure to watch ahead. Boaters on all sections should be aware of logs and other debris that tend to build up around bridge pilings during high water.

After Cliff Swallow the serious rapids subside, and skilled intermediate to expert canoeists can try their skills. It's about a 10-mile run from Cliff Swallow to Absaroka, with mostly strong Class II water. It's the same story from Absaroka to Whitebird: solid Class II whitewater, nothing outrageous. Immediately downstream from Absaroka, take the right channel to avoid a dangerous concrete slab in the river. Also look out for a decent drop with a big wave about 1 mile upstream from Whitebird. At low to moderate flows, this rapid douses many boaters. At high water it gets washed out.

Finally, there's the 4-mile trip between Whitebird and Fireman's Point. Just above Swinging Bridge FAS start the Swinging Bridge Rapids, solid Class II rapids that are usually fun for all. Watch out for a big hole less than 1 mile downstream from Swinging Bridge. This hole, Mad Max, is just past the private Beartooth Ranch Bridge (actor Mel Gibson's ranch) on river left and is big enough to swamp the best. When flows are up, it is Class IV; at normal flows it's a solid Class III. Avoid it by taking the right channel.

Because most of the ore in this complex is low grade, fluctuating metal prices have dictated the level of mining, which has been ongoing for nearly a century. Mining has taken off again recently. While the federal Mining Law of 1872 grants the miner his discovery, Montana state law clearly speaks to preserving natural ecosystems. Is it possible to balance a free-flowing, unpolluted stream with mines, mills, and tailing dumps? The questions are difficult, but one thing is certain: If those who care about rivers aren't involved, there won't be any balance.

Float fishing: Between Cliff Swallow and the confluence with the Yellowstone, float fishing on the Stillwater can be quite effective. In fact, the only way to fish much of the Stillwater is by boat, because private property lines most of this fast-moving stream, and wade fishing is a recipe for a long swim. Float fishing usually comes into shape by mid-July and can be especially productive mid-August when the cool waters of the Stillwater attract eager Yellowstone browns. Think about using big foam grasshoppers or yellow streamers.

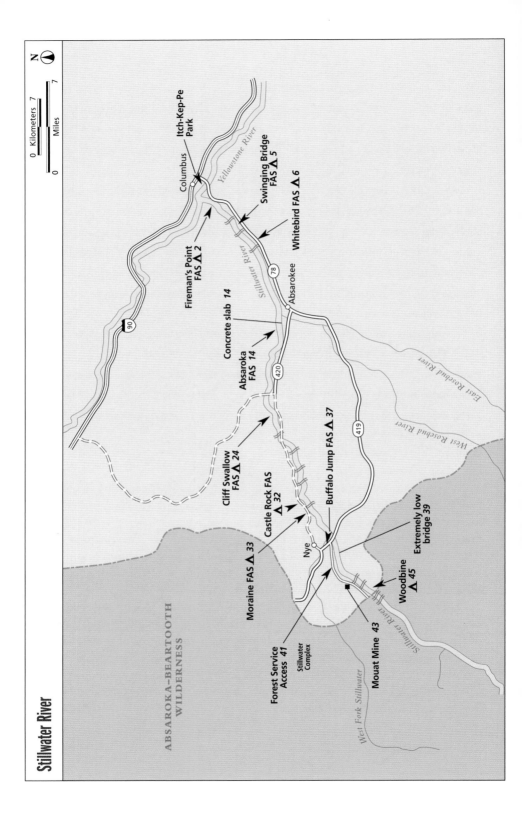

Stillwater River

ABSAROKA-BEARTOOTH
WILDERNESS

Moraine FAS △ 33

Cliff Swallow
FAS △ 24

Castle Rock FAS
△ 32

Forest Service
Access 41

Stillwater
Complex

Mouat Mine 43

Nye

Buffalo Jump FAS △ 37

Woodbine
△ 45

Extremely low
bridge 39

Absaroka
FAS 14

Concrete slab 14

Fireman's Point
FAS △ 2

Swinging Bridge
FAS △ 5

Whitebird FAS △ 6

Absarokee

Columbus

Itch-Kep-Pe
Park

Yellowstone River

Stillwater River

Stillwater River

West Fork Stillwater

West Rosebud River

East Rosebud River

90

78

420

419

0 Kilometers 7

0 Miles 7

N

Key Access Points along the Stillwater River

Access Point	Access Type	(River Mile)
Woodbine	Hand Launch	(45)
Forest Service Access	Hand Launch	(41)
Buffalo Jump FAS	Hand Launch	(37)
Moraine FAS	Hand Launch	(33)
Castle Rock FAS	Hand Launch	(32)
Cliff Swallow FAS	Hand Launch	(24)
Absaroka FAS	Hand Launch	(14)
Whitebird FAS	Ramp	(6)
Swinging Bridge FAS	Hand Launch	(5)
Fireman's Point FAS	Raft Slide Launch	(2)
Itch-Kep-Pe Park	Ramp	(0) (Yellowstone River)

31 Sun River

The Sun River starts in a deep canyon, runs through prairie grasslands, and finally meanders past cottonwood bottoms on its way to the Missouri. In the upper river, horizontal upthrusts create ledges of rock that cross the river and create challenging rapids.

Vital statistics: 101 miles from Gibson Reservoir to the Missouri River at Great Falls.

Level of difficulty: Class I and II at normal flows with occasional harder spots. Very difficult water (Class V) for 2.5 miles immediately below Gibson Dam. Excellent canoeing stream for solid intermediate paddlers.

Flow: Annual mean flow: 696 cfs near Vaughn. Gibson Dam has erratic flows. Flows may be low during spring runoff and high in the fall. Minimum floating level is 400 cfs. Anything over 3,000 cfs is for experts only and canoes are discouraged.

Recommended watercraft: Canoes, kayaks, small rafts.

Hazards: Rock gardens, ledges, standing waves, diversion dams, and snags; big winds, grizzly bears.

Where the crowd goes: Access below diversion dam to Highway 287 bridge.

Avoiding the scene: Between US 287 and Vaughn, where you'll find only an occasional angler or ranch hand cooling off.

Inside tip: When many other streams are high and muddy with spring runoff, the Sun may be perfect.

Maps: USFS: Lewis and Clark (Rocky Mountain Division), Bob Marshall Complex; USGS: Choteau, MT; Great Falls, MT.

Shuttle information: None; find a friendly local in Augusta or bring two vehicles.

River rules: Mostly private land; camp within the high-water mark. If you camp or hike on state land, a recreational-use permit is required.

For more information: FWP, Great Falls; Medicine River Canoe Club, Great Falls, (406) 788-8326.

The Paddling

The Sun River cuts a handsome swath through a narrow canyon, unlike any other in Montana, as it winds its way out of the remote Bob Marshall Wilderness. Many historians have remarked on the beauty of this stream as it plunges out of the mountains. Its towering sandstone formations, multicolored rocks, occasional waterfalls, and parched surroundings make it look like a river of the southwestern United States. The canyon between the diversion dam access and US 287 is a geologist's delight of thrusts, folds, uplifts, and layers of sedimentary rock. They tell a story of how this land was formed. The area surrounding the river has special significance to the Blackfeet Indians, who defended it fiercely.

The Blackfeet knew the Sun as the Medicine River, reportedly because of unusual mineral deposits along its banks that possessed remarkable medicinal properties. One can only speculate on how the river came to be known as the Sun. The river flows directly east, causing it to reflect the sun in the morning and evening hours. Viewed from afar it often appears as a ribbon of light.

What must once have been a bronco of a river has since been tamed and bridled. Gibson Dam, built in 1913, blocks the river's flow. Four miles below Gibson there's a large diversion dam. Approximately 97 miles of the Sun remain free flowing, but they, too, have felt the hand of man.

The river remains strikingly beautiful as it leaves the sheer walls of the majestic Rocky Mountain Front. Sawtooth Ridge rises prominently from the south side of the river, and Castle Reef juts just as spectacularly to the north. If the river weren't so tricky, there would be a real temptation to float down the river backward.

Along parts of the upper river, the stream bottom is solid bedrock and smooth as a pool table. In other places, reefs of rock cross the river, creating ledges and sharp drops. Experienced hands can maneuver around most of the ledges, but some drop several feet and require caution, especially for canoeists. Rocky riffles alternate with large, extremely deep pools that are excellent swimming holes in the heat of summer. Surrounding cliffs make good jumping platforms. The water is deep, emerald green, and usually quite clear.

With the towering Castle Reef in the background, the Sun River is an often overlooked multi-day float.

The canyon section of the Sun starts immediately below the diversion dam (a short distance above an old bridge) and continues for about 25 river miles to the bridge over US 287. When water flows are low, it's a long 2-day trip, as the river meanders a great deal. The constant maneuvering will wear you down. When the water is high, it's a rip-roaring whitewater trip that can be done in 6 to 8 hours. Be aware of two diversions, a diversion at mile 81 and the Floweree Diversion at mile 74. The first can be run with caution, but Floweree may have to be portaged on river right.

Floaters should also be keenly aware that grizzly bears heavily occupy the Sun River's willow and cottonwood bottoms. Bear attacks have occurred with floaters in this section, despite caution and experience. Make sure to keep a clean camp and always carry bear spray.

The narrow canyon of the upper river eventually gives way to open agricultural land after the Highway 287 bridge. Rolling, grass-covered hillsides dominate the landscape, and deer, antelope, and coyotes can often be seen from the river. While the river generally gets easier, several difficult rapids can be found about 4 or 5 miles below the Highway 287 bridge.

Floating on the Sun begins just downstream of the Diversion Dam at the base of the massive rock face known as Castle Reef.

About halfway between the Highway 287 bridge and Simms, cottonwood groves become denser and willows thicken, creating excellent fish and wildlife habitat that lasts all the way to Vaughn. Fishing for brown trout can be good when the river isn't seriously dewatered. The river bottom between the Highway 287 bridge and Vaughn is isolated and largely undeveloped, even though civilization isn't far away. Most of the land along the river is privately owned, and access comes via county bridges. Be careful of the Fort Shaw Diversion, 3.5 miles above Lowry Bridge. Portage on river left.

Below the town of Sun River, the water slows, then becomes heavily silted at Vaughn with the entry of Muddy Creek. It's not really very scenic after this—the river more closely resembles a big ditch. Rocky Reef, a major diversion 2.5 miles above Fort Shaw, needs to be portaged on river right.

The entire Sun River receives only moderate floating pressure. Access is limited, and the scarcity of public land limits the amount of overnight camping (although stream access law permits camping within the high-water mark of major rivers provided you aren't within sight, or within 500 yards, of an occupied dwelling).

The Sun's difficulty is directly proportional to its flows, which can be irregular. Although the Sun is a sizable river, it has frequent agricultural diversions, and the releases from Gibson Dam are unpredictable. In some years even spring flows may be too low for floating. In other years the river may be bank-full and very challenging. Check flows before you go by calling the numbers or checking the website listed in appendix A. Minimum floating level is 400 cfs. If you prefer, go low-tech and take a look at the river gauge on the northwest side of the Highway 287 bridge near the old bridge abutments. If the gauge reads below 2 feet, forget it. At 2 feet it's marginal floating, but possible if you read water well.

While intermediate canoeists and rafters will find the rock gardens and ledges of the upper Sun great fun, these hazards will eat up beginners. Much of the upper river calls for quick maneuvering and excellent boat control. Some of the runs should be scouted. When the river is high, large standing waves can spell trouble for open canoes. Below the Highway 287 bridge, the rapids and ledges gradually give way to occasional cottonwood snags and numerous diversion dams. It's easier, but still too much for beginners. Anyone can handle the river below the town of Sun River.

Much of the land surrounding the Sun is used intensively for irrigation. The frequent diversion dams take large gulps of water out of the river, sometimes leaving it almost completely dry. Erratic flows not only limit recreation, but they hurt wildlife as well. Fluctuating flows from the dam may keep a healthy riparian zone from establishing and may hurt aquatic insect populations, to the detriment of species further up the food chain like beaver, mink, waterfowl, and trout. This river sorely needs consistent flows as well as regulations that retain a minimum amount of in-stream water.

Float fishing: Despite the erratic flows coming out of Gibson Reservoir, heavy irrigation, sedimentation, and few tributaries, the Sun is still a productive fishery.

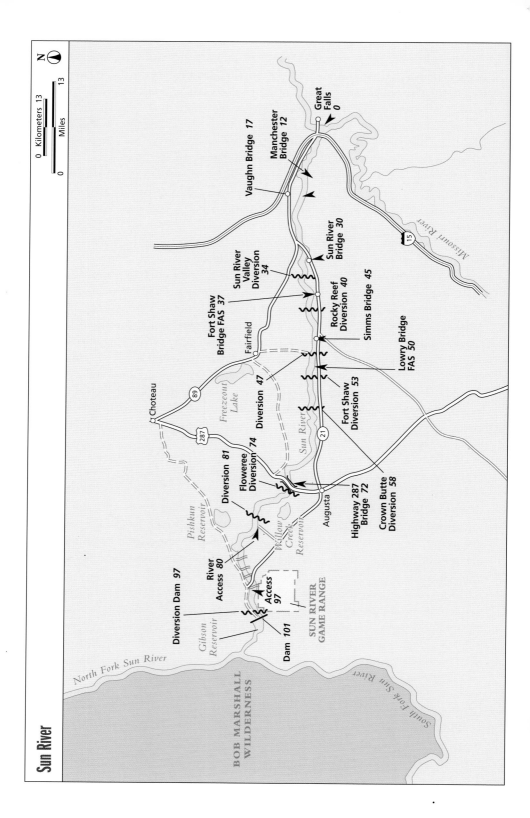

Sun River

Brown trout are voracious in the spring months and can grow well over 20 inches. Above the reservoir, as you would guess, both forks of the Sun contain healthy fish populations. The Sun River is in dire need of improved management to restore the historical in-stream flow that native fish depend upon.

Key Access Points along the Sun River

Access Point	Access Type	(River Mile)
Access below diversion dam	Hand Launch	(97)
River Access (BLM road)	Hand Launch	(80)
Highway 287 bridge	Ramp	(72)
Lowry Bridge FAS	Ramp	(50)
Simms Bridge	Hand Launch	(45)
Fort Shaw Bridge FAS	Hand Launch	(37)
Sun River Old Railroad Bridge	Hand Launch	(30)
Vaughn Bridge	Hand Launch	(17)
Manchester Bridge	Hand Launch	(12)
Missouri River at Great Falls	Hand Launch	(0)

32 Swan River

The sparkling Swan flows through pine forests and cottonwood bottoms, providing occasional views of spectacular mountain ranges on both sides of the river.

Vital statistics: 93 miles (15 miles of lakes and reservoirs) from its headwaters above Lindbergh Lake to Flathead Lake.

Level of difficulty: Mostly Class I water except for a difficult 1-mile Class V section immediately below Bigfork Dam. Wicked logjams limit most of the Swan to intermediates, but practiced beginners can handle specific sections. Very dangerous at high flows.

Flow: Annual mean flow: 1,155 cfs near Bigfork. Above Point Pleasant it can get too low by mid-August. A gauge at Piper Creek Bridge should read at least 2.25 feet to float the river above Point Pleasant.

Recommended watercraft: Canoes, kayaks.

Hazards: Numerous logjams and sharp bends.

Where the crowd goes: Fatty Creek Road Bridge to Point Pleasant.

Avoiding the scene: Lindbergh Lake to Condon.

Inside tip: Include huckleberry picking in the nearby woods with an August float.

Maps: USFS: Flathead; USGS: Choteau, MT; Cut Bank, MT; Kalispell, MT.

Shuttle information: Try Swan Mountain Outfitters, Swan Lake, (406) 387-4405; or the Mission Mountain Mercantile, Condon, (406) 754-2387.

River rules: Piper Creek to Swan Lake is catch-and-release for cutthroats and rainbows with artificial lures only.

For more information: Bigfork Chamber of Commerce; FWP, Kalispell.

The Paddling

Any mountains as spectacular as the Missions would have to spawn a beautiful stream, and the Swan River is that gem. The Swan springs out of Crystal and Grey Wolf Lakes and then dashes wildly down the mountains until it reaches Lindbergh Lake on the valley floor. Then it flows more placidly for about 60 river miles northward before entering Swan Lake. After Swan Lake it meanders slowly for about 13 miles before entering Flathead Lake near Bigfork.

Thick timber and abundant vegetation characterize the Swan Valley, which generally ranges from about 4 to 16 miles wide. This valley receives nearly 25 inches of precipitation per year, significantly more than most other western Montana valleys. The moisture creates a thick mantle of pines that frequently extend right to the river's edge. Nearly every coniferous tree native to Montana can be found close to the Swan River.

Early logging companies tried to use the river to float logs, but it was too small. Above Condon it's barely large enough to float a canoe. The abundant trees make continual contributions to the river; numerous logjams and downed trees are the Swan's claim to fame. This creates difficult and hazardous floating.

At peak flows Swan River float trips can be hair-raising and dangerous. Sharp bends in the river hide impenetrable logjams, and the river frequently braids into

Due to numerous portages and logjams, canoes and kayaks are the craft of choice on the Swan River. TIM PALMER

small, ever-changing channels. Expect to encounter jams that completely block the river. This river's many blind corners require excellent boat control.

About 2 or 3 miles above Swan Lake, the river slows down and begins to flow in wide, easy meanders. Beginners can handle this section if they start at the first county bridge upstream from the lake—Porcupine Creek Road Bridge. This section includes part of the Swan River National Wildlife Refuge, which supports large populations of waterfowl and shorebirds, as well as deer, mink, and muskrat. This area receives heavy hunting pressure in the fall.

Swan River

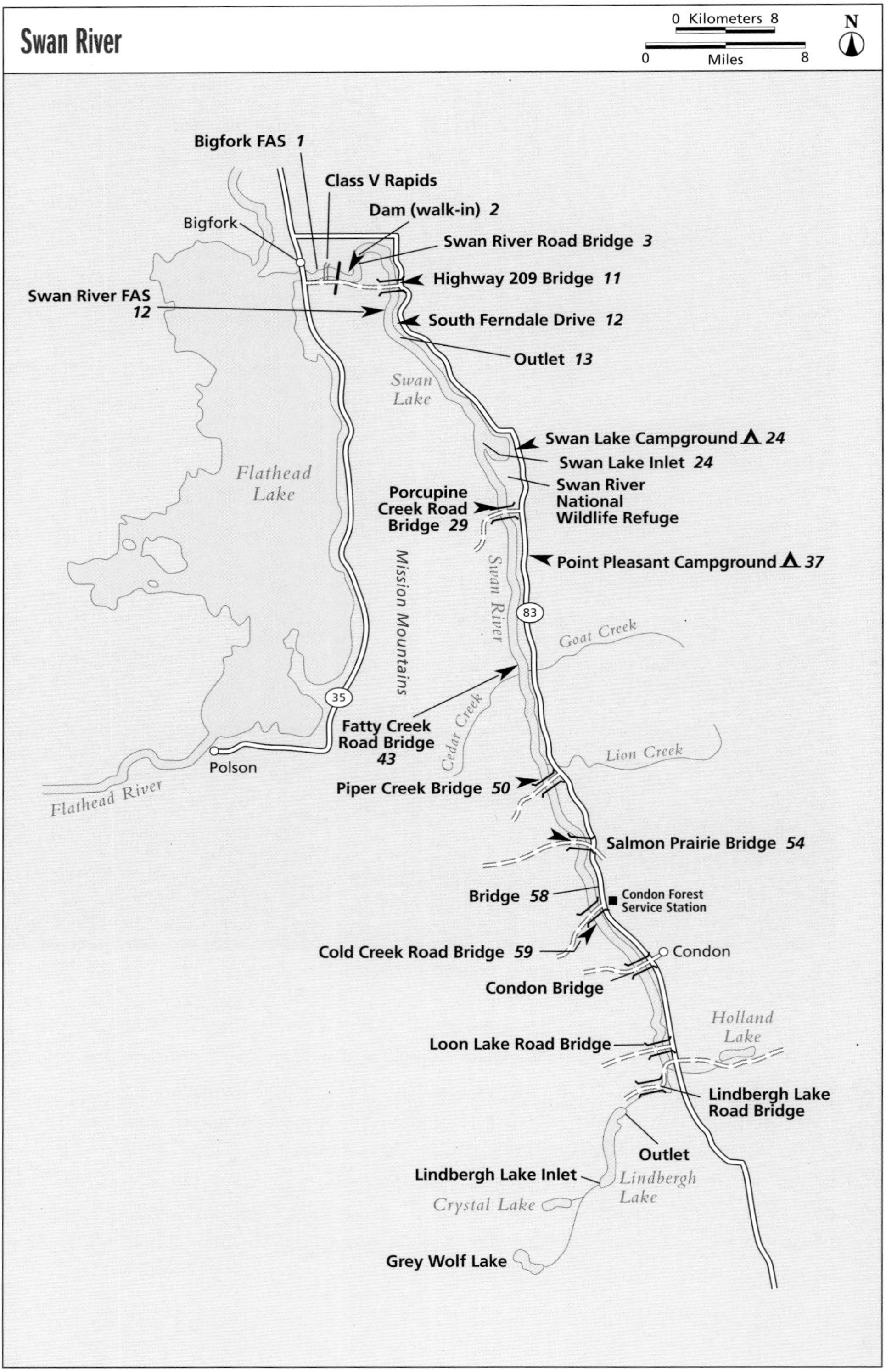

0 Kilometers 8
0 Miles 8
N
Bigfork FAS 1
Class V Rapids
Dam (walk-in) 2
Bigfork
Swan River Road Bridge 3
Highway 209 Bridge 11
Swan River FAS 12
South Ferndale Drive 12
Outlet 13
Swan Lake
Swan Lake Campground 24
Swan Lake Inlet 24
Swan River National Wildlife Refuge
Flathead Lake
Porcupine Creek Road Bridge 29
Point Pleasant Campground 37
Mission Mountains
Swan River
83
Goat Creek
35
Fatty Creek Road Bridge 43
Cedar Creek
Lion Creek
Polson
Flathead River
Piper Creek Bridge 50
Salmon Prairie Bridge 54
Bridge 58
Condon Forest Service Station
Cold Creek Road Bridge 59
Condon
Condon Bridge
Holland Lake
Loon Lake Road Bridge
Lindbergh Lake Road Bridge
Outlet
Lindbergh Lake Inlet
Lindbergh Lake
Crystal Lake
Grey Wolf Lake

Those floating the last few miles of the upper river above Swan Lake have to paddle across the lake for about a mile to reach the take-out point at Swan Lake Campground. Stick close to the shore when strong winds are blowing.

Except for the last few miles, the entire river above Swan Lake requires at least intermediate canoe skills. The logjams make it perilous for rafts, too. The upper Swan gobbles up boats every year and occasionally claims lives, so note water conditions carefully. Peak runoff usually occurs around the first week in June. Since the area receives heavy snowfall, high flows may continue into July. When the runoff subsides, the river is safer. Spills that might be catastrophic in June will likely mean only wet feet in August.

Except for ever-increasing subdivisions, much of the upper Swan River bottom remains undeveloped. It's a great place to see wildlife such as white-tailed deer and black bears. A few grizzlies prowl the valley, but they're rarely seen because of the lush vegetation. While the Swan has great birdlife, this river's namesake is not common.

There's also floating downstream from Swan Lake. For the first several miles below the lake, the river flows briskly and has some tricky rapids. Beginners should steer clear.

The Swan River is well known for being very woody. Don't despair, pack light and be prepared for portages. TIM PALMER

A float popular with Bigfork residents is the 8-mile trip beginning at the Highway 209 bridge east of Ferndale. From here the river takes a giant loop, and floaters end this tranquil trip at the Swan River Road Bridge. This section of river is a popular spring and fall float-fishing section, suitable for beginners.

The Bigfork Dam blocks the river a couple of miles above where the Swan empties into Flathead Lake. Right below the dam flows an unbroken stretch of extremely difficult whitewater. Every spring the Swan River is host to the Bigfork Whitewater Festival, where experienced kayakers try their luck at the "Mad Mile." The river plummets 100 feet in 1 mile. This section is for expert boaters, and scouting is essential. It's difficult to catch an eddy to size up the next rapid. Additionally, many rocks along this stretch have sharp edges. In sum, wear a good life jacket and helmet, use quality equipment, and be careful.

Since white people first settled the Swan Valley in the late 1800s, towering trees have attracted timber cutters. The Forest Service approved the first timber sale in the Swan in 1907, and the cutting continues both on public and private lands. Scars on the land bear testimony to past abuses. Thankfully, forest management practices have changed, and fewer broad-brush clear-cuts occur. Many of the last big trees remain along scenic MT 83. They line the road like a Hollywood set, hiding the hatchet job behind.

Float fishing: Floaters can expect to encounter anglers on foot. The Swan retains one of the nation's best populations of bull trout, an imperiled fish species. There are also good populations of rainbows (about 800 per mile) and whitefish. All but the slowest stretches are challenging to float fish because of the constant maneuvering this river demands. Turn your eye to a rising fish and end up underneath a logjam. The cool, clear waters have healthy bug life and plenty of hiding places for big fish. Getting to them is the challenge.

Key Access Points along the Swan River

Access Point	Access Type	(River Mile)
Cold Creek Road Bridge	Hand Launch	(59)
Salmon Prairie Bridge	Hand Launch	(54)
Piper Creek Bridge	Hand Launch	(50)
Fatty Creek Road Bridge	Hand Launch	(43)
Point Pleasant Campground	Hand Launch	(37)
Porcupine Creek Road Bridge	Hand Launch	(29)
Swan Lake Campground	Ramp	(24)
South Ferndale Drive	Hand Launch	(12)
Swan River FAS	Hand Launch	(12)
Highway 209 bridge	Hand Launch	(11)
Swan River Road Bridge	Hand Launch	(3)
Bigfork Dam	Walk-In	(2)
Bigfork FAS	Ramp	(1)

33 Tongue River

A true prairie river, the Tongue River winds through narrow canyons and cotton-wood bottoms, the only moist spot in a parched landscape.

Vital statistics: 207 miles (8 reservoir miles) from Tongue River Reservoir to the Yellowstone River near Miles City.
Level of difficulty: Class I all the way, suitable for beginners.
Flow: Annual mean flow: 389 cfs near Birney. Usually floatable all year, although irrigation diversions may dewater the river in dry years, especially in the lower 20 miles. A minimum of 150 cfs is needed (Miles City gauge).
Recommended watercraft: Canoes.
Hazards: Diversion dams, irrigation jetties, cables, barbed wire, and rattlesnakes.
Where the crowd goes: Nowhere. Between the dam and Birney gets the most traffic.

Avoiding the scene: Not to worry. Try downstream from the Highway 332 bridge.
Inside tip: A good early season float (April and May) in an area that tends to be hotter and drier than most of Montana. If you hit it just right, the river may even be clear.
Maps: USFS: Custer (Ashland Division); USGS: Hardin, MT; Forsyth, MT; Miles City, MT.
Shuttle information: Check with FWP in Miles City.
River rules: Mostly private land; respect private landowner rights.
For more information: Custer National Forest, Ashland; FWP, Miles City.

The Paddling

The Tongue River may be Montana's most overlooked float stream. It provides easy paddling, excellent fishing, fine scenery, and almost unexcelled solitude. This prairie stream flows from Wyoming into Montana and provides a unique perspective for observing eastern Montana's quiet beauty. The Tongue offers more than 100 miles of quality floating before joining the Yellowstone River near Miles City.

Scholars argue about how the Tongue got its name. Some say the river was named for the prominent buttes on the upper sections of the river, which resemble tongues. Others say Native Americans named the meandering river the Tongue because it goes in every direction. Still others say the river derived its name from Native Americans who thought it looked like a protruding tongue when viewed from the Bighorn Mountains, the river's birthplace.

Floating on the Tongue starts right below the Tongue River Dam near the Montana-Wyoming border. For the first 10 miles below the dam, the river winds through a narrow canyon that some consider the most scenic section of the river. Persistent anglers might even catch a few trout here. After exiting the canyon, the river winds through lush cottonwood bottoms. These big trees stand in marked contrast to their sparsely vegetated, parched surroundings. Sometimes visible along the riverbanks are thick seams of coal, which have spelled trouble in regard to coal development in the region.

The Tongue River is a remote prairie stream lined with red sandstone cliffs. CAROL FISCHER

Wildlife thrives in the cottonwood bottoms. Whitetails are plentiful, as are ducks and beaver. The river has some exceptionally large turtles. Birdlife includes double-crested cormorants, vultures, white pelicans, and sandhill cranes.

The Tongue provides easy floating even for beginners, but beware of cables, barbed wire, and occasional diversion dams. Access is extremely limited, consisting mostly of county road bridges.

Because of the massive coal reserves that lie nearby, the Tongue is one of the most endangered rivers in Montana. Luckily coal markets have continued to decline and have provided a respite from continued mining and development.

Although relatively undeveloped right now, the Tongue's water is in demand. Developers of irrigation projects, coal gasification and liquefaction plants, and coal slurry pipelines all would like to remove water from the river.

Float fishing: The Tongue River contains one of Montana's few quality small-mouth bass fisheries. The river also provides habitat for northern pike (some as large as 15 pounds!), walleye, sauger, and catfish. It is the only river in the state with rock bass. In the lower river near Miles City, anglers pursue such oddities as the paddlefish and shovelnose sturgeon, two ancient fish species. Sturgeon in the 15-pound class have been netted by fisheries workers. Paddlefish may exceed 100 pounds. A diversion dam 12 miles above Miles City blocks the migration runs of these species.

Although the Tongue is frequently turbid, it often clears in August, especially in the upper reaches. But the sunshine in the water can result in thick algae growth, which can impede fishing. The algae usually diminish after a couple of hard freezes, and fishing usually reaches its peak around mid-September and remains good until freeze-up. Anglers can sometimes find clear water in late April and early May, before spring runoff.

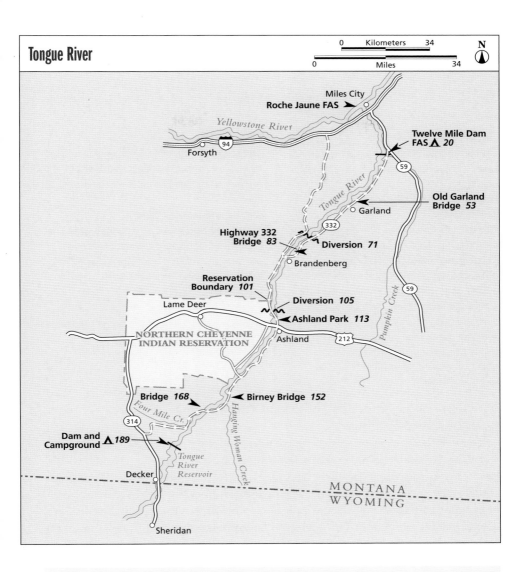

Key Access Points along the Tongue River

Access Point	Access Type	(River Mile)
Tongue River Dam	Hand Launch	(189)
Bridge	Hand Launch	(168)
Birney Bridge	Hand Launch	(152)
Ashland Park	Hand Launch	(113)
Highway 332 bridge	Hand Launch	(83)
Old Garland Bridge	Hand Launch	(53)
Twelve Mile Dam FAS	Hand Launch	(20)
Roche Jaune FAS (Yellowstone River)	Ramp	(0)

34 Two Medicine River

The scenic Two Medicine flows calmly through isolated cottonwood bottoms and prairies west of Glacier National Park.

Vital statistics: 95 miles from Two Medicine Lake to its juncture with Cut Bank Creek near Cut Bank.
Level of difficulty: Class II-III, suitable for intermediates.
Flow: Annual mean flow: 338 cfs near Browning. Often too low to float by August.
Recommended watercraft: Canoes, rafts.
Hazards: Fences, irrigation diversions, numerous logjams, debris, and grizzly bears.
Where the crowd goes: You'll be lucky to see another floater.
Avoiding the scene: No scene here.
Inside tip: A wonderful overnight float is possible between Heart Butte Bridge and the Highway 89 bridge.

Maps: USGS: Cutbank; USFS: Lewis and Clark. Pick up a free Blackfeet Reservation visitor map when you purchase your recreation/fishing license.
Shuttle information: None.
River rules: When floating, camping, or fishing on Blackfeet tribal lands, a tribal recreation permit is required. Pick one up in Teeples IGA in Browning or the Bear Track Travel Center in East Glacier.
For more information: Blackfeet Fish and Wildlife Department, Browning; FWP, Great Falls.

The Paddling

The Two Medicine River begins at Two Medicine Lake and flows through an isolated canyon past East Glacier for 20 miles before crossing under the Heart Butte Bridge, where most floating begins. The upper section of this stream remains largely unexplored due to Two Medicine Falls upstream of East Glacier. This river reportedly earned its name from Two Medicine Lake, where early settlers came upon the remains of two Blackfeet medicine lodges. The lake was first called "lake of two medicine lodges" and later shortened to reflect its current name.

Present-day explorers will likely have the Two Medicine all to themselves, as it receives very little floating pressure. Downstream from the Heart Butte Bridge, the "Two Med" meanders through thick willow and cottonwood bottoms. Paddlers will have to resist the urge to float backward and take in the magnificent scenery of Glacier Park to the west. Keep your eyes open for wildlife, in particular grizzly bears, as they are commonly sighted along the upper Two Med. Make sure to bring along bear spray and hang your food or bring a bearproof container if camping.

Highway and county bridges provide some access to the river, but the put-ins can be tricky. Some bridges provide two-track roads down to the water, while others are less developed, so be prepared to carry your gear down to the river. Six miles upstream from the Highway 89 bridge, paddlers must portage (right) around a river-wide diversion dam. While this diversion may look harmless, it has some dangerous hydraulics below. It is possible to use a rope and line an unmanned raft over the diversion to avoid a full portage.

Below the Highway 89 bridge, the river changes somewhat in character as it carves its way east to the plains. The mud banks of the Two Med are laden with history. Bison bones, remnants of the Great Plains herds that were extirpated 100 years ago, jut haphazardly from the banks. Recent efforts are underway to restore a trans-boundary bison population on tribal lands. Hopefully, in the near future, floaters will witness live bison instead of their bleached bones.

The river is fairly mild mannered until the Lenoir Road Bridge. This section has little public access and even fewer floaters. Downstream of the bridge the Two Med picks up some steam, and there are numerous Class II-III rapids. Intermediate canoeists shouldn't have too much difficulty, but make sure your gear is well secured. A final rapid immediately upstream of the Highway 358 bridge may require a portage and

Although much of the paddling on the Two Med is Class I, there are several rock ledges that deserve a closer look before running in a loaded canoe. CAROL FISCHER

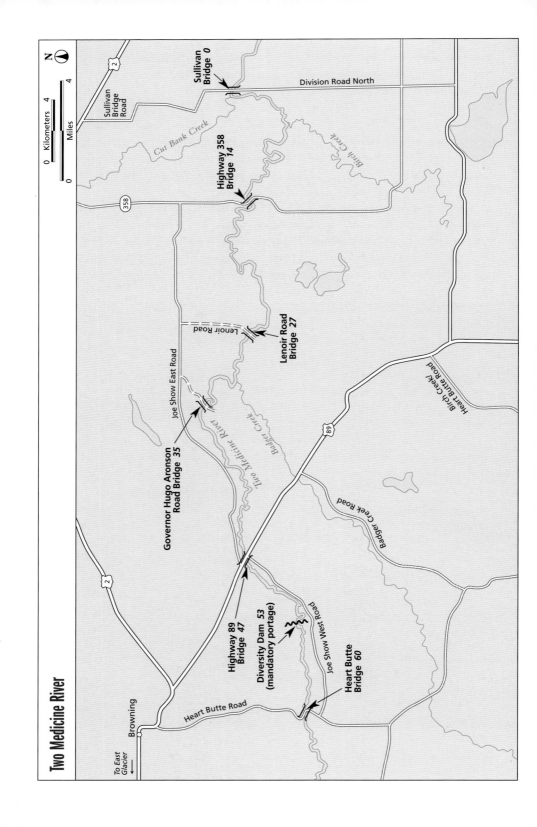

Two Medicine River

Keep an eye out for grizzly bears on the Two Medicine. They use the rivers flowing east from the Rocky Mountain Front as their main travel corridors. CAROL FISCHER

is a Class III-IV. Below the Highway 358 bridge the river flows through magnificent limestone formations. Several more Class III rapids should signal caution to paddlers who explore this isolated section of stream, as there is limited cellphone reception and few houses if disaster strikes.

Float fishing: Most folks traveling to the Blackfeet Reservation focus on the abundant and equally enormous rainbows that are stocked in the various lakes. Few anglers take the time to explore the waters of the Two Medicine, though the trout are plentiful. Rainbows and cutthroats are fairly abundant and eager to feed on top. The hopper fishing in the summer can be lights-out, and anglers will be kept busy with numerous cutthroats in the 14-inch range. To augment the fish population, the US Fish and Wildlife Service actively stocks the Two Med with fish originating from the Creston hatchery. The best fishing is found in the upper sections of the river because the Two Med warms considerably in the summer months.

Key Access Points along the Two Medicine River

Access Point	Access Type	(River Mile)
Heart Butte Bridge	Hand Launch	(60)
Highway 89 bridge	Hand Launch	(47)
Governor Hugo Aronson Road Bridge	Hand Launch	(35)
Lenoir Road Bridge	Hand Launch	(27)
Highway 358 bridge	Hand Launch	(14)
Sullivan Bridge	Hand Launch	(0)

35 Whitefish River

The slow-moving Whitefish River meanders past grassy meadows and willow-lined banks, providing a quiet escape close to town.

Vital statistics: 26 miles from Whitefish Lake to its juncture with the Stillwater River near Kalispell.

Level of difficulty: Class I, suitable for beginners.

Flow: Annual mean flow: 190 cfs near Kalispell. Sufficient water for floating all year except in driest years.

Recommended watercraft: Canoes, kayaks.

Hazards: Fences, irrigation jetties, numerous logjams, and debris.

Where the crowd goes: Not a busy river. Whitefish Lake to the Highway 40 bridge is the most popular section.

Avoiding the scene: Bowdish Road to Kalispell.

Inside tip: Perfect spot to take nervous-Nellie relatives. No dunking danger.

Maps: USFS: Flathead; USGS: Kalispell, MT.

Shuttle information: Check with Invert Sports, Whitefish, (888) 205-7119.

River rules: None. Nonmotorized only in the first few miles between the lake and Whitefish.

For more information: Sportsman and Ski Haus, Kalispell; FWP, Kalispell.

The Paddling

The Whitefish River begins at Whitefish Lake and flows for nearly 26 miles before joining the Stillwater River about a mile north of Kalispell (near where US 2 crosses the Stillwater). The Stillwater's juncture with the Flathead River lies another 3 miles downstream.

The Whitefish flows through agricultural land that's gradually being converted to homesites and golf courses. It's a deep river with a sandy streambed that frequently has thick vegetation along its shoreline. Occasional pine groves alternate with willows and marsh grasses. The water moves slowly and the banks are undercut, creating excellent beaver habitat. The Whitefish River is an excellent spot for a quiet, after-work float. The thick vegetation effectively screens the not-too-distant city life. Abounding with wildlife, the birdlife is excellent. Access is good, as county bridges cross the river at regular intervals. This river is almost all flatwater and can be handled by beginners. Because there's minimal current, a canoe or kayak is the craft of choice.

The Whitefish's claim to fame is its annual lake-to-lake (Whitefish Lake to Flathead Lake) canoe race. In past years the race started at Whitefish Lake, proceeded for the length of the Whitefish River, went for a short distance on the Stillwater River, continued down the main stem Flathead River to Flathead Lake, and ended with a short paddle across the lake to Bigfork, a distance of almost 53 miles. In recent years the race has been abbreviated and comprises only 12 miles of the Whitefish River.

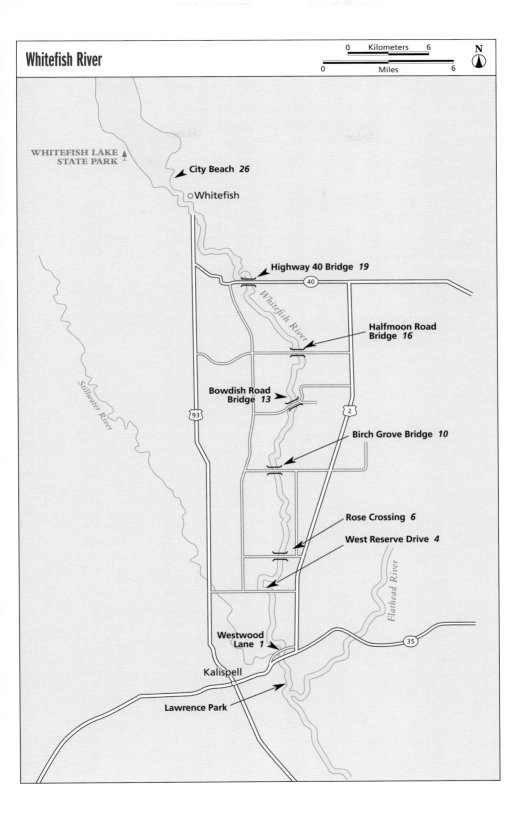

Whitefish River

WHITEFISH LAKE STATE PARK

City Beach *26*

○ Whitefish

Highway 40 Bridge *19*

Whitefish River

Halfmoon Road Bridge *16*

Stillwater River

Bowdish Road Bridge *13*

Birch Grove Bridge *10*

Rose Crossing *6*

West Reserve Drive *4*

Flathead River

Westwood Lane *1*

Kalispell

Lawrence Park

0   Kilometers   6

0   Miles   6

N

This river is a popular stopping place for ducks and geese during migration, providing both viewing and hunting opportunities. Floating pressure on the entire river is minimal.

Float fishing: Besides a few worm dunkers, few anglers focus on the Whitefish River. The prolific tuber hatch deters most anglers in the summer. Some decent fishing can be had at the mouth of Whitefish Lake for those who want to avoid the crowds.

Key Access Points along the Whitefish River

Access Point	Access Type	(River Mile)
City Beach	Ramp	(26)
Highway 40 bridge	Ramp	(19)
Halfmoon Road Bridge	Hand Launch	(16)
Bowdish Road Bridge	Hand Launch	(13)
Birch Grove Bridge	Hand Launch	(10)
Rose Crossing	Hand Launch	(6)
West Reserve Drive	Hand Launch	(4)
Westwood Lane	Hand Launch	(1)

36 Yaak River

One of the few floatable streams in the far northwest corner of Montana, the Yaak meanders its way through lush forests in an often forgotten corner of the state.

Vital statistics: 53 miles from its headwaters in British Columbia to the confluence with the Kootenai River.
Level of difficulty: Class I-II water; downstream from Yaak Falls is Class IV-V.
Flow: Annual mean flow: 885 cfs. Sufficient water for floating all year except in driest years.
Recommended watercraft: Canoes, kayaks, small rafts.
Hazards: Numerous logjams and sharp turns. Yaak Falls is the start of an impressive Class IV-V whitewater section and should only be attempted by expert kayakers.

Where the crowd goes: Not a busy river. Whitetail Campground to Hellroaring Creek.
Avoiding the scene: Above Yaak Village.
Inside tip: Rent and stay in one of the numerous fire lookouts in the area.
Maps: USFS: Kootenai; USGS: Yaak.
Shuttle information: Check with one of the Forest Service campground hosts or ask at the Yaak Mercantile, (406) 295-5159.
River rules: None.
For more information: Yaak Mercantile, Yaak; Tim Linehan Outfitters, Yaak; FWP, Kalispell.

The Paddling

The Yaak earned its name from the Kootenay Indians, who called it *Yhak*, meaning arrow or bow. The Kootenai River similarly was named Yhak by Native Americans, and when looking on a map, the Yaak appears like an arrow strung on the bow of the Kootenai.

The Yaak is a region of Montana lost in time. Tucked into the southern end of the Purcell Mountains, the Yaak River valley is one of the lowest-elevation river systems in the state. In addition, this area is one of the wettest in the state. If there was ever a place to believe in Sasquatch, this would be it. Inhabitants of the Yaak River valley don't live there for the nightlife. It is a place where people go to disappear and find true solitude—the nearest cellphone service is over 60 miles away. Enormous western red cedars, hemlock, ponderosa pines, and grand fur line the river bottom. Abundant populations of elk, deer, lynx, and wolverines thrive in this region. Woodland caribou once inhabited this region and unfortunately are now virtually extinct from this region. Geologists note that the Yaak region was the last area in Montana to thaw after the last ice age. As a result the mountains in this area lack the stunning peaks and jagged ridges found in the Bitterroots or the Missions. Ice thousands of feet thick slowly eroded the landscape into gentler knobs and broad, wide valleys.

The Yaak has a long history of logging. As you drive up the valley, the scars on the mountains are a stark reminder of a resource that lacks protection. The valley has reportedly seen more logging activity than any other area in the state. Logging has

Near the village of Yaak, the river attracts a variety of boaters. Further downstream, don't expect any company.

slowed considerably in recent years, and like-minded conservationists formed the Yaak Valley Forest Council to protect the resource. If you are interested in seeing this spectacular region preserved, consider supporting their efforts (see appendix B for contact info).

Floating can begin as high as the Upper Ford Bridge, about 10 miles north of Yaak Village. This section of stream is somewhat braided and more challenging to navigate, but you are likely guaranteed to have the river to yourself. Be prepared for a couple of portages over logjams or beaver dams. Most floating begins below the bridge at Yaak Village behind the Mercantile. This isn't legally a public launch site, so buying a few supplies in the store is appreciated. While you're in Yaak Village, it would just be a dirty shame if you didn't stop by the famous landmark, the Dirty Shame Saloon.

Between Yaak Village and the falls, the river meanders slowly and is suitable for beginners. Unlike the torrent that rages just miles downstream, the upper Yaak is fairly placid, and in many places the current seems to stop altogether as the river becomes broad and deep. Below Whitetail Campground small motorboats can even handle the river. By the Seventeen Mile Creek Bridge the river begins picking up a bit more steam. Four miles farther downstream the stream plummets over the 50-foot Yaak Falls and continues to cascade through nearly continuous Class IV-V whitewater until reaching the Kootenai, 9 miles downstream. The whitewater section should only be attempted by extremely accomplished kayakers.

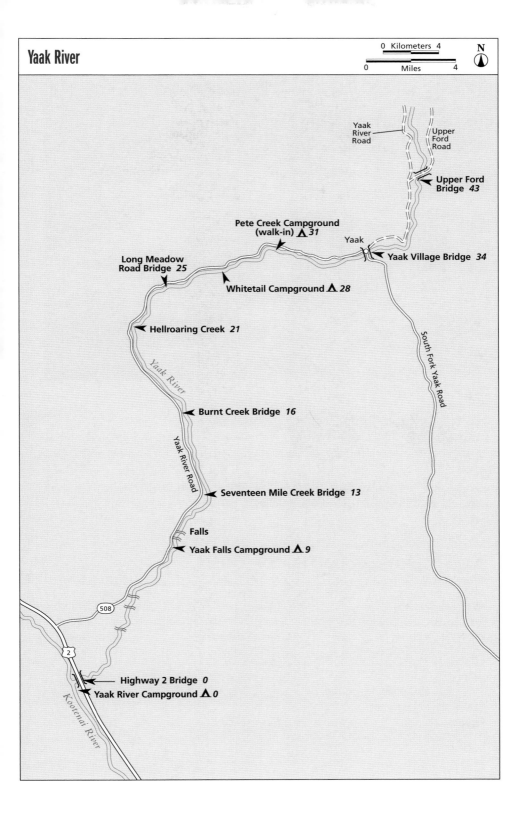

Yaak River

0 Kilometers 4

0 Miles 4

N

Yaak River Road

Upper Ford Road

Upper Ford Bridge *43*

Pete Creek Campground (walk-in) ▲ *31*

Yaak

Yaak Village Bridge *34*

Long Meadow Road Bridge *25*

Whitetail Campground ▲ *28*

Hellroaring Creek *21*

Yaak River

South Fork Yaak Road

Burnt Creek Bridge *16*

Yaak River Road

Seventeen Mile Creek Bridge *13*

Falls

Yaak Falls Campground ▲ *9*

508

2

Highway 2 Bridge *0*
Yaak River Campground ▲ *0*

Kootenai River

Upstream of Yaak Falls the stream is suitable for intermediate and advanced paddlers.
CAROL FISCHER

Float fishing: The Yaak isn't a hugely popular fishing stream. While decent numbers of rainbows and cutthroats inhabit the river system, it has never become a destination fishing location and the size of fish will not make any records, unlike the Kootenai downstream. Bull trout inhabit the river system, so be aware and don't mistake them for a brook trout if you're looking for a quick meal. All bull trout must be released.

Key Access Points along the Yaak River

Access Point	Access Type	(River Mile)
Upper Ford Bridge	Hand Launch	43)
Yaak Village Bridge	Ramp	(34)
Pete Creek Campground	Walk-In	(31)
Whitetail Campground	Hand Launch	(28)
Long Meadow Road Bridge	Hand Launch	(25)
Hellroaring Creek	Ramp	(21)
Burnt Creek Bridge	Hand Launch	(16)
Seventeen Mile Creek Bridge Hand	Launch	(13)
Yaak Falls Campground	Walk-In	(9)
Highway 2 bridge	Hand Launch	(0)

37 Yellowstone River

The longest free-flowing river in the Lower 48 at over 500 miles long, the Yellowstone tumbles down a mountain valley, traverses prairie grasslands, and meanders through cottonwood groves on its way to meeting the Missouri River. The only physical evidence of the Lewis and Clark Expedition in Montana—Captain Clark's name carved on a rock—can still be seen near the Yellowstone east of Billings.

Vital statistics: 554 miles from the Montana/Wyoming border to the North Dakota border.
Level of difficulty: Class I at normal flows except for the first 20 miles below Gardiner, where it is Class II and Class III (Class IV at peak flows).
Flow: Annual mean flow: 6,947 cfs at Billings. A big river with strong flows all year. Exercise extreme caution in Yankee Jim Canyon with flows over 15,000 cfs (Corwin Springs gauge).
Recommended watercraft: Drift boats; canoes in lower river.
Hazards: Logjams, tricky currents, and diversion dams.
Where the crowd goes: Mill Creek to Carter's Bridge in the Paradise Valley.
Avoiding the scene: Terry to Glendive.
Inside tip: Spend a month and take a Lewis and Clark trip from Billings to the North Dakota border.

Maps: BLM: Yellowstone River Floaters Guide; USGS: Bozeman, MT; Billings, MT; Forsyth, MT; Miles City, MT; Glendive, MT; FWP: Treasure of Gold (Billings to Missouri River); Montana Afloat: #12 (The Yellowstone River from Gardiner to Big Timber), #13 (The Yellowstone River from Big Timber to Huntley).
Shuttle information: Yellowstone Raft Company, Gardiner, (406) 848-7777; B & G River Shuttle, Livingston, (406) 222-3174; Stillwater Anglers, Columbus, (406) 322-4977.
River rules: 10 horsepower limit above Highway 89 bridge near Livingston.
For more information: Dan Bailey's Fly Shop, Livingston; Parks' Fly Shop, Gardiner; Sweet Cast Angler, Big Timber; Yellowstone Raft Company, Gardiner; FWP, Billings.

The Paddling

King of Montana rivers, the Yellowstone flows clean and free for over 678 miles, making it the nation's longest free-flowing river outside Alaska. This meandering ribbon of water, which the Indians knew as the Elk River, originates high in the mountains of Wyoming and flows for about 100 miles through Yellowstone National Park, forming such landmarks as Yellowstone Lake and the Grand Canyon of the Yellowstone. It then flows across central and eastern Montana before meeting the Missouri River just over the Montana–North Dakota border.

The Yellowstone is steeped in early Montana history. Early explorers and fur trappers—including Lewis and Clark, John Colter, Jim Bridger, and Jed Smith—all used this pathway to the wilderness. With their bullboats, pirogues, and hollowed-out logs, they explored the river's most remote points. Barges and even steamboats later

Flowing north from Yellowstone Park, the river is extremely popular during the summer months. In the winter, floaters can finally enjoy a brief respite from the crowds. JOSH CONNER

arrived on the Yellowstone, providing passage for miners, cowboys, soldiers, home-steaders, and other pioneers intent on opening the West.

Since no floating is allowed on this river in Yellowstone National Park, the first access point is near Gardiner, the start of the 100-mile "mountain" section of the river, which extends to Big Timber.

Float fishing (upper): The upper Yellowstone is nationally renowned for its trout fishery. Biologists estimate fish populations as high as 500 fish per 1,000 feet of stream. In the 50-mile stretch between Gardiner and Livingston, this translates into more than 50 tons of trout! Those who want to see how big the fish can get should visit the "Wall of Fame" in Dan Bailey's Fly Shop in Livingston. The wall displays outlines of hundreds of Yellowstone trout over 4 pounds, all taken on flies.

"YANKEE JIM" GEORGE

Yankee Jim Canyon deserves special mention for its colorful history. The area was named for an enterprising pioneer named "Yankee Jim" George, who built a cabin at the mouth of the canyon in 1872. Yankee Jim charged a toll to anyone wanting to use the narrow road through the canyon. Since this was the main route to Yellowstone National Park, the ex-miner had constructed a veritable "gold mine." Like St. Peter guarding the pearly gates, Yankee Jim became known as the guardian of Yellowstone National Park. He was such a character that famous people (including Teddy Roosevelt and Rudyard Kipling) often stopped to visit him. Kipling respectfully called the yarn-spinning Yankee Jim "the biggest liar I ever met."

The Yellowstone is the country's longest free flowing river, with over 500 miles of floating possible in Montana. JOSH CONNER

Conservation-minded anglers release large fish, which account for most of the reproduction. It's key to maintaining healthy populations.

The appropriately named Paradise Valley lies between Gardiner and Livingston. Cold, clear water and cobbled bottoms characterize the river, which alternates between long riffles and deep pools. The Yellowstone is shaded by the saw-toothed Absaroka Mountains to the east and the Gallatin Range to the west. Locals joke that these mountains cast shadows bigger than many eastern states. Canada geese nest along the river bottom, golden and bald eagles patrol the skies, and deer and elk haunt the willow thickets and aspen stands.

The upper river flows north from the park until it reaches Livingston, where it turns east at the point the Lewis and Clark Expedition termed "the Great Bend." Just upstream is the narrow spot in the Allenspur Canyon that for two decades marked the location of the proposed Allenspur Dam, which would have flooded 31 miles of the Paradise Valley. Fortunately, in the late 1970s, sanity prevailed.

The Yellowstone's only whitewater lies in the first 20 miles of river below Gardiner. Between Tom Miner Bridge and Livingston, practiced beginners can handle the Yellowstone at low flows. Beware of downed trees and snags. Canoeists should watch for big standing waves.

Numerous access points contribute to the upper Yellowstone's popularity, and they help distribute use. All sections of river in the Paradise Valley receive heavy floating pressure in summer. One method for avoiding summer crowds: Go early in the morning—at sunrise—on a long section of river that doesn't have intermediate access points. You will have solitude, because most of the boat traffic will be behind you.

YELLOWSTONE WHITEWATER

While the Yellowstone is best known for its fishing and wildlife, both the 8-mile stretch between Gardiner and Corwin Springs and the 4-mile section through Yankee Jim Canyon offer good whitewater excitement.

Gardiner to Corwin Springs has become increasingly popular with intermediate rafters and canoeists. Access is excellent, and much of the land along the river is publicly owned. A standard access point is an undeveloped site in the town of Gardiner. Take Park Street east off US 89 in town. Go 2 blocks to a dead-end turnaround. Carry 100 yards down to the river. The best whitewater lies in the first 3 or 4 miles below town. Not overwhelmingly difficult, this run contains solid Class II water that becomes Class III at peak flows. Look for a steep gradient, many rocks, and numerous sharp turns. This stretch has more rapids than Yankee Jim Canyon, but they aren't as big.

Yankee Jim Canyon starts about 13 miles below Gardiner and lasts only 4 miles. Most runs start near Corwin Springs. Although it's flatwater for the first 4 or 5 miles, the scenery is exceptional. Those interested in whitewater only should launch at the Joe Brown access, which lies immediately upstream from Yankee Jim Canyon. The standard take-out point is about 4 miles downstream at Tom Miner Bridge. The Tom Miner access is private, so be especially considerate. There's a public access only 0.25 mile below Tom Miner Bridge at Carbella.

Yankee Jim offers exciting but not particularly difficult water at normal summer flows (Class II and easy Class III). Intermediate rafters and kayakers can handle it then with little trouble, and beginners will have fun if they go with outfitters. Canoeists in open boats should stay clear unless they are experts.

At peak flows (over 15,000 cfs at the Corwin Springs gauge), a large volume of water gets squeezed into a very narrow canyon. The waves get big and the holes get deep, and at least two of the rapids become Class IV. Two anglers drowned in the canyon in 1998.

Between Livingston and Big Timber, the fishing remains good and boat traffic decreases. Floating gets a little more hazardous, however, as the river frequently braids and creates tricky currents where the channels rejoin. Side channels may be blocked by trees, so be careful when you wander off the main channel. Practiced beginners can handle this section at low flows if they remain alert. During spring runoff, the river can be extremely dangerous and should be avoided for pleasure floating as swift currents, hydraulics, and wood can cause serious problems.

The 165-mile-long "transition" section of the river runs from Big Timber to the Yellowstone's confluence with the Bighorn River near Custer. Here the river changes from a mountain stream to a prairie river. The water gets warmer, the river valley

Yankee Jim Canyon consists of three major rapids. The first is known as either Yankee Jim's Revenge or Boateater. Outfitters say it flips more boats than any other rapid. At high flows Revenge consists of a long tongue of water that leads directly into a huge standing wave. If boaters aren't set up right for the wave, it's swim time. This rapid has a reputation for taking the unwary by surprise.

The second major rapid is the easily identified Big Rock Rapid. You can guess what to look for. While not technically difficult, a dangerous hole forms behind the rock at high flows. At peak flows the river goes over the rock and forms a huge standing wave. Under normal conditions it's a straight shot past the rock that makes you wonder what all the fuss is about.

The final major whitewater in the canyon is known as Boxcar Rapids. At high water it's generally considered the toughest, and some outfitters say it's unrunnable at peak flows. The river constricts considerably at this point, and huge standing waves develop. The higher the water, the higher the waves—and the higher the likelihood of an upset.

The lesson of Yankee Jim is the same as for other free-flowing rivers: Conditions change dramatically with spring runoff. In August the river may move at a placid 3 miles per hour and hit temperatures as high as 60 degrees Fahrenheit. In June the river may roar by at 7 miles per hour with temperatures in the upper 30s. Don't forget that it's hard to define an "average" year. High water may extend until late July, or it may not happen at all.

Those interested in up-to-date water conditions can call the Yellowstone Raft Company in Gardiner, a local outfitting company that works the river regularly. The company's number is in appendix A.

opens up, and yellowish bluffs (the river's namesake) and rocky cliffs flank the stream. On a rock outcropping east of Billings, you can find the only physical evidence of Lewis and Clark's journey through Montana—the words "Wm Clark, July 25, 1806" scrawled on the rock. Clark named this particular rock formation Pompeys Pillar in honor of the infant son of the party's guide, Sacagawea.

The river in this section frequently braids and changes its channel, as free-flowing rivers typically do. Peak flows in spring create islands, bars, backwaters, and the kind of riparian diversity that makes ideal wildlife habitat. This is still the excellent beaver country that early fur trappers told tall tales about and risked their own hides for. Furbearers such as mink, muskrat, and a few otters lurk in the cottonwood and willow

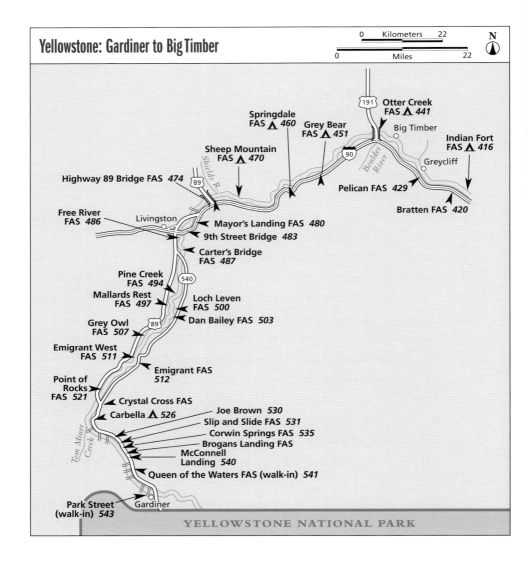

0   Kilometers   22

0   Miles   22

N

Springdale FAS ▲ 460

Grey Bear FAS ▲ 451

Otter Creek FAS ▲ 441

Big Timber

Indian Fort FAS ▲ 416

Sheep Mountain FAS ▲ 470

Greycliff

Highway 89 Bridge FAS 474

Pelican FAS 429

Free River FAS 486

Livingston

Mayor's Landing FAS 480

9th Street Bridge 483

Bratten FAS 420

Carter's Bridge FAS 487

Pine Creek FAS 494

Mallards Rest FAS 497

Loch Leven FAS 500

Grey Owl FAS 507

Dan Bailey FAS 503

Emigrant West FAS 511

Emigrant FAS 512

Point of Rocks FAS 521

Crystal Cross FAS

Carbella ▲ 526

Joe Brown 530

Slip and Slide FAS 531

Corwin Springs FAS 535

Brogans Landing FAS

McConnell Landing 540

Queen of the Waters FAS (walk-in) 541

Park Street (walk-in) 543

Gardiner

Shields R.

Boulder River

Tom Miner Creek

YELLOWSTONE NATIONAL PARK

bottoms that border the river. Geese, ducks, turkeys, and ungulates raise their young on the islands, and great blue heron rookeries can be found in isolated pockets. Whistling swans and sandhill cranes use the river heavily during migration. For foragers, morel mushrooms and asparagus are plentiful during April and May; just be aware and respectful of private property.

It was on this section of the Yellowstone that Captain Clark finally was struck silent by the incredible numbers of wildlife the Corps of Discovery observed. He wrote in his journal in 1806, "for me to mention or give an estimate of the different Species of wild animals on this particularly Buffalow, Elk Antelopes & Wolves would be increditable. I shall therefore be silent on the subject further. So it is we have a great abundance of the best of meat."

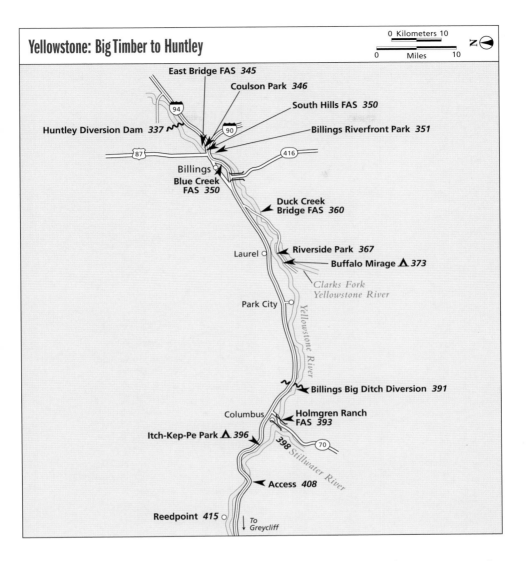

Yellowstone: Big Timber to Huntley

0 Kilometers 10

0 Miles 10

N

East Bridge FAS 345

Coulson Park 346

South Hills FAS 350

Huntley Diversion Dam 337

94

90

Billings Riverfront Park 351

87

416

Billings

Blue Creek
FAS 350

Duck Creek
Bridge FAS 360

Laurel

Riverside Park 367

Buffalo Mirage ▲ 373

Clarks Fork
Yellowstone River

Park City

Yellowstone River

Billings Big Ditch Diversion 391

Columbus

Holmgren Ranch
FAS 393

Itch-Kep-Pe Park ▲ 396

398 Stillwater River

70

Access 408

Reedpoint 415

To
Greycliff

Although the trout fishing is not quite as good below Big Timber, scenery remains superb. The FWP access points provide good river entry. Although I-90 and I-94 parallel the Yellowstone for its entire run across Montana, they're usually unnoticeable.

Each July a Livingston-to-Billings float trip attracts hundreds of participants, and the overloaded beer coolers give a literal twist to the notion of getting "Yellowstoned." Beginners can handle this section if they are cautious and don't drink too much. Watch for occasional weirs and diversions.

The "prairie" section of the Yellowstone flows for about 350 miles from the mouth of the Bighorn River to the North Dakota border, where the Yellowstone joins the Missouri. It provides one of Montana's most exceptional floating opportunities, following the same route Captain Clark and his men followed when crossing

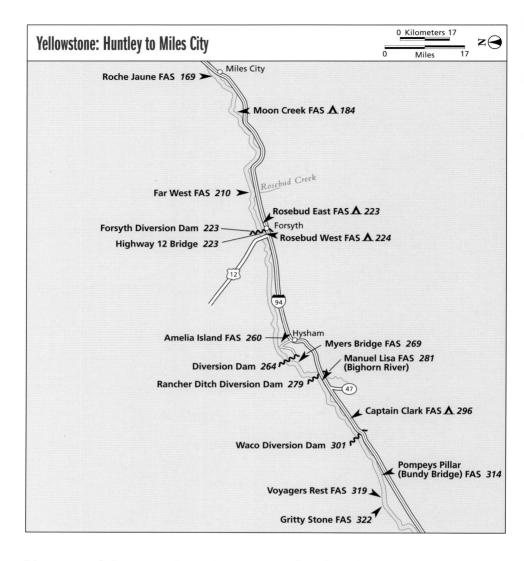

0 Kilometers 17

0 Miles 17

N

Roche Jaune FAS *169* ➤

Miles City

Moon Creek FAS ▲ *184*

Rosebud Creek

Far West FAS *210* ➤

Rosebud East FAS ▲ *223*

Forsyth Diversion Dam *223*

Forsyth

Highway 12 Bridge *223*

Rosebud West FAS ▲ *224*

12

94

Amelia Island FAS *260*

Hysham

Myers Bridge FAS *269*

Manuel Lisa FAS *281*
(Bighorn River)

Diversion Dam *264*

Rancher Ditch Diversion Dam *279*

47

Captain Clark FAS ▲ *296*

Waco Diversion Dam *301*

Pompeys Pillar
(Bundy Bridge) FAS *314*

Voyagers Rest FAS *319*

Gritty Stone FAS *322*

Montana on their return to St. Louis in 1806. Winding through wooded bottomlands shaded by rocky bluffs, a lower Yellowstone trip offers solitude and easy floating. It's an excellent choice for an extended boat trip.

Float fishing (lower): Despite its aridity the prairie section of the Yellowstone contains a greater diversity and abundance of wildlife than any other part of the river. The river itself supports at least forty-five species of fish, including two ancient rarities (the paddlefish and the shovelnose sturgeon) and a freshwater cod (the burbot, or ling). Walleye, sauger, northern pike, and channel catfish add to the angler's smorgasbord. Fishing can be quite good, particularly where tributaries enter the river.

The lower river often sustains unexpected avian species, including white pelicans, eared grebes, and double-crested cormorants. Endangered whooping

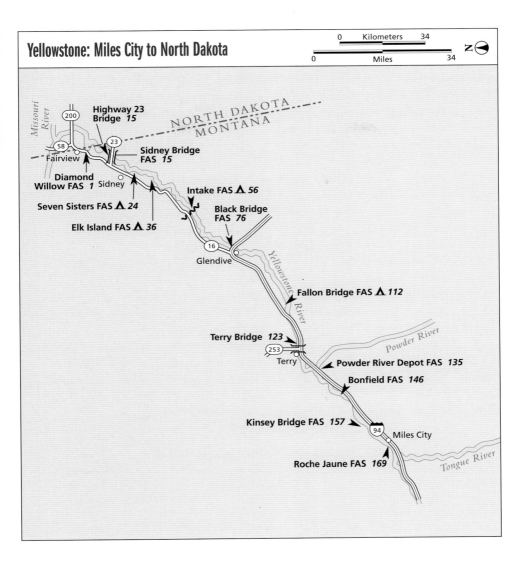

0   Kilometers   34

0   Miles   34

N

Missouri River

200

Highway 23 Bridge *15*

NORTH DAKOTA
MONTANA

58

23

Fairview

Sidney Bridge
FAS *15*

Diamond
Willow FAS *1*   Sidney

Intake FAS ▲ *56*

Seven Sisters FAS ▲ *24*

Black Bridge
FAS *76*

Elk Island FAS ▲ *36*

16

Glendive

Yellowstone River

Fallon Bridge FAS ▲ *112*

Terry Bridge *123*

Powder River

253

Terry

Powder River Depot FAS *135*

Bonfield FAS *146*

Kinsey Bridge FAS *157*

94   Miles City

Roche Jaune FAS *169*

Tongue River

cranes occasionally visit the river during migration, and sandhill cranes and whis-tling swans are common. Antelope can often be seen from the river. Turkeys are abundant.

Although a few organized float trips are conducted each year between Forsyth and Miles City, the lower river is usually devoid of people. While access isn't as good as on the upper river, highway bridges and occasional FWP access sites suffice. Begin-ners can handle the lower river except during runoff. The only real hazards are occa-sional weirs and diversions. The five most dangerous diversions are at Huntley, Waco, Rancher Ditch, Forsyth, and Intake. Be prepared for difficult, unmarked portages at Forsyth and Intake; portage river right (south bank) for both. There are channels around the diversions at Huntley and Waco, but no signs marking them.

The most serious environmental threat to the Yellowstone is clearly visible along the banks of the lower river: thick, black-banded layers of coal. Captain Clark observed these "straters" of coal, as did an 1876 journalist by the name of Finerty. He predicted, "Someday, I think, when the Sioux are all in the happy hunting ground, this valley will rival the Lehigh of Pennsylvania." Industrial forces that want the Yellowstone's limited water have tried their best to make Finerty's woeful forecast come true.

They suffered a strong setback in 1978 when the Montana Board of Natural Resources and Conservation decided that substantial amounts of water must remain in the Yellowstone for the benefit of fish and wildlife and water quality. Unless the legislature changes this decision, it means Montana has rejected massive industrial development of the Yellowstone. Instead the state has chosen to emphasize the river's natural values while maintaining present agricultural uses. If trout could cheer or beaver could applaud, their clamor would be heard for the length of the river.

Sadly, fish and floaters alike were shaking their heads in dismay when a pipeline running underneath the Yellowstone ruptured outside of Laurel in 2011. Although big oil fronted the bill for the cleanup (after a lengthy delay), the river and its wildlife felt the toll. High waters have washed most of the oil away in recent years, but the river is still recovering.

The Yellowstone River has consistently been mentioned as a prime candidate for the National Wild and Scenic Rivers System. Such designation would protect the river from inappropriate shoreline development, dams, and spills. Those who would like to help write the final chapter on Yellowstone River conservation should stay alert for new developments in the long battle to keep the river free.

Key Access Points along the Yellowstone River

Access Point	Access Type	(River Mile)
Park Street	Hand Launch	(543)
Queen of the Waters FAS	Walk-In	(541)
McConnell Landing	Ramp	(540)
Brogans Landing FAS	Ramp	(536)
Corwin Springs FAS	Hand Launch	(535)
Slip and Slide FAS	Hand Launch	(531)
Joe Brown	Ramp	(530)
Carbella	Ramp	(526)
Crystal Cross FAS	Hand Launch	(525)
Point of Rocks FAS	Ramp	(521)
Emigrant FAS	Ramp	(512)
Emigrant West FAS	Hand Launch	(511)
Grey Owl FAS	Ramp	(507)
Dan Bailey FAS	Walk-In	(503)
Loch Leven FAS	Ramp	(500)
Mallards Rest FAS	Ramp	(497)
Pine Creek FAS	Ramp	(494)
Carter's Bridge FAS	Ramp	(487)

Free River FAS	Walk-In	(486)
Ninth Street Bridge	Hand Launch	(483)
Mayor's Landing FAS	Ramp	(480)
Highway 89 bridge FAS	Ramp	(474)
Sheep Mountain FAS	Ramp	(470)
Springdale FAS	Ramp	(460)
Grey Bear FAS	Ramp	(451)
Otter Creek FAS	Ramp	(441)
Pelican FAS	Ramp	(429)
Bratten FAS	Ramp	(420)
Indian Fort FAS	Ramp	(416)
Access	Hand Launch	(408)
Itch-Kep-Pe Park	Ramp	(393)
Holmgren Ranch FAS		(396)
Billings Big Ditch Diversion	Hand Launch	(391)
Buffalo Mirage FAS	Ramp	(373)
Laurel Riverside Park	Ramp	(367)
Duck Creek Bridge FAS	Ramp	(360)
Blue Creek FAS	Ramp	(350)
Billings Riverfront Park	Ramp	(351)
South Hills FAS	Walk-In	(350)
Coulson Park	Ramp	(346)
East Bridge FAS	Ramp	(345)
Gritty Stone FAS	Hand Launch	(322)
Voyagers Rest FAS	Ramp	(319)
Bundy Bridge FAS (Pompeys Pillar)	Ramp	(314)
Captain Clark FAS	Ramp	(296)
Manuel Lisa FAS	Ramp	(281)
Myers Bridge FAS	Ramp	(269)
Amelia Island FAS	Walk-In	(260)
Rosebud West FAS	Ramp	(224)
Rosebud East FAS	Ramp	(223)
Far West FAS	Ramp	(210)
Moon Creek FAS	Ramp	(184)
Roche Jaune FAS	Ramp	(169)
Kinsey Bridge FAS	Ramp	(157)
Bonfield FAS	Ramp	(146)
Powder River Depot FAS	Ramp	(135)
Terry Bridge	Hand Launch	(123)
Fallon Bridge FAS	Ramp	(112)
Black Bridge FAS	Ramp	(76)
Intake FAS	Ramp	(56)
Elk Island FAS	Hand Launch	(36)
Seven Sisters FAS	Hand Launch	(24)
Sidney Bridge FAS	Ramp	(15)
Diamond Willow FAS	Hand Launch	(1)

Providing a Future for Montana's Treasured Streams

*Swift or smooth, broad as the Hudson or narrow enough to scrape your gunwales,
every river is a world of its own, unique in pattern and personality. Each mile on
a river will take you further from home than a hundred miles on a road.*

—Bob Marshall

Montana is blessed to have so many free-flowing and undisturbed rivers. The forces
that have killed many of America's spectacular waterways have been slow to reach
the Treasure State. Now, however, threats to Montana's rivers are building. Energy
development, mining, streamside subdivisions, water depletion, and pollution hang
like dark clouds over these sparkling streams.

Most Montana streams do not face problems with overuse. So why write a floaters' guide and risk promoting more use? If floating in Montana gets too popular, it
could lead to use restrictions and limitations, just as it has in many other western
states.

The answer is simple. Limiting the number of boats going down a river is easy
compared to preventing impoundment, channelization, depletion, or pollution of
wild waterways. It takes overwhelming public pressure to deny such tragedies. Rivers
have no voice of their own, so people who value rivers must speak for them. Time
and again, the people who use these streams and appreciate their natural qualities arise
as the rivers' defenders.

There are several important aspects of river protection. First and foremost is keep-
ing sufficient water in streams, not only for floating but also to protect fish and wildlife
and maintain water quality. Several of Montana's most outstanding rivers—including
the Big Hole, Jefferson, Bitterroot, Sun, and Beaverhead—suffer from serious dewatering problems. Luckily a few conservation organizations are working directly with
irrigators to lease water rights and develop irrigation systems that keep more water
instream. Trout Unlimited and the Clark Fork Coalition are doing fantastic work
across the state to keep more, cooler water in streams.

In addition to maintaining adequate in-stream flows, the habitat and shorelines
adjacent to rivers need protection from inappropriate development. Streamside subdivisions not only destroy a river's naturalness, they also provide the impetus for riprapping, channelization, and levees. These problems can be tackled on a local level by
regulating building activities in the floodplain. Contact your county commissioners.

A tactic that has been used successfully on the Blackfoot River is cooperative management. Landowners, concerned citizens, and appropriate state agencies
get together and work out agreements whereby the river corridor is preserved and
opened to carefully managed recreation. In areas where local landowners are strongly
concerned about protecting natural attributes, this system has real potential.

Those concerned about the future of Montana's rivers should help support the efforts of citizens' organizations working to protect them. These include the Clark Fork Coalition, Trout Unlimited and the Montana Council of Trout Unlimited, the Montana Audubon Society, the Montana Wilderness Association, and the Montana Wildlife Federation. National organizations such as the National Audubon Society, the American Rivers Conservation Council, the American League of Anglers, American Rivers, and the National Wildlife Federation have also been involved and deserve support.

Most often, however, the work is done by local groups and individual citizens, who seem to pop up like mushrooms when they learn their river is threatened. These organizations always need help, both physical and financial. Lend a hand so that future generations have the same opportunities to enjoy the clean and free rivers that you've enjoyed.

Appendix A: For More Information

Flow information for these rivers is available from the US Geological Survey (USGS) by calling the Helena USGS office at (406) 457-5900 or visiting the website at http://waterdata.usgs.gov/MT/nwis/current/?type=flow. Additional sources for flow and other information are listed in the entries below.

1. Beaverhead River

Flow information: Bureau of Reclamation, Billings; (406) 247-7318
Four Rivers Fishing Company, Twin Bridges; (888) 4-RIVERS (474-8377)
Frontier Anglers, Dillon; (800) 228-5263
Montana Fish, Wildlife and Parks, Bozeman; (406) 994-4042

2. Big Hole River

Big Hole River Outfitters, Wise River; (406) 832-3252
Sunrise Fly Shop, Melrose; (406) 835-3474
Four Rivers Fishing Company, Twin Bridges; (888) 4-RIVERS (474-8377)
Montana Fish, Wildlife and Parks, Bozeman; (406) 994-4042

3. Bighorn River

Bighorn Angler, Fort Smith; (406) 666-2233
Bighorn Trout Shop, Fort Smith; (406) 666-2375
Flow information: Bureau of Reclamation, Billings; (406) 247-7318
Montana Fish, Wildlife and Parks, Billings; (406) 247-2940
National Park Service, Fort Smith; (406) 666-2412
Quill Gordon Fly Fishers, Sheridan; (406) 666-2253

4. Bitterroot River

Grizzly Hackle, Missoula; (406) 721-8996; www.grizzlyhackle.com
Missoulian Angler, Missoula; (406) 728-7766; www.missoulianangler.com
Montana Fish, Wildlife and Parks, Missoula; (406) 542-5500

5. Bitterroot River, West Fork

Chuck Stranahan's Flies and Guides, Hamilton; (406) 363-4197
Missoulian Angler, Missoula; (406) 728-7766; www.missoulianangler.com
Montana Fish, Wildlife and Parks, Missoula; (406) 542-5500

6. Blackfoot River

Grizzly Hackle, Missoula; (406) 721-8996; www.grizzlyhackle.com
Missoulian Angler, Missoula; (406) 728-7766; www.missoulianangler.com
Montana Fish, Wildlife and Parks, Missoula; (406) 542-5500

7. Boulder River

Montana Fish, Wildlife and Parks, Bozeman; (406) 994-4042
Sweetwater Angler, Big Timber; (406) 932-4469

8. Bull River

Kootenai River Outfitters, Troy; (406) 295-9444
Montana Fish, Wildlife and Parks, Kalispell; (406) 752-5501

9. Clark Fork River

Grizzly Hackle, Missoula; (406) 721-8996; www.grizzlyhackle.com
Lewis & Clark Trail Adventures, Missoula; (800) 366-6246; www.trailadventures.com
Montana Fish, Wildlife and Parks, Missoula; (406) 542-5500
Montana Fish, Wildlife and Parks, Missoulian Angler, Missoula; (406) 728-7766; www
.missoulianangler.com
Montana River Guides, Missoula; (800) 381-RAFT (7238); www.montanariver
guides.com
10,000 Waves–Raft & Kayak Adventures, Missoula; (800) 537-8315
University of Montana Campus Recreation Outdoor Program, Missoula; (406)
243-2802
Western Waters, Missoula; (877) 822-8282

10. Clarks Fork of the Yellowstone

Montana Fish, Wildlife and Parks, Billings; (406) 247-2940

11. Clearwater River

Lolo National Forest, Seeley Lake; (406) 677-2233
Montana Fish, Wildlife and Parks, Missoula; (406) 542-5500
Missoulian Angler, Missoula; (406) 728-7766; www.missoulianangler.com

12. Dearborn River

Montana Fish, Wildlife and Parks, Great Falls; (406) 454-5840
Montana Fly Goods, Helena; (800) 466-9589
The Trout Shop, Craig; (406) 235-4474

13. Flathead River, Main Stem

Confederated Salish and Kootenai Tribes, Pablo; (406) 675-2700
Flathead Raft Company, Polson; (800) 654-4359
Kerr Dam, Polson; (406) 883-4450
Montana Fish, Wildlife and Parks, Kalispell; (406) 752-5501

14. North Fork Flathead River

Flathead National Forest, Hungry Horse; (406) 387-5243 (flow information also available from this number)
Glacier Raft Company, West Glacier; (800) 235-6781; www.glacierraftco.com
Montana Fish, Wildlife and Parks, Kalispell; (406) 752-5501
Montana Raft Company, West Glacier; (800) 521-RAFT (7238); www.glacierguides.com

15. Middle Fork Flathead River

Montana Raft Company, West Glacier; (800) 521-RAFT (7238); www.glacierguides.com
Glacier Raft Company, West Glacier; (800) 235-6781; www.glacierraftco.com
Great Northern Whitewater, West Glacier; (800) 735-7897; www.gnwhitewater.com
Flathead National Forest, Hungry Horse; (406) 387-5243 (flow information also available from this number)
Montana Air Adventures, Kalispell; (406) 755-2376

16. South Fork Flathead River

Flathead National Forest, Hungry Horse; (406) 387-5243 (flow information also available from this number)
Spotted Bear Ranger Station; (406) 758-5376 (summer only)
Bob Marshall Wilderness Outfitters, Charlo; (406) 644-7889

17. Gallatin River

Montana Fish, Wildlife and Parks, Bozeman; (406) 994-4042
Montana Whitewater, Bozeman; (800) 799-4465
Northern Lights Trading Company, Bozeman; (406) 586-2338

18. Jefferson River

Four Rivers Fishing Company, Twin Bridges; (800) 4-RIVERS (474-8377)
Frontier Anglers, Dillon; (800) 228-5263
Montana Fish, Wildlife and Parks, Bozeman; (406) 994-4042

19. Judith River

Bureau of Land Management, Lewistown; (406) 538-7461
American Prairie Reserve PN Ranch, Winifred; (877) 273-1123

20. Kootenai River

Kootenai Angler, Libby; (406) 293-7578
Montana Fish, Wildlife and Parks, Kalispell; (406) 752-5501
Kootenai National Forest, Libby; (406) 293-6211
US Army Corp of Engineers, Libby Dam; (406) 293-5577

21. Madison River

Madison River Fishing Company, Ennis; (800) 227-7127
The Tackle Shop, Ennis; (800) 808-2832
Montana Fish, Wildlife and Parks, Bozeman; (406) 994-4042
Bureau of Land Management, Dillon; (406) 683-2337

22. Marias River

Bureau of Land Management, Havre; (406) 265-5891
Coyotes Den Sports, Chester; (406) 759-5305
Flow information: Bureau of Reclamation, Tiber Dam
Montana Fish, Wildlife and Parks, Great Falls; (406) 454-5840

23. Milk River

Bureau of Land Management, Havre; (406) 265-5891
Flow information: Bureau of Reclamation, Billings; (406) 247-7318
Montana Fish, Wildlife and Parks, Glasgow; (406) 228-3700

24. Missouri River

Bureau of Land Management, Lewistown; (406) 538-7461; or Fort Benton; (406) 622-5185
Lewis and Clark Trail Adventures, Missoula; (800) 366-6246; www.trailadventures.com
Missouri River Outfitters, Fort Benton; (406) 622-3295
Montana River Outfitters, Great Falls; (406) 761-1677

25. Powder River

Bureau of Land Management, Miles City; (406) 233-2800
Montana Fish, Wildlife and Parks, Miles City; (406) 232-0900

26. Red Rock River

Flow information: Bureau of Reclamation, Billings; (406) 247-7318
Montana Fish, Wildlife and Parks, Bozeman; (406) 994-4042
Red Rock Lakes National Wildlife Refuge, Lima; (406) 276-3536

27. Rock Creek

Grizzly Hackle, Missoula; (406) 721-8996; www.grizzlyhackle.com
Missoulian Angler, Missoula; (406) 728-7766; www.missoulianangler.com
Montana Fish, Wildlife and Parks, Missoula; (406) 542-5500
Rock Creek Mercantile, Rock Creek; (406) 825-6440

28. Ruby River

Four Rivers Fishing Company, Twin Bridges; (800) 4-RIVERS (474-8377)
Harmon's Fly Shop, Sheridan; (406) 842-5868
Montana Fish, Wildlife and Parks, Bozeman; (406) 994-4042

29. Smith River

Amy's Think Wild Shuttle Service, White Sulphur Springs; (406) 547-2215
Montana Fish, Wildlife and Parks, Great Falls; (406) 454-5840; or Camp Baker; (406) 547-3893
Montana River Outfitters, Great Falls; (406) 761-1677
US Weather Service, Great Falls; (406) 453-2081; http://nimbo.wrh.noaa.gov/greatfalls

30. Stillwater River

Absaroka River Adventures, Absarokee; (406) 328-7440
Adventure Whitewater, Red Lodge; (800) 446-3061
Beartooth Whitewater, Red Lodge; (800) 799-3142
Custer National Forest (Beartooth Division), Red Lodge; (406) 446-2103
Montana Fish, Wildlife and Parks, Billings; (406) 247-2940

31. Sun River

Montana Fish, Wildlife and Parks, Great Falls; (406) 454-5840

32. Swan River

Bigfork Chamber of Commerce; (406) 837-5888
Montana Fish, Wildlife and Parks, Kalispell; (406) 752-5501
Swan Mountain Outfitters, Swan Lake; (406) 387-4405

33. Tongue River

Custer National Forest, Ashland; (406) 784-2344
Montana Fish, Wildlife and Parks, Miles City; (406) 232-0900

34. Two Medicine River

Blackfeet Fish and Wildlife Department, Browning; (406) 338-7207
Montana Fish, Wildlife and Parks, Great Falls; (406) 454-5840

35. Whitefish River

Montana Fish, Wildlife and Parks, Kalispell; (406) 752-5501
Sportsman and Ski Haus, Kalispell; (406) 755-6484

36. Yaak River

Montana Fish, Wildlife and Parks, Kalispell; (406) 752-5501
Yaak Mercantile, Yaak; (406) 295-5159
Tim Linehan Outfitters, Yaak; (406) 295-4872

37. Yellowstone River

Dan Bailey's Fly Shop, Livingston; (406) 333-4401
Montana Fish, Wildlife and Parks, Billings; (406) 247-2940
Parks' Fly Shop, Gardiner; (406) 848-7314
Sweet Cast Angler, Big Timber; (406) 932-4469
Yellowstone Raft Company, Gardiner; (800) 858-7781

Appendix B: Conservation Organizations

Local Organizations

Big Blackfoot Chapter of Trout
  Unlimited
P.O. Box 1
Ovando, MT 59854
(406) 240-4824
www.bbctu.org

Big Hole River Foundation
P.O. Box 3894
Butte, MT 59702
www.bhrf.org

Bitterroot Water Forum
178 S. 2nd St.
Hamilton, MT 59840
(406) 375-2272
www.brwaterforum.org

Clark Fork Coalition
P.O. Box 7593
Missoula, MT 59807
(406) 726-3247
www.clarkfork.org

Jefferson River Watershed Council
P.O. Box 550
Whitehall, MT 59759
(406) 579-3762
www.jeffersonriverwc.org

The Jefferson River Chapter of the Lewis
  and Clark Trail Heritage Foundation
P.O. Box 697
Pony, MT 59747
(406) 685-3222

North Fork Preservation Association
P.O. Box 4
Polebridge, MT 59928
www.gravel.org

Rock Creek Trust
P.O. Box 8953
Missoula, MT 59807
www.rockcreektrust.org

Yaak Valley Forest Council
11896 Yaak River Rd.
Troy, MT 59935
(406) 295-9736
info@yaakvalley.org

State Organizations

Montana Audubon Society
324 Fuller Ave.
Helena, MT 59624
(406) 443-3949
www.mtaudubon.org

Montana Trout Unlimited
312 N. Higgins Ave.
Missoula, MT 59802
(406) 543-0054
www.montanatu.org

Montana Wilderness Association
80 S. Warren St.
Helena, MT 59624

(406) 443-7350
www.wildmontana.org

Montana Wildlife Federation
616 Helena Ave.
Helena, MT 59624
(406) 458-0227
www.montanawildlife.com

Northern Plains Resource Council
220 S. 27th St.
Billings, MT 59101
(406) 248-1154
www.northernplains.org

National Organizations

American Recreation Coalition
1200 G St. NW #650
Washington, DC 20005
(202) 682-9530
www.funoutdoors.com

American Rivers
1101 Fourteenth St. NW, Ste. 1400
Washington, DC 20005
(202) 347-7550
www.americanrivers.org

Backcountry Hunters and Anglers
725 W. Alder
Missoula, MT 59802
(406) 926-1908
www.backcountryhunters.org

National Audubon Society
225 Varick St.
New York, NY 10014
(844) 428-3826
www.audubon.org

National Wildlife Federation
11100 Wildlife Center Dr.
Reston, VA 20190
(800) 822-9919
www.nwf.org

River Network
P.O. Box 21387
Boulder, CO 80308
(303) 736-2724
www.rivernetwork.org

Trout Unlimited
1777 N. Kent St. #100
Arlington, VA 22209
(703) 522-0200
www.tu.org

The Wilderness Society
1615 M St. NW
Washington, DC 20036
(800) 843-9453
www.wilderness.org

Appendix C: Map Resources

Bureau of Land Management Maps

5001 Southgate Dr.
P.O. Box 36800
Billings, MT 59107-6800
(406) 896-5000

Forest Service's Forest Visitors Series

USDA Forest Service
Northern Region Headquarters, Federal Building
P.O. Box 7669
Missoula, MT 59807
(406) 329-3511

Lewis and Clark Maps

Portage Route Chapter
Lewis & Clark Trail Heritage Foundation, Inc.
P.O. Box 2424
Great Falls, MT 59403
www.corpsofdiscovery.org

Montana Recreation Map and Fishing Guide

Montana Fish, Wildlife and Parks
1420 E. Sixth Ave.
P.O. Box 200701
Helena, MT 59620-0701
(406) 444-2535
https://fwp.mt.gov/conservation/landowner-programs/fishing-access-site-program

Red Rock River Map

Red Rock Lakes National Wildlife Refuge
Monida Star Route
Lima, MT 59739

USGS Topographical Maps

US Geological Survey
Branch of Information Services

P.O. Box 25286
Denver, CO 80225-0286
(800) USA-MAPS (872-6277)
store.usgs.gov

Yellowstone River Map

Montana Fish, Wildlife and Parks
2300 Lake Elmo Dr.
Billings, MT 59105

Specialty Maps

Specialty maps are available for certain rivers, including:

Bighorn River—The National Park Service produces a free map of Bighorn Canyon National Recreation Area that includes the portion of river from Afterbay to Bighorn. The map is not very detailed. It's available at the Park Service visitor center. Montana Fish, Wildlife and Parks produces a free map with river regulations and access points. It can be picked up at the FWP's Billings office.

Blackfoot River—Montana Fish, Wildlife and Parks has a small brochure on the Blackfoot River Recreation Corridor (Russell Gates to Johnsrud Park). The free brochure provides regulations and a small map that shows campsites and day-use areas.

Flathead River—The Glacier Natural History Association (in cooperation with the Flathead National Forest and Glacier National Park) has produced an excellent map of the three forks of the Flathead. *Three Forks of the Flathead Wild & Scenic River Float Guide* can be purchased at Forest Service offices or Glacier National Park.

Madison River—The Bureau of Land Management's *Bear Trap Canyon Wilderness Visitor's Guide* is available for free at the Powerhouse access or by contacting the BLM at its Dillon office, 1005 Selway Dr., Dillon, MT 59725, (406) 683-2337.

Missouri River—The Bureau of Land Management has a special waterproof floaters' map for the Wild and Scenic section of the Missouri River. It comes in two parts and provides information about making the trip as well as a mile-by-mile report. The maps are inexpensive and available at most BLM offices. (Maps 1 and 2 are printed back-to-back and cover Fort Benton to the Slaughter River. Maps 3 and 4 cover the Slaughter River to James Kipp State Park.) Request one directly from the BLM office in Fort Benton (see appendix A).

Red Rock River—Red Rock Lakes National Wildlife Refuge has a refuge map that shows the river between Upper and Lower Red Rock Lakes. It's free and available at the contact listed in appendix A.

Yellowstone River—Montana Fish, Wildlife and Parks has an excellent publication with a map of the Yellowstone River from Billings to the Missouri confluence titled *Treasure of Gold*. This small book contains detailed maps, historical information, and biological details. It's free by writing to the FWP office in Billings (see appendix A). A more detailed and updated version of this guide is in the works.

Lewis and Clark—To see where the Corps of Discovery camped along the Beaverhead, Jefferson, and upper Missouri Rivers, consult the maps in *Lewis and Clark in the Three Rivers Valley*, published by The Patrice Press (Tucson, Arizona). It's available from the Lewis & Clark Trail Heritage Foundation, P.O. Box 2424, Great Falls, MT 59403.

Appendix D: Stream Access

This appendix summarizes how Montana's 1985 stream access law affects the recreational use of the state's streams and rivers. Please read the following definitions carefully; they are important in determining the recreational uses that require permission. The information in this appendix is taken from the Montana Fish, Wildlife and Parks brochure titled "Stream Access in Montana."

The law says that, in general, all surface waters capable of recreational use may be so used by the public without regard to the ownership of the land underlying the waters. It also states that recreationists can use rivers and streams up to the ordinary high-water mark. The law does not address recreational use of lakes; it applies only to rivers and streams.

The law defines surface water, recreational use, and the ordinary high-water mark as follows:

Surface water means a natural river or stream, its beds, and banks up to the ordinary high-water mark.

Recreational use means fishing, hunting, swimming, floating in small craft or other flotation devices, boating in motorized craft (except where prohibited by law), boating in craft propelled by oars or paddles, other water-related pleasure activities, and related unavoidable or incidental uses. The law imposes certain restrictions on some forms of recreation. These restrictions are listed later in the appendix.

Ordinary high-water mark means the line that water impresses on land by covering it for sufficient time to cause different characteristics below the line, such as deprivation of the soil of substantially all its terrestrial vegetation and destruction of its value for agricultural vegetation. Floodplains next to streams are considered to be above the ordinary high-water mark and are not open for recreation without permission.

Water Classification

Class I waters are defined as those that are capable of recreational use and have been declared navigable or that are capable of specific kinds of commercial activity, including commercial outfitting with multiperson watercraft. Montana Fish, Wildlife and Parks (FWP) has developed a preliminary list of rivers that meet at least one of the criteria listed in the law for Class I rivers. This preliminary list includes the main stems of the following waters, as described:

Kootenai River Drainage: Kootenai River—from Libby Dam to the Idaho border; Lake Creek—from the Chase cutoff road to its confluence with the Kootenai River; Yaak River—from Yaak Falls to its confluence with the Kootenai River.

Flathead River Drainage: South Fork of the Flathead—from Youngs Creek to Hungry Horse Reservoir; Middle Fork of the Flathead—from Schafer Creek to its confluence with the main stem of the Flathead River; North Fork of the

Flathead—from the Canadian border to its confluence with the main stem of the Flathead River; Flathead River (main stem)—to its confluence with the Clark Fork River.

Clark Fork of the Columbia River Drainage: Clark Fork River—from Warm Springs Creek to the Idaho border; North Fork of the Blackfoot—from MT 200 east of Ovando to its confluence with the main stem of the Blackfoot River; Blackfoot River—from the Cedar Meadow FAS west of Helmville to its confluence with the Clark Fork; Bitterroot River—from the confluence of the East and West Forks to its confluence with the Clark Fork; Rock Creek—from the mouth of the West Fork to its confluence with the Clark Fork.

Missouri River Drainage: Missouri River—from Three Forks to the North Dakota border; Beaverhead River—from Clark Canyon Dam to its confluence with the Jefferson; Big Hole River—from Fishtrap FAS downstream from Wisdom to its confluence with the Jefferson; Gallatin River—from Taylors Fork to its confluence with the Missouri; Jefferson River—from the confluence of the Big Hole and Beaverhead to its confluence with the Missouri at Three Forks; Madison River—from Quake Lake to its confluence with the Missouri; Dearborn River—from the Highway 434 bridge to its confluence with the Missouri; Sun River—from Gibson Dam to its confluence with the Missouri; Smith River—from Camp Baker FAS near Fort Logan to its confluence with the Missouri; Marias River—from Tiber Dam to its confluence with the Missouri; Judith River—from the mouth of Big Spring Creek to its confluence with the Missouri.

Yellowstone River Drainage: Yellowstone River—from Yellowstone National Park to the North Dakota border; Bighorn River—from Yellowtail Dam to its confluence with the Yellowstone; Tongue River—from Tongue River Dam to its confluence with the Yellowstone.

Keep in mind that this list is preliminary and that other waters may be added to it in the future as other criteria listed in the law for determining Class I waters are addressed. Also keep in mind that there may be times during a year when the flow and physical condition of these waters may not permit their use for certain kinds of recreation.

Class II waters are all rivers and streams capable of recreational use that are not Class I waters.

Activities Requiring Landowner Permission

What types of activities between the ordinary high-water marks require landowner permission?

On Class I streams, landowner permission is required for the following recreational activities, even if these activities take place between the high-water marks:

- Overnight camping, unless necessary for the enjoyment of the water resource and it is done out of sight of, or more than 500 yards from, an occupied dwelling.

- Big-game hunting.

- Making recreational use of stock ponds or private impoundments fed by intermittent streams.

- Making recreational use of water diverted from a stream, such as an irrigation canal or drainage ditch.

- The placement or creation of a permanent duck blind, boat moorage, or any other permanent object.

- The placement or creation of any seasonal objects, such as a duck blind or boat moorage, unless necessary for the enjoyment of that particular water resource and they are placed out of sight of, or more than 500 yards from, any occupied dwelling.

- Using a streambed as a right-of-way for any purpose when no water is flowing.

On Class II waters no overnight camping is permitted without landowner permission.

On both Class I and Class II waters, landowner permission is required for the following recreational uses:

- Operating all-terrain vehicles or other motorized vehicles not intended for use on the water.

- Making recreational use of stock ponds or private impoundments fed by intermittent streams. Although this restriction deals specifically with only those stock ponds or impoundments fed by intermittent streams, it's recommended, as a matter of courtesy, that recreationists obtain permission from landowners before using any private ponds.

- Making recreational use of water diverted away from a stream, such as an irrigation canal or drainage ditch.

- Big-game hunting.

- Overnight camping, unless necessary for the enjoyment of the water resource and it is done out of sight of, or more than 500 yards from, any occupied dwelling. For example, camping is allowed if you are around a river bend and out of sight of a home, but only 200 yards away. It is also allowed if you are more than 500 yards away, but still within sight of a home.

- The placement or creation of any permanent duck blind, boat moorage, or any other permanent object.

- The placement or creation of any seasonal objects, such as a duck blind or boat moorage, unless necessary for the enjoyment of that particular water resource and they are placed out of sight of, or more than 500 yards from, any occupied dwelling. Any necessary placement of seasonal objects on Class I waters within sight of or within 500 yards of an occupied dwelling (whichever is less) requires landowner permission.

- Using a streambed as a right-of-way for any purpose when no water is flowing.

In addition, on all Class II waters, the following activities require landowner permission.

- Overnight camping.
- The placement or creation of any seasonal objects, such as a duck blind or boat moorage.
- Any other pleasure activities not primarily water related.

These restrictions apply to streams flowing through privately owned land. Of course, if the landowner grants permission for any of the activities mentioned, they would be permitted. Recreation on public lands may take place in accordance with the regulations of the agencies managing these lands.

Portage

The stream access law says that floaters using a stream may go above the ordinary high-water mark to portage around barriers but must do so in the least intrusive manner possible, avoiding damage to the landowner's property and violating his rights. A "barrier" is defined by the law as an artificial obstruction (like a fence or a bridge) that totally or effectively obstructs the recreational use of the surface water. The law does not address portage around natural barriers and does not make such a portage either legal or illegal.

If a landowner puts a fence or other structure across a stream, such as a float-over cable or a float-through gate, and it does not interfere with the recreational use of the water, the public does not have the right to go above the ordinary high-water mark to portage. In all cases, recreationists must keep portages to a minimum and should realize that landowners may place fences and other barriers across streams for purposes of land or water management or to establish landownership, if otherwise allowed by law.

Portage Routes

The law sets out a process by which either a landowner or a member of the public may, if necessary, request that a portage route over or around a barrier be established. Montana FWP encourages, however, that portage problems be resolved through other means if at all possible. If establishing a portage route is deemed the only workable solution, the request would have to be submitted to the board of supervisors of the local conservation or grazing district, or to the board of county commissioners. For assistance in determining where to file a request, or for other information regarding establishment of a portage route, maintenance, and signing, contact the FWP's Landowner/Sportsmen Coordinator at (406) 444-3798.

Liability

The legislature has limited the situations in which a landowner may be liable for injuries to people using a stream flowing through his or her property. This limitation on liability applies not only to the landowner but also to his or her agent or tenant and to supervisors who participate in a decision regarding a portage route. The law states that landowners and others covered by the restriction on liability are liable only for acts or omissions that constitute "willful or wanton misconduct."

Prescriptive Easements and Land Title

The legislature previously stated that a prescriptive easement cannot be acquired through recreational use of rivers and streams, the beds and banks, portage routes, or property crossed to reach streams. A 2014 Supreme Court ruling, however, overturned previous rulings and affirms that once a prescriptive easement is established, recreational use is included.

Trespass Legislation

This legislation states that a member of the public has the privilege to enter or remain on private land by the explicit permission of the landowner or his or her agent or by the failure of the landowner to post notice denying entry onto the land. The landowner may revoke the permission by personal communication.

The law states that notice denying entry must consist of written notice or of notice by painting a post, structure, or natural object with at least 50 square inches of fluorescent orange paint. In the case of a metal fencepost, the entire post must be painted. This notice must be placed at each outer gate and all normal points of access to the property and wherever a stream crosses an outer boundary line.

Access from County Roads at Bridge Crossings

Recreationists may gain access to streams and rivers from a county road right-of-way at bridge crossings. However, recreationists should be aware that access at a bridge could be restricted by a county commission for public safety.

About the Author

Kit Fischer, a conservation professional and river enthusiast, grew up paddling and rafting rivers across Montana with his parents, Hank and Carol Fischer, the original authors of *A Floaters Guide to Montana (Paddling Montana)*. A Montana native, Kit has explored nearly every mile of floatable river in Montana from Ekalaka to Eureka. He lives in Missoula, Montana, with his wife and young daughter, where he is the Director of Wildlife Programs for the National Wildlife Federation.